Japanese Mythology

Nichibunken Monograph Series No. 10

and in

Religion in Culture: Studies in Social Contest and Construction

Series Editor: Russell T. McCutcheon, University of Alabama

This series is based on the assumption that those practices we commonly call religious are social practices that are inextricably embedded in various contingent, cultural worlds. Authors in this series therefore do not see the practices of religion occupying a socially or politically autonomous zone, as is the case for those who use "and" as the connector between "religion" and "culture." Rather, the range of human performances that the category "religion" identifies can be demystified by translating them into fundamentally social terms; they should therefore be seen as ways of waging the ongoing contest between groups vying for influence and dominance in intra- and inter-cultural arenas. Although not limited to one historical period, cultural site, or methodological approach, each volume exemplifies the tactical contribution to be made to the human sciences by writers who refuse to study religion as irreducibly religious; instead, each author conceptualizes religion—as well as the history of scholarship on religion—as among the various *arts de faire*, or practices of everyday life, upon which human communities routinely draw when defining and reproducing themselves in opposition to others.

Published titles in the Religion in Culture series:

*Religion and the Domestication of Dissent:
Or, How to Live in a Less than Perfect Nation*
Russell T. McCutcheon

*The Symbolic Jesus: Historical Scholarship, Judaism and
the Construction of Contemporary Identity*
William E. Arnal

Representing Religion: Essays in History, Theory and Crisis
Tim Murphy

Situating Islam: The Past and Future of an Academic Discipline
Aaron W. Hughes

Myth and the Christian Nation: A Social Theory of Religion
Burton L. Mack

Forthcoming:

It's Just Another Story: The Politics of Remembering the Earliest Christians
Willi Braun

Rethinking Hindu Identity
Dwijendra Narayan Jha

Japanese Mythology
Hermeneutics on Scripture

Jun'ichi Isomae

Translated by Mukund Subramanian

FRED L. MATHEWS LIBRARY
SOUTHWESTERN MICHIGAN COLLEGE
DOWAGIAC, MI 49047

LONDON OAKVILLE

INTERNATIONAL RESEARCH CENTER FOR
JAPANESE STUDIES
KYOTO

First published 2009 by Equinox Publishing Ltd
UK: Unit 6, The Village, 101 Amies Street, London, SW11 2JW
USA: DBBC, 28 Main Street, Oakville, CT 06779

www.equinoxpub.com

In cooperation with
International Research Center for Japanese Studies (Nichibunken)
3-2 Oeyama-cho, Goryo
Nishikyo-ku, Kyoto 610-1192
Japan

www.nichibun.ac.jp

© Jun'ichi Isomae 2010
This translation © Equinox Publishing Ltd 2010

All rights reserved. No part of this publication may be reproduced or transmitted in any form or by any means, electronic or mechanical, including photocopying, recording or any information storage or retrieval system, without prior permission in writing from the publishers.

British Library Cataloguing-in-Publication Data

A catalogue record for this book is available from the British Library.

ISBN 978 1 84553 182 9   (hardback)
ISBN 978 1 84553 183 6   (paperback)

Library of Congress Cataloging-in-Publication Data

Isomae, Jun'ichi, 1961-
  Japanese mythology: hermeneutics on scripture / Jun'ichi Isomae; translated by Mukund Subramanian.
    p. cm. — (Religion in culture: studies in social contest and construction)
Includes bibliographical references and index.
  ISBN-13: 978-1-84553-182-9 (hb)
  ISBN-13: 978-1-84553-183-6 (pbk.)
  1. Mythology, Japanese. I. Title.
  BL2203.I8213 2010
  299.5'6113—dc22
                         2007050696

Typeset by S.J.I. Services, New Delhi
Printed and bound in the United States of America by The Maple-Vail Book Manufacturing Group, Lakeville, MA.

Contents

Preface	vii
Introduction: Hermeneutics on the Theory of Sacred Texts and Nostalgia toward Historical Origins	1

Chapter 1
National History, Shintō, and Myth: General Remarks on the History of the Interpretation of the Kiki — 17

Chapter 2
The Canon and Variants: An Examination of the Mythology of Susanowo — 35

Chapter 3
Myth in Metamorphosis: Ancient and Medieval Versions of the Yamatotakeru Legend — 66

Chapter 4
Myth and Rationality: Understanding God in the Early-Modern and Modern Periods — 85

Chapter 5
Myth and Nationalism: Motoori Norinaga's Creation Myths — 108

Chapter 6
The Space of Historical Discourse: Ishimoda Shō's Theory of the Heroic Age — 126

Notes — 156

Index — 175

Preface

"Singing to you like this is my only way to reach you." Bryan Ferry

In looking back at the history of mankind, first and foremost, each of us must uphold an astute perception of our own past, whether this concerns one nation or something as vast as all of humanity. I do recall a time ten years back while I was immersed in the process of documenting this work in Japanese, when I realized that I faced the inevitable challenge to meditate over what is called the past, what becomes the representation of that which has actually passed, and what this actually implies for me in seeking to ascertain the present.

Realistically, can one really retrieve the lost time of the past? Is not our memory of the past, that which involves each of us, inevitably torn in the process? Perhaps, one can say, feeling this type of uneasiness is not surprising. For example, even if lovers who have separated while retaining feelings for each other miraculously meet again, will they be making up for the time that they have lost? Will they be able to again walk toward the future? Or can the memory that has been lost during the separation of the lovers be brought definitively to this irreconcilable ground? In another sense, can we actually say that we were sharing time together from the very beginning? Is not the idea of sharing time an illusion woven in a period that lapses disparately? Do people who bond for the second time, feeling a form of nostalgia, have the chance to construct a communion while facing the future?

Akin to this line of thought, the essays included in this book are the tracks of my struggle to answer the recurring emotions in my heart. Certainly, in this place, there are no clear answers that exist. This is because the practice of historical inquiry is not meant to bring everyone into agreement, so as to reach a definitive answer. Rather, the act of reflecting on history and immersing oneself in the space of the past signifies the experience of struggling in conjunction with others. Suppose, for example, that you and I momentarily crossed paths and never met again. The feeling that we shared a struggle cannot but have a fragile existence as we are thrown into the prolonged movement of time where different people's emotions intersect.

This book is an experiment in the vein of interpretive history, elucidating its influence and function. The original Japanese texts that are the basis of this work include *Kiki shinwa no metahisutori* (Tokyo: Yoshikawa Kōbunkan, 1998), and "Hyōshō no rikigaku toshite no Kikiron" (Rekishi Hyōron, 623), published in 2002. In the process of editing these works, I am grateful for the guidance and advice offered by several scholars: on Japanese literature, Kōnoshi Takamitsu of the University of Tokyo; on religious studies, Shimazono Susumu of the University of Tokyo, and Kubota Hiroshi of Rikkyo University; and on Japanese history, Yoshie Akio and Miyachi Masato, both of the University of Tokyo. I am especially indebted to Professor Kōnoshi's recent epochmaking contribution to the interpretation of the *Kojiki* and the *Nihon shoki*, and Professor Kubota's insight into current trends in the theory of the canon in the West.

Earlier versions of four chapters have previously been translated and published in English:

"Myth in Metamorphosis: Ancient and Medieval Versions of the Yamatotakeru Legend," *Monumenta Nipponica*, 54:3 (1999). (Translated by Kate Wildman Nakai.)

"Re-appropriating the Japanese Myths: Motoori Norinaga and the Creation Myths of the Kojiki and Nihon Shoki," *Japanese Journal of Religious Studies*, 27:1-2 (2000). (Translated by Sarah Thal.)

"The Space of Historical Discourse: Ishimoda Shō's Theory of Heroic Age," *Positions: East Asia Cultures Critique*, 10:3 (2002). (Translated by Richard Calichman.)

"Japanese Mythology," in *Encyclopedia of Religion*, 2nd edn, New York: Macmillan, 2004. (Translated by Trent Maxy.)

I would like to thank the translators, Richard Calichman (City University of New York), Trent Maxy (Amherst College), Kate Wildman Nakai (Sophia University), and Sarah Thal (University at Wisconsin-Madison). In addition, I would like to thank Gary Ebersole (University of Missouri-Kansas City), Naoki Sakai (Cornell University), and Paul Swanson (Nanzan University), who urged me to publish the articles in English.

In re-editing and completing the work in English, I have considerably changed and added to the content and notes. In this regard, I would like to thank Orikasa Megumi, Tsuda Yuko, and Wada Mitsutoshi in helping me through the process. I would like to extensively thank Mukund Subramanian (former postdoctoral fellow at Harvard University) for translating the newly added chapters, and for editing the entire book—including the retranslation and editing of previously translated chapters. In this endeavor to appeal to the English reader, I am especially indebted to Patricia Fister and Sandra Margolies, without whom this work would not have been possible to complete. Finally, I would like to profusely thank Russell McCutcheon (University of Alabama) and Janet Joyce (Equinox Publishing) for their encouragement with regard to this publication.

Jun'ichi Isomae
Tokyo, 2007

Introduction: Hermeneutics on the Theory of Sacred Texts and Nostalgia toward Historical Origins

The *Kojiki* (712 C.E.; Record of Ancient Matters) and the *Nihon shoki* (720 C.E., Chronicle of Japan) were compiled in the eighth century under the auspices of the Yamato court, during one of the most powerful reigns in ancient Japan. The texts have been perceived as being central for the people of Japan because they are the oldest books describing the birth of the nation. Henceforth, from the perspective of hermeneutics on the theory of sacred texts, I centrally situate and analyze the *Kojiki* and the *Nihon shoki* (which I refer to as the Kiki hereafter) as a part of what are generally referred to as the ancient myths of Japan.

My perspective here relates to how the Kiki have been interpreted rather than to what is actually written in the texts. In other words, I ask why is it that the texts have continued to be read over the ages. Since the *Kojiki* and the *Nihon shoki* were both written as historical accounts of the very same kingdom, there are several overlapping descriptions of events in both texts. Yet, despite this fact, the texts contain several descriptions that vary, which signify differences in relating distinct events of the past. This is especially apparent with the *Nihon shoki*, which includes many different versions of a given story, followed by inscriptions as evident in the *ujibumi* (the legend held by a given clan, such as *Kogoshūi*) and the *fudoki* (regional records on the origins of geographic names). The debate as to what is written in the Kiki, and moreover which text reflects an authentic account of history, has persisted over the past 1300 years. Following their compilation, the interpretation of the texts shifted over the ages under the influence of Buddhism, Confucianism (Jukyō), Nativism (Kokugaku), and Western philosophy.

Thus, a huge gap, with regard to the vocabulary utilized and the worldview propounded, emerged between the texts and their interpreters. In this context, the history of Kiki interpretation developed to fill the gap between such differences, namely, between texts and the discrepancy between their interpreters, by discovering and tracing the "authentic" origins of the "truth" that was inscribed therein.

Certainly, as becomes apparent from the existential hermeneutics originating with Martin Heidegger,[1] there is no form of evidence that allows one to clearly grasp and confirm the meaning of historical texts as such, prediscursively. Therefore, the interpreter has to believe in the unstated presupposition that there is a clear meaning in the internal structural form of the texts, which is all the more reason why the interpreter is able to reinterpret its meaning. Yet, even if by chance the intended interpretation of the text accurately hits the mark (so to speak), there is no means of confirming this fact. In other words, unlike face-to-face conversations, one cannot determine whether an interpretation of texts from the past is right or wrong *per se*. In fact, if we reflect on the long history of Kiki interpretation, regardless of the transition in time period or the diverse strands of thought, there has never been an instance in which the various claims and opinions of researchers have coincided. This is applicable to our current period as well.

One could suggest that by considering the underlying gap between object and interpreter, research on the Kiki has been radically transformed. In this light, the aim of research to date has been criticized as one proclaiming a self-evident and direct means of comprehension, which in fact lopsidedly tells us more about the interpreter's worldview. In turn (ironically), research has focused narrowly on the epistemological horizon, if you will, which informs the interpreter's perception.

By putting an end to the diatribe over claims to "truly" understand the texts, in terms of historical interpretation, one can conjecture how this traditional text is in fact an axis located within a discursive realm comprised of multifarious thoughts and worldviews.[2] In particular, even within this formulation, the main argument propelling the history of Kiki interpretation concerns the centripetal force that the texts exude with regard to their sacredness. One is thus inclined to delve into the source of this authority and ask: why did different classes of people, through distinct periods, reflect their thoughts and worldviews in terms of a text that belonged to an ancient kingdom? Furthermore, why do we continue to look to a textual interpretation that is so removed from ourselves? Herein, there arises my methodological reasoning underlying a hermeneutics on the theory of sacred texts.

As is generally known about the study of Western religion, from the 1980s to the beginning of the 1990s, theories on scriptures reached their peak, being published one after another in succession. For the most part, Western researchers, rooted in their own religious history founded in Protestantism, freely interpreted the methodology of the comparative study of religion so as to formulate a critical perspective on the Bible. Generally speaking, their primary concern was influenced by the following three factors. First, restoring the viewpoint of written texts in the light of oral texts, including ways of interpreting the Koran or the Vedas, as thoroughly researched by William A. Graham and Miriam Levering.[3] What this clarified was that sacred texts, like the Bible, were not merely written records. Rather, before they were written down, oral religious traditions, as apparent in Islam's Qur'an or the Hindu Vedas, were directly connected to ritual practices in light of the foundation of human memory.[4]

This makes more sense if one bears in mind the form of the legend that signified the myth of primitive society, whereby religion did not attain its significance through a foundation in texts. In other words, if one were to conjecture a step further, although most sacred texts of religious traditions, including Christianity,[5] were inscribed, people would read the texts out loud (rather than merely reading silently), with a sense of rhythm, to a community of believers. Therefore, scriptures rarely obey the dichotomy between silent reading and oral history. Rather, as pointed out by the Annales school of historians, such as Roger Chartier (although not in reference to sacred texts),[6] the general form and style of reading in pre-modern France was apparent in situations whereby the minority of literate people, rather than engaging in silent reading, read texts aloud to illiterate people. The fact that there was a marked shift which gradually transformed this situation into one where individual silent reading was the norm, provides a richer perspective to the theory of sacred texts.

Second, as commonly seen in the analysis of sacred texts, the central matter in embodying truth is presumed to substantiate the privileged canon rather than help restore the significance of marginalized scriptures. From the point of view of the theory of sacred texts, at any given point in the movement of history, the actual canon is the scripture that is artificially selected and fixed by a community of believers, regardless of their attitudes or belief in its revelations. Prior to this moment, it can be stated that several sacred texts, with a contentious relationship, mutually attained significance.

Even if one were to examine the history of Christianity, one begins to understand this notion when investigating those texts, other than the fixed canons like the Bible, which were deemed heretic or false. In this regard, critical research by Wilfred Cantwell Smith or James Bar[7] can be added to the previously mentioned work by Levering. However, the theory of sacred texts does not claim that, because of the artificial nature of sacred texts, as having been invented by human beings, all texts are devoid of a revelatory quality (which in itself can be conceived as being sacred). Rather, the theory opposes the exclusive dogma propounding a self-proclaimed faith in the canon which monopolized this very revelatory quality.[8]

In unraveling the claim to the paramount status of texts, the theory of sacred texts focuses on the historical process of canonization itself, whereby the sacredness monopolized through a particular canon attains its distinction from other sacred texts. It becomes clear that this status of the canon, rather than resulting from what can be claimed as the work of its "holy spirit," emerges out of an artificial process within different historical circumstances.

This process of canonization is apparent not only in Christianity, but within Islam, Buddhism, and Confucianism. In this regard, the comparative study of Confucianism and Christianity by John B. Henderson deserves special mention.[9] However, as discussed later, the conundrum that continues to thrive concerns the manner by which this revelatory quality or even the sacredness is born. Researchers have failed to seriously discuss this "secret" imbedded in the sacredness that constitutes such texts.[10]

This question regarding the theory of sacred texts naturally raises qualms about the methodology of comparative religions. In other words, it raises the following concern: Is the sacredness in all sacred texts the same thing? Is the revelatory quality synonymous with sacredness?

Although it has been suggested that the various texts of different religious traditions reveal many distinct qualities,[11] in actuality, the question as to what concrete values these diverse qualities uphold has not been addressed. The reason for this is that the predominant mode of comparison in the study of sacred texts has been framed by Protestantism's canonical worldview. Therefore, all the schemes in the argument are reconceived to fit the contentious dualism between Protestantism, on the one hand, and the various other religions, on the other hand. In turn, the differences between religions have not been seen as the primary subject of concern.[12] What this implies is that the theory of sacred texts aims to make relative the emergence of Protestantism, and in particular the stark revelatory quality of the self-proclaimed Abraham-based religions. We have to await a viewpoint that elucidates the authority of sacred texts by upholding the secret in the sacredness, so that the differences between various religious traditions become the main subject of concern.

Third, I would like to raise the possibility of a discourse that interconnects the canon and its interpreters from subsequent periods by focusing on the interpretive style of the commentary. Generally speaking, once the canon is fixed as authoritative, it is considered difficult to shift. It therefore creates a gap for subsequent interpreters, often at the risk of their misunderstanding a scenario. As pointed out by Jonathan Z. Smith,[13] the form of commentary is a way of describing the means of filling the gap between the canon and the interpreter. This in turn enables the self-proclaimed canon to move beyond any notion of historicity or class, and in turn adapt and become relevant for people under various historical circumstances.

As a result, the canon, bequeathed with a trans-historical authority, which is sustained by the work of commentary, attains its significance so as to make people commit to it for the first time. By focusing on the form of the commentary, the aforementioned perspective is in fact subjected to criticism, as in the notion that the canon crosses historical periods to directly address its interpreters in the storehouse of "universal truth."

The privilege that the canon holds in the form of religious authority was overthrown by historical discourse. Although it cannot be claimed that the theorists who studied the topic of sacred texts were that self-aware, the theory of sacred texts opened the path into the evolution of existential hermeneutics through the discourse on commentary. Consequently, this not only put to question the authority of the space of the sacred text, but even more situated the interpreter's existence in the light of distinctive historical circumstances. It becomes possible to read the history of the human pursuit of interpreting sacred texts as a hermeneutics on the history of sacred texts.[14]

In Jon Davis and Isabel Wollaston's edited volume,[15] vibrant theories examining ideal sacred texts under historical circumstances are prevalent. Yet again, the history of acceptance in the Old Testament and Deuteronomy in particular, as explicated in Bernard M. Levinson's fascinating research,[16] unravels the dynamic relationship between the regulative power of the narrative in the text confirmed as the canon and the discursive possibility of transforming its meaning from the perspective of the interpreter. However, in such research on the form of commentary transforming alongside modernity, the process of dissipation in the authority of sacred texts, leading to its final end, has not been questioned. Therefore, one can argue that by not analyzing the debut process of the commentary transforming into the thesis, such works fail to problematize the form of the commentary as an emergent mode of thought.

Criticism of a Protestant-based view of the Bible, as the canon written by the spirit, runs through the three aforementioned arguments; namely, the belief in the canon as extending across periods and direct human sensorial experience, and as that which manifests only in the midst of its self-proclaimed exclusive desire for truth. Such a perspective of the canon, in terms of what is called Protestantism, amounts to a worldview that is signified in terms of a more confined and local form of religion which does not surmount historical and regional factors. In this manner, the theory of the canon is unmasked by utilizing the method of comparative religious studies, by comparing Islam, the religions of India, and of China.

This being the case, if one were to entertain the argument that sacred texts have arisen from inside European society, principally in the United States, then, on the one hand, what might be called "reflective scholarly activity," in terms of one's own religious tradition, begins to attain credence. On the other hand, as a result of this form of self-criticism, an uninformed methodology, irrespective of the religious and historical context, surfaces within religious studies—one which conflates non-Western religions and pre-Protestant Christianity's perspective on the sacred texts. Furthermore, with regard to the limited and fixed authority of the canon working to confine the confrontational tactics of pluralism in sacred texts, we are still left with an issue that has not been accounted for to the extent that it has been beyond the scope of examination—namely, what is the emergent form of the sacredness of the sacred text, or its revelatory quality, or the importance of annotating the historical circumstances of the interpreter's human condition? In order to overcome the methodological problems that are inherent within historical studies of religion, it becomes critical to address these concerns.

As we enter the twenty-first century, the theory of sacred texts has reached a point of stagnation. Unlike earlier periods, it has become difficult to sustain its relevance at the forefront of religious studies. Yet, in confronting the three main issues discussed above, and by going beyond the long-established criticism of Protestantism, it is possible to hope that the theory of sacred texts will again acquire a new significance in research. In this regard, this book focuses on exploring Japanese mythology and ancient oral texts. In doing so, it does not merely aim to elucidate supplementary material which uncovers a theoretical gap prevalent within studies of Islam, or of religion in India and China: areas which have been proclaimed as quintessential within research on sacred texts. Rather, it aims to open a new horizon for conceiving a method for comparative religious studies, and especially the inherited theoretical framework of Western-centric sacred texts, through a distinctively context-sensitive argument.

While various texts by the ancient Japanese royal court highlight the *Nihon shoki* and the *Kojiki*, the question arises whether a new significance can be upheld in researching the hermeneutics of the sacred texts, particularly in terms of the stagnation seen in the Western-centric theory of sacred texts. Herewith, I expound on this possibility as to how research on the Kiki can contribute a new dimension to research on Western sacred texts, along three lines of argument.

The first point concerns the capacity for restoring the comparative analysis of oral and written texts. It was the predominant belief that the *Kojiki*'s and *Nihon shoki*'s origin rested in an oral tradition, that they were originally developed as a form of recitation, and were gradually replaced by the written text, a view formally discussed in Watsuji Tetsurō's (1889–1960) *Nihon kodai bunka* (Japan's Ancient Culture).[17] Although in ancient Japan, with the influx of kanji characters from mainland China, a written culture existed for the first time among the intelligentsia in the country's culturally prosperous regions, the process of including the content rooted in a primordial Japanese culture resulted in a national attempt to interconnect the Kiki (at its origin) and the idea of a "Pure Japanese Culture." In other words, a retroactive mode of thought focused on these written records prior to being influenced by Chinese culture, whereby the pre-inscribed legend of each text would emerge.

Against this predominant movement from oral tradition to written record, while claiming to restore the historical process of the formation of the text in terms of the emergence of its inscription, there materializes a new point of view, one structurally proclaiming that the Kiki display the consistency of a distinct unified work. This perspective has been addressed by Kōnoshi Takamitsu,[18] among others, and has attained strong support today. According to this perspective, to inscribe implies that one has decided to fix the content of the text, in terms of the fluid and fragmentary form of various texts that have mutual relevance, in order to form an edited, unified, systematic text. Certainly, on the one hand, the script as imbibed, fixed, and formalized enabled the formation of the canon. Yet, on the other hand, it is important not to forget the dynamism and fluidity embodied and instilled by new historical records or oral texts. It is apparent that even after the configuration of the canon, there were various texts that existed simultaneously and which, even if inscribed at a given time, were not completely fixed as a result.[19]

Second, with regard to the prospect of restoring numerous sacred texts as opposed to the distinctive canon, it can be said that in Japan, in a parallel sense to Western sacred texts, the canon signified the text which was coterminous with national history, as apparent in the *Kojiki* and the *Nihon shoki* (the edited texts dealing with the eighth-century Yamato reign). Yet, prior to this reign, myths or traditions were preserved within each family clan, as explicated by Miyake Kazuo, among others, which attested to the existence of diversity and of distinctive texts which bore historical authority.[20]

Certainly, this line of argument begs us to ask: amidst various sacred texts, how did the canon (namely, the *Kojiki* or the *Nihon shoki*) come to be selected and edited? I am alluding here to the process of canonization, which Tsuda Sōkichi (1873–1961) discusses in his classical study *Nihon koten no kenkyū* (Research on Japanese Classics)[21] with regard to research on the Kiki. Furthermore, in taking the argument one step further, one is prompted to ask: how should we see the various sacred texts as gaining mutual relevance while existing at the same time, particularly in the periods preceding and following the formation of the canon?[22] In this light, along the lines of Ishimoda Shō's (1912–86) work, why was it important for the canon (as the *Kojiki* and the *Nihon shoki*) to be crystallized in the eighth century, and in what way did the political argument for the formation of the canon become connected to the history of the formation of the ancient nation? Furthermore, once the authority of the canon materialized (alongside the ancient nation's collapse), in what way did it relate to the new social environment? Investigating the canon's role and social function from a historical point of view, as a text located at the core of national authority upholding a political ideology, is an important specialization in historical research on Japan.[23] In fact, such inquiry has attained its relevance in the wider social context today when one examines the prevalent views that advocate a literal interpretation of the Bible, as in the close connection between American Evangelism and Bush's power, or the relationship between Islamic fundamentalism and terrorism.

Henceforth, in connection to Evangelism, especially in terms of the contemporary period, I would like to point out that Japanese researchers examining sacred texts dating from ancient times to the middle ages (namely, the *Kojiki* or the *Nihon shoki*) have founded themselves on the belief that the motive for the formation of the canon can "actually" be unearthed. In other words, between the text and the interpreter there comes about an estrangement in meaning, and this very impossibility to clarify meaning has not been sufficiently recognized, given that the text is only partially comprehensible within a distinct historical perspective, the horizon, as it were, of the interpreter, namely, where an individual is situated.[24]

In this vein, it becomes critical to contend that a text's literal meaning has a predetermined existence. In other words, one can infer that the interpreter's wish to embrace this literal meaning is synonymous to a naive positivism. Furthermore, if one were to argue along the lines of the theory of sacred texts, this disposition is no better than a believer's literal interpretation of a text, which enables him to listen to a divine voice directly (namely, prediscursively). As explicated below, today's researchers have to recognize, more than ever, the implications of the impossibility of determining the meaning of a text via any method of comprehension.

Third, I shall discuss the function of commentary as it gains significance in terms of the manner that the canon has endured through different eras. One can state that regardless of the restrictions due to canon fixation, the interpreter or even the reader becomes tied to a given period. In this regard, the formation of the canon in disparate periods gets intertwined with a given form which adapts to each era's categorization of the means of comprehension. Kōnoshi Takamitsu's ambitious work[25] outlining a means of interpreting the Kiki's annotated history attains its critical significance for having raised this perspective.

Certainly, the function of commentary for the most part concerned a connection to rationality. Yet, conversely, as Maruyama Masao elaborates pertinently,[26] this principle or essentialist movement emerges because the sacredness of the canon serves to protect the impairment of reason. In any case, by focusing on the commentary style and form, it becomes critical to examine the vantage point from which research on the Kiki to date has occurred; research transformed from asking what is actually written in the Kiki (amounting to an essentialist form of questioning), to how the Kiki is interpreted (amounting to a hermeneutic form of questioning).

However, even if one were to use the method of historical interpretation discussed thus far, it becomes impossible to re-experience the self as being inherent to a given commentary of the texts. Therein, it is important to be aware of the fact that the depiction which constitutes the interpreted history is in itself nothing other than that which is precisely constituted in terms of the immediacy of the contemporary moment. The gap between the text and the interpreter is not one that translates merely as the fissure between the canon or sacred texts and the interpreter, but also, without exception, includes the latent gap between the commentary and the interpreter, and the practice of reading various texts and especially the practice of writing a variety of texts. Furthermore, what becomes important here is to be careful not to restore the historical transformation in the interpreter's worldview as a part of the conclusion in the interpretive history of the commentary on the canon and other sacred texts. If one were to construct such an argument, the annotated study would become solely a means of elucidating a period- or class-based worldview.

Why is it that in the midst of a long history, we tend to lose sight of the peculiar form of thought which constitutes the commentary? Or yet, within the practice of commentary, why is it that we lose sight of the transformation of idealistic thought? In this regard, it becomes important to distinguish clearly the style of commentary constituting the history of interpretation and the consequence of accepting an interpreter's worldview. This is relevant because of the belief that it is impossible to violate the sacredness of the text through a form of commentary. By this, I am not implying that the practice of interpreting the texts should be to explicate the point of view of the interpreter. Rather, it is to elucidate the interpreter's act of entering the world of the sacred text, which can minimally be understood as resonant with an interpreter's consciousness. Yet, once having reached this point, and given the lack of concern over such matters within contemporary research on the Kiki, it is difficult to restore the text in terms of the interpreter's historical circumstances and in turn to re-read with a set disposition.

In the current age, to generalize, a dissertation-like style of thought has emerged, instead of and amidst the dissipation of the commentary style, which dismantles the authority of sacred texts and instills the practice of making relevant and comprehending the interpreter's perspective. In comprehending the past, textual descriptions have been thought of as bare facts. While only fragmentary facts are described in the text, by combining various pieces from different texts, the interpreter's perception proceeds to discover a means of understanding the real truth underlying the text—namely, a hypothetical invisible space whereby "history" gets severed from the text and a belief in the historical credibility of the sacred text itself is undermined. If one were to return to the dilemma regarding the authority of sacred texts, the sacredness upheld by the texts in the past, at least in terms of Japanese mythology and oral traditions, ruptures with modernity when the space of "history" fractures into independent historical truths, in other words, which was sustained by the thought that the facts imagined as historical origin and the texts are synonymous.[27]

In this manner, while the theory of the sacred text from the past is continually reinterpreted, the question as to what constitutes sacredness surfaces as a large thematic issue.[28] In considering the challenges in the study of the Kiki, an interest in the historical origin of the distinct name "Japan" keeps emerging as an issue in terms of the authenticity of sacred texts. This prompts one to ask: what does the desire to return to the origin, which Mircea Eliade termed "nostalgia,"[29] actually amount to? In other words, what is the desire to endorse the appropriation of what constitutes "Japan" as a living world, in terms of historical truths? Certainly, as a result of contact with the modern Western world, Japanese mythology, an idea often linked to the Kiki, emerges as the result of two Western concepts—nationalism and mythology.[30]

The concept of nation or mythology, on one hand, is nothing more than a modern invention or artificial product. Yet, on the other hand, it is an indisputable fact that the historical origin of the concept of "Japan" is precisely what the majority of people have clung to across different periods. Surely, what the term "Japan" constitutes at any given period cannot be imagined as anything other than a phantasmal discourse,[31] namely, a motivational force in the discursive space spanning the history of Kiki interpretation which repeatedly adheres to a sense of origin. After all, interpreters of sacred texts (and people at large interpreting such texts) are always impelled to elucidate an unsolvable riddle in order to surpass the impossibility of extracting meaning from texts. Even if this were the case, we should not conceive their interpretation as prejudice or illusion, given that the idea of Japan's historical origin (a common notion ceaselessly alluring people) is not predetermined and does not characterize a permanent substance. Rather, the resonance in the voices of various interpretations with regard to one subject, an idea echoing Hans-Georg Gadamer's notion of "the working history of interpretation,"[32] makes it critical to examine the discursive space (on origins) accumulating over 1300 years or more.

In hermeneutics to date, the question as to how diligently one reads the texts emerges in the continual attempt to retrieve the original text. In contrast, "the working history of interpretation" draws out the reciprocal function of interpreting the subject and object without restoring the issue as being one-sided in its relevance, so that, in the act of the subject engaging with the object, a shared mutual space is established. In turn, the reciprocating functional movement is witnessed when the textual meaning evoked transforms at the same time as the interpreter's horizon.

Publishing this book in English significantly strengthens the possibility of reframing the debate over the study of Kiki and situating the persistent fascination with origins within a comparative framework. The relationship of legends and the identity of a people is a subject that has been and continues to be discursively constructed and invoked with a lurid sense of power across geographies and religious traditions. To shape a theoretical lens for analyzing the various interpretations of the Kiki over the ages, in the form of a discourse and the materiality of its content, allows a comparative commentary on the way that the "sacredness" of sacred texts withstands the test of time and the space of origins.

At this point, I would like to outline the contents of this book. Chapter 1, "National History, Shintō, and Myth: General Remarks on the History of the Interpretation of the Kiki," is a broad outline of the entire argument of the book, as apparent from the subtitle. The chapter describes how the Kiki was understood in terms of the horizon of interpretation that emerged following the act of fixing the canon in ancient times, the medieval period, and the modern period, arguing that the study of the sacred text developed in the progression from its being upheld as the "canon," a "sacred text," a "commentary," and a "dissertation." Although the history of interpreting the Kiki is complex, in a general sense, in accordance with the actual circumstances of the different eras, the sacred text attained authority as "national history" in ancient times, as "Shinto" in medieval times, and as "myth" in modern times.

The political authority associated with the Kiki's ancient regal power, whereby a literal belief in its textual descriptions ensured its credibility in the ancient social arena, diminishes in the transition to medieval times. In a gradual process, the textual content begins to bear greater religious implication in terms of the human heart. Subsequently, in modern times, by fully differentiating itself from the question of historical credibility, the Kiki comes to be perceived as fiction or as human invention. Over the course of time, through this process whereby the ancient political authority loses control over the canon, the Kiki diffuses into Japanese society through various agents who freely interpret and compile the edited versions. Although this process shows the trials and tribulations of excavating, yet admonishing, the ancient political authority, these various acts of reconciling the gap between the sacred text and the interpreter (in accordance with each period) amount to a reflection on the continual desire to find the historical origin of contact. Finally, with the debut of modern history, the authority of sacred texts is thoroughly criticized, and a "historical" space that is completely separate from the descriptions in the texts emerges. Yet, one must not ignore the fact that the desire to return to historical origins continues to be preserved.

Chapter 2, "The Canon and Variants: An Examination of the Mythology of Susanowo," discusses the apparent form of ancient mythology and oral tradition as typified in the Kiki. There has been a debate for over 1300 years, from the Kiki's inception up until the current age, as to why the successively edited *Kojiki* and *Nihon shoki* of the seventh century reveal a conflict in their descriptive content despite being edited versions of the very same Yamato royal prerogative. In this context, and consistently, the implicit presupposition is that the *Kojiki* and the *Nihon shoki* were originally based on the same mythology and legend which, as time elapsed, adopted different means of transmission and as a result were differentiated. In that respect, the history of Kiki interpretation has been engaged in restorative work based on the belief that if one were to tactfully combine the *Kojiki* and the *Nihon shoki*, then it would become possible to retrieve the original genuine myth and legend. In contrast, I explicate in this chapter that the Yamato kingdom's mythology and legend, from its inception, while centering on the same theme, inhabited a differentiated structure. Despite the fact that the various texts were perceived as being equally relevant, the respective holders' conscious orientation supposed that the differentiated structure amounted to a form of corruption that was derivative of the genuine myth and legend. In turn, they propounded the belief that their own textual form or interpretation would make it possible to restore the unadulterated content. In this form of textual differentiation, the discrepancy between the objective condition and an interpreter's subjective consciousness all the more provokes the desire to return to the original text, which never actualizes. This desire fermenting in successive generations of interpreters sustains the perpetually unaccomplished task of interpreting the Kiki.

Chapter 3, "Myth in Metamorphosis: Ancient and Medieval Versions of the Yamatotakeru Legend," elaborates the manner in which the various texts dating back to the origin of the ancient period and invoking the legendary hero Yamatotakeru as their subject material, which legitimated the status of the *Nihon shoki* as the ancient regime's canon, depreciated in social standing from the latter part of the ancient period to the medieval period. In accordance with this shift in significance, the chapter questions the way that the text which highlights Yamatotakeru was re-edited; how this involved incorporating the *Kojiki* or even the *fudoki*, compiled in accordance with the ancient regime, and the distinct *ujibumi* held by each clan which were written down in the latter part of the ancient period. In the ancient period, the canon was fixed through its unyielding power to literally regulate a character or phrase. In turn, alongside the royal kingdom's political plight, it can be surmised that alternative textual phraseology attained more credence, whereby the canon's legend was reinterpreted into other successively emerging texts which resonated with a differing narrative. Yet again, in the midst of the reign, the story of Yamatotakeru, the protagonist, and his father, and the narrative logic of his emotional conflict, were considered an important subject; it might be called the ancient royal kingdom's claim to rule via the process of instilling reality into political advocacy.

Subsequently, as the ancient regime was dismantling, what is deemed to be the character Yamatotakeru decreases in interest, while the text's primary theme and leveraging point transforms to focus on the cultural dimension of what is considered his most treasured possession, the sword Kusanagi-no-Tsurugi. This refers to the historical legitimacy bequeathed in exposing the treasured sword, which is considered an object with supernatural powers, or symbolizing greater spirituality. This chapter unravels the power-ridden dynamics to control and interpret the canon of ancient Japan alongside the real circumstances underwriting historical transitions.

Chapter 4, "Myth and Rationality: Understanding God in the Early-Modern and Modern Period," elucidates the movement to rationalize the Kiki legend in pre-modern and modern times. In the pre-modern period, the *Nihon shoki*'s canonical power to regulate concretely slackens when the actual existence of different deities, namely, the credible description of the age of the gods, is put in doubt by Confucian scholars unraveling a rationalist critique. However, this process does not completely refute the description of the age of the gods. Rather, the deities depicted in the Kiki are thought to connote an honorific means of describing people who actually existed, and through the act of engaging in interpretation, a sense of authenticity (as bestowed upon the texts) is maintained. Nonetheless, this form of interpretation, by what might be called a Confucian intelligentsia, is opposed by Kokugaku, Nativism that resembles a type of romanticism, claiming that human reason is nothing other than a form of overconfidence and arrogance. Even if one did not comprehend this rationally, this form of essentialist interpretation, leading to the emergence of a belief in the literal interpretation of the Kiki, admonishes excessive modes of reasoning. Herein, an aporia surfaces, whereby one would have to sacrifice an interpreter's ability to reason in order to preserve the Kiki's literal credibility.

In the modern period, this question critically problematizes the prerogative of the national government or the conservative ruling class constituting the citizen's identity as founded in the Kiki. Yet, in the period beginning in 1910 and leading into the 1920s, the historian of East Asia Tsuda Sōkichi's notion of a psychological interpretation influenced by Western mythology allows for a credible means of reinterpreting the Kiki's description of the age of gods regardless of its physical existence. From this perspective, such descriptions are conceived as a mental production of the sixth-century Yamato kingdom, whereby the fiction that is contained as a part of the psychological reality is reinterpreted to co-exist alongside the criticism grounded in modern reasoning. In other words, in the period from the pre-modern to the modern era, as rationalism deepens, the authority of the Kiki, which at one point confronts a crisis, is sustained. Through this process, in terms of absolute rationalism, mythology in the modern period is regenerated. Yet, Tsuda's criticism does not merely pertain to the age of the gods. Rather, its immeasurable influence concerns the entire narrative of the Kiki, inclusive of the age of humanity, which is surmised as an artificial invention of the intelligentsia during the sixth-century Yamato reign rather than being the fruition of a nationalistic spirit. In this manner, the chapter relates how, beginning in the pre-modern era, a conundrum surrounding the Kiki and its credibility unfolds in light of the physical existence of the various mythologized gods, which resurfaces in terms of constituting the story of national character as a part of modern national identity.

Chapter 5, "Myth and Nationalism: Motoori Norinaga's Creation Myths," traces the Kiki legend during the transition from the pre-modern to the modern era, from having been under the custody of the ancient royal class to beginning to appeal to a national subjectivity and consciousness, in terms of the interpretation of Motoori Norinaga's (1730–1801) creation myth by pre-modern proponents of Nativism. Originally, the Kiki legitimates the ascendance of the ruling class under the Yamato royalty, who gain control over the Japanese archipelago and the southern part of the Korean peninsula. The body of the legend concerns one specific region limited to the Yamato reign and its span of control over the people residing in the Japanese archipelago. Therein, Motoori's commentary attempts to induce a re-reading of the text as the tale of historical origin concerning the entire population residing in the Japanese archipelago. In other words, in order to reconstitute the legend so that it pertains to the entire national community, it becomes critical to make it possible for the respective constituents, belonging to distinct communities, to withstand at their own volition that which is construed as being fundamental to the Japanese people, namely, two emotional dispositions that are seen as being original and authentic, *mono no aware* (the emotional feeling aroused when moved by something, what can be termed "an aesthetic empathy toward things") and *makoto no michi* (the path of sincerity). The former notion implies an acute sensitivity to the expression of one's feelings and, at the same time, the capacity to sympathize with others. Through the act of being self-aware within such dynamics, the entire nation materializes into an empathizing community. On the other hand, the latter notion espouses a fair-minded attitude toward others and in doing so advocates national authority under the emperor, as a central figure, and his surrounding subordinates. Consequently, this formulation allows one to imagine the original and authentic national community referred to as "Japan," which becomes emotionally bound and reciprocally filled with compassion. For Motoori, "the aesthetic empathy toward things" and "the path to sincerity" refer to a natural characteristic of the people of Japan, whereby he expounds on the history of the imperial theocracy as a model that reflects the emotional disposition of the populace, which in turn bestows credence on the *Kojiki* and the *Nihon shoki* as sacred texts. In this manner, the Kiki are reinterpreted by Motoori as texts asserting the historical origins of the national community which transforms with the imminent modern era. Coterminously, through this process, the imperial theocracy that marks the central axis in the Kiki's depictions is conceived as and designated to be a national symbol aligning the modern nation state.

Chapter 6, "The Space of Historical Discourse: Ishimoda Shō's Theory of the Heroic Age," is set in the period following Japan's defeat in World War II, with the Allied Occupation as its backdrop. It expounds on how Marxist historiography, introduced into Japan in order to critique the imperial claim to an ethnic identity, began to sink into nationalism again through its interpretation of the Kiki. In this period, the leading Marxist historiographer, Ishimoda Shō, constitutes an argument in his article "Eiyujidairon" (On the Heroic Age in Ancient Japan), which incorporates the Marxist line of critique over imperial theocracy. In this work, Ishimoda attempts to reveal the tenacity with which the orientation rooted in the ubiquitous desire to return to historical origins prevails. As a result, this inclination that Ishimoda establishes, which he claims results from an awareness of the individualized personal dimension to national history, critically contributes to postwar historical discourse leading up to that point in terms of its narrative framework.[33] This process of historical etymology that explores origins, and entices a people's imagination to reach beyond the memory ascertainable through written records, constitutes an imaginary space reflecting an interpreter's ideal community. For Ishimoda, this implies the Heroic Age commencing in the ancient period, or what might be called the golden age, that propounds a balance between individual autonomy, as embodied by the patriot, and the whole community, as its beneficiary.

This orientation to historical origins focuses on the *Kojiki* and the *Nihon shoki* as being the oldest historical documents of Japan, which engage not merely Marxist historiographers but a plethora of interpreters successively from the ancient period to modern times. The *Kojiki* and the *Nihon shoki*, which bestow historical truth on an ethnic national identity and additionally legitimate the imperial theocracy, uphold a hidden dimension concerning the nostalgia for historical origins with respect to a given period and sustain the meaning of national existence (in spite of its transformations) over a long period of time. Above all else, the texts provide evidence that an orientation to historical origins has always existed within people in a resolute manner. As elaborated in this book, one can surmise that the history of the interpretation of the Kiki demonstrates the manner in which a new era comes to be accepted through the trials of grasping one's conscience and the ability to establish critical distance in terms of the orientation to historical origins. In becoming self-aware of one's relentless desire to return to historical origins, namely, of an impulse critically constituting primordial elements as the truth, the practice of historical inquiry sets itself free from the notion of historical essentialism which espouses an incessant link to the primal. Consequently, the meaning of existence is positioned variously, in terms of the distinct moments that make up what is considered "current times." This formulation points to the dynamic elements at the forefront of what might be termed "immanent historiography."[34]

1 National History, Shintō, and Myth: General Remarks on the History of the Interpretation of the Kiki

Approaches to Japanese Mythology

Japanese mythology is typically identified with the *Kojiki* (Record of Ancient Matters) and *Nihon shoki* (Chronicle of Japan), which together are referred to as the Kiki. The works record the history of the Yamato kingdom and its rule, which extended throughout the Kinki region of Japan. Both were compiled, the *Kojiki* in 712 and the *Nihon shoki* in 720, when the Ritsuryō state (statutory system), which adopted the Chinese legal codes and institutions, was nearing completion. Both texts begin with tales of deities, narratives that are understood as myths today. Moreover, in the modern period, the Kiki texts have been understood in relation to the Western notion of "myth." This urges us to question the way that this concept has been applied (noting that the term "myth" is not contained in the Kiki), and, consequently, how our understanding of the texts has been transformed.

Until recently, the study of Japanese mythology has been guided by the question of how to read the *Kojiki* and *Nihon shoki* in a self-referential manner. In other words, the texts alone have provided the assumed framework for all readings, and their significance within the discursive space of distinct historical periods has rarely been examined. This issue has been neglected by the two primary streams of interpretation in the postwar period. One stream, involving the Marxist historians Ishimoda Shō (1912–86) and Tōma Seita (1913–), who were influenced by Hegel, invokes a perspective on the materiality that originates from "the theory of the Heroic Age."[1] This resulted from their re-reading the Kiki texts in terms of the memory of a primitive ethnic community dating back to pre-imperial times. The second stream involves Kōnoshi Takamitsu (1946–), a scholar of Japanese literature, and Mizubayashi Takeshi (1947–), a political historian.[2] Their orientation distinguishes the *Kojiki* and *Nihon shoki* as texts, attributing a distinct structure and coherence that one can say informs today's main current of thought.

While issues of memory and amnesia within historical discourse, like the revisionist debate over the Holocaust or the Nanking Massacre, have been extensively discussed within the field of modern history,[3] likewise, regardless of the theme or time period, the predicament resulting from the annihilation of historical material confronts all fields of research. In this regard, one can conjecture that many written and orally transmitted narratives that have not been preserved must have existed alongside the Kiki texts. While the Kiki represented just one part of the whole discursive space of history in the ancient period, it worked to regulate other writings and oral traditions in an overarching manner.

Current research methods that discuss ancient Japanese mythology by focusing solely on the Kiki betray a textual approach that was once representative of the modern nation-state. An early manifestation of this textual approach can be seen in the works of Yoshimi Yoshikazu (1673–1761), a late Tokugawa period scholar belonging to Yamazaki Ansai's Suika Shintō school. Yoshimi distinguished historical sources that clearly stated the date of composition and the names of authors from texts, including oral transmissions, whose origins were uncertain. For example, he rejected the Ise Shintō[4] claim that the enshrined deity of the Outer Shrine, a shrine with close ties to the imperial house, was in fact Kuni-Tokotachi-no-mikoto by appealing to classical sources whose dates of composition were certain:

> It is clear that the Outer Shrine originally did not enshrine Kuni-Tokotachi-no-mikoto. Those who make such claims believe only unofficial histories and mixed theories; they do not consult the state histories and official pronouncements...Not a single word that pronounces Kuni-Tokotachi-no-mikoto the enshrined deity of the Outer Shrine can be found in the true material records.[5]

As a result, it was determined that the Five Books of (Ise) Shintō (*Shintō gobusho*) and the Shintō texts of the Yoshida house, contrary to what was proclaimed, were not ancient. Instead, the *Nihon shoki* was granted higher status and proclaimed to be an authentic ancient source. Yoshimi declared that the familial documents which had been submitted to the court and the clan (*uji*) records that originally functioned to connect specific groups to the Kiki texts were inauthentic. During the early-modern period, the Kiki were separated from clan and family transmissions. In the process these texts became the repositories of national memory that was no longer connected to specific groups or families.

Subsequently, after Yoshimi, there was a time when scholars of Nativism applauded the *Kojiki* above all other texts. As the modern state founded on the imperial system (*tennōsei kokka*) took shape in the nineteenth century, accounts derived from the Kiki appeared as official history in state-sponsored textbooks. Thus, the Kiki functioned as the source of historical identity among national subjects (*kokumin*) and as the memory of a pure and continuous ethnic community (*minzoku*). One can say that already, by the late eighteenth century, Motoori Norinaga (1730–1801) had reinterpreted the Musuhi-no-kami (the deity enabling creation) in the Kiki as signifying the origin of all things, including human beings,[6] stating:

> All living things in this world…instinctively know well and perform those acts which they must each perform, and this all comes about through the august spirit of the Musuhi-no-kami. Human beings are born into this world as especially gifted beings.[7]

Let us now turn to the question of how the Kiki texts functioned in the ancient and medieval periods. What follows is an examination of how the Kiki were related to clan traditions (*ujibumi*) and familial records (*kachō*), Kiki commentaries, and Shintōist texts (*Shintōsho*). In the process, we will also discuss the transformation of the discursive space that signified these works over time.

Kōnoshi Takamitsu[8] and Isomae Jun'ichi, among others, have researched the history of Kiki interpretation in order to trace the distinct worldviews that have been reflected onto the texts. Such approaches have tended to compare individual texts in a chronologically arranged fashion. However, non-Japanese scholars of world religions have brought to light the discursive space of interaction surrounding such written documents by introducing the three textual categories of canon, scripture, and commentary. As a result, texts such as the Bible or Confucian classics, which had previously been considered orthodox in an unchallenged manner, have been re-examined.[9] Thus, scholars today refer to the "canonization process" rather than to the notion of a predetermined canon. It became apparent that applying this methodological approach to the Kiki would yield critical insights. Henceforth, in order to understand the historical nature of our present-day understanding of the Kiki, which also informs the horizon of our own contemporary research, the modern textual category referred to as the "scholarly essay" (constituting the fourth textual category) will also be examined.

The Ancient Discursive Space

As already noted, the Kiki were compiled in close relation to the establishment of the Ritsuryō state's ruling structure. Although scholars have pointed out structural differences in the stories of the *Kojiki* and *Nihon shoki*, both texts sought to legitimate the hegemonic rule of the state founded on the imperial system. Let us first examine the foundational myth.

In the beginning, the order-less world divided into heaven and earth, and in the midst a solitary deity emerged. After several generations, the male deity Izanagi and the female deity Izanami materialized and gave birth to all things, including the land which was the Japanese archipelago, with its mountains, rivers, grass, and trees. In addition, three additional principal gods, Amaterasu Ōmikami, Tsukiyomi-no-mikoto, and Susanowo-no-mikoto, were born. Amaterasu ruled the heavens as the sun goddess and provided order to the mythical world of the Kiki, as the ancestral deity to the imperial house. The story goes on to provide an account of the origin of mortal death in the conflict between Izanagi and Izanami, and furthermore elaborates on the cycle of day and night as emerging from the battle between Tsukiyomi-no-mikoto, the moon god, and Amaterasu, the sun goddess.

Eventually, the grandson of Amaterasu, Ho-no-Ninigi-no-mikoto (a name referring to maturing ears of rice) descended from the heavenly realm to the earthly sphere, where he pacified the deities of the earth, represented by Ōkuninushi-no-mikoto. The stories involving the *kami* end by demonstrating that the descendants of Ho-no-Ninigi-no-mikoto (i.e., the emperors) possess the authority to rule the Japanese archipelago. The narrative then moves from the age of deities to the age of humans, recounting how successive emperors, beginning with Emperor Jimmu, and princes, such as Yamatotakeru, brought the Japanese islands (and perhaps even the Korean peninsula) under military, religious, and political control.

We should note from the outset that the texts were not intended for the subservient population but rather the aristocracy and the officials in the Yamato court. As Tsuda Sōkichi (1873–1961) has pointed out, the concept of divinity (*kami*) within the Kiki reveals a strong influence of Chinese Confucianism and is indicative of a clear conceptual bent that should have differed significantly from popular notions of the divine at the time.[10] Furthermore, the characters within the Kiki belong largely to the imperial house and to the ruling elite, whereas other groups merely appear as objects of conquest.[11]

From the Nara period (710–84) through the early Heian period (794–1185), lectures on commentaries of the Japanese Chronicles (*Nihongi kōsho*, approximately dated 721–965) were produced periodically for the central aristocracy in order to create a unified textual understanding of the Ritsuryō state.[12] There is no evidence that the commoners in regional villages, or the *bemin* slaves belonging to particular clans, read or were even informed about the Kiki.

In other words, the Kiki texts did not propagate the cultural unity of the subservient masses from the perspective of the ruling elite, as apparent in the modern nation-state. Rather, the texts were compiled to shape the communal memory of the ruling class. This is also apparent from the fact that the imperial chronicles (*teiki*) and ancient tales (*kuji*), which originally formed the basis for the Kiki texts, were selected from familial documents belonging to distinct clans (*shizoku/ujizoku*). This is how it is described in the *teiki* and *kuji* in relation to Emperor Tenmu's reign.[13]

Let us further examine the relationship between the Kiki and the ruling class of the Yamato court. At the time, the term Kiki was never employed. Instead, six texts were referred to as "state histories" (*kokushi*), which included the *Nihon shoki* but not the *Kojiki*. To be precise, the status of the *Nihon shoki* as opposed to the *Kojiki* was evident. The *Nihon shoki* was included as the first book of Six National Histories (*rikkokushi*), while the *Kojiki*, regardless of the original intent behind its compilation, was understood merely as a variant of the *Nihon shoki*.[14] In fact, by late antiquity, the *Kojiki* was hardly read at all.

At the same time, the historical discourse propounded by the Ritsuryō state was not restricted to state histories, but included familial records (*kachō*) and clan transmissions (*ujibumi*). As stated in the *Shoku Nihon shoki* "these things [articles of *Shoku Nihon shoki*] are recorded in detail in the state histories and familial records."[15] Each clan possessed its own tradition that had been transmitted and had thereby incorporated passages from the *Nihon shoki*. As a result, the clan claimed to hold an intimate relationship with the imperial house, which then extended to include the state. We can see this structure within the *Kogoshūi* (Gleanings from Ancient Stories; compiled 807) of the Inbe clan,[16] in the *Takahashi ujibumi* (compiled approximately 789) of the Takahashi clan,[17] and in the familial histories included in the *Shinsen shōjiroku* (compiled 815)[18] and the Six National Histories. To illustrate such textual relations, let us examine a passage from the *Nihon shoki* alongside the corresponding passage from the *Kogoshūi*.

> Takamimusubi-no-mikoto spoke and said, "we have raised *Amatsuhimoroki* (tree to worship heavenly deities) and *Amatsuiwasaka* (rock to worship heavenly deities) to bless our descendants. You two deities, Ame-no-Koyane-no-mikoto and Futodama-no-mikoto, descend to the Middle Land of the Reed Plains and bless our descendants. You two deities, both serve within the palace and guard it well." He also spoke and said, "Take the ear of rice from the sanctified garden of our Plain of High Heaven and give it to our children."....For this reason, Ame-no-Koyane-no-mikoto and Futodama-no-mikoto, and the gods of the leading families with them, gave rice to all. (*Nihon shoki*)[19]

In comparison, *Kogoshūi* states:

> Amatsumioya Amaterasu Ōhokami, Tamamimusuhi-no-mikoto thus spoke and said, "We have raised Amatsuhimoroki and Amatsuiwasaka to bless our descendants. You two deities, Ame-no-Koyane-no-mikoto and Futodama-no-mikoto, descend to the Middle Land of the Reed Plains and bless our descendants. You two deities both serve within the palace and guard it well. Take the ear of rice from the sanctified garden of our Plain of High Heaven and give it to our children. *Futodama-no-mikoto, lead the gods of the leading*

families and serve your lord, and do according to the command of heaven." Thus the various gods also came to serve.[20]

In this passage that closely mirrors the language of the *Nihon shoki*, the *Kogoshūi* inserts a section (italicized in the original) wherein only the ancestor of the Inbe clan, Futodama-no-mikoto, is honored. Previous research has tended to view sections that do not overlap with the Kiki as the actual transmissions of the clans, while the overlapping sections have been understood as falsifications produced subsequent to the Kiki texts. However, such an understanding reflects the unconstructive effects of modern-day research that focuses solely on the Kiki, which at the same time treats the clan transmissions as mere variants of the Kiki, thereby overlooking the differences that are prevalent with regard to the social function of the two texts. The function of the clan transmissions and the familial records was to chronicle the history of each group's service to the court, which as a result fulfilled a political purpose in advocating the legitimacy of a given clan's respective social position within the court. Although the example above comes from the Heian period, there are many cases recorded in the Six National Histories, including a dispute between the Takahashi clan and the Azumi clan[21] concerning the office of the imperial messenger who delivered offerings to Ise Shrine, and with regard to the alteration of clan names, whereby clan and familial records were appealed to as substantial documents. The state's basis for arbitrating such disputes concerned the extent to which a given clan's traditions concurred with the Six National Histories, including the *Nihon shoki*, and the Ritsuryō code.

Against this backdrop, the Six National Histories including *Nihon shoki*, which were proclaimed to be the "historical canon" of the state, came to control the historical consciousness in clan and familial records belonging to members of the court (via the terms/words utilized).[22] However, conversely, given that the familial records and clan transmissions (unlike the Kiki) were not closed records, they developed their own unique narratives which were not included in state histories and consequently devised connections to passages in the Six National Histories. As long as the group that was represented actually existed, the records remained open texts which accumulated new narratives through time while being reformulated at each opportunity (enabled, for example, via submitting records to the state). The structure of the *Takahashi ujibumi* (a document explaining the origins of court offices held by the Takahashi clan) and the production process of the *Nakaomi honkeichō* (the genealogy of the Nakaomi clan) both exhibit a configuration of ongoing supplementation.

The expansion of the Ritsuryō state was accompanied by an increase in the number of officials. As the state's rule reached into the lower strata of society, the number of familial traditions that were regulated by the authority professed through the Six National Histories seem to have increased as well. This is evident from the large number of familial traditions included in the *Shinsen shōjiroku*, compiled in 815.

In summary, as national histories such as the *Nihon shoki* materialized, the memory of the state solidified as the canon within the ruling class, while individual clan histories developed in a distinct yet conjunctive manner. The clan records and familial documents submitted to the court functioned as a bridge between the constitutive memory of the state and the disparate memory of clans. Consequently, due to the manner that memory in the ancient period extensively spread to include clan records and familial documents that existed concurrently, national histories were proclaimed as authoritative texts, denoting that the quintessential lineage of the ancient court was justified to grant social legitimacy to a distinct clan. In other words, only when the memory of each family was woven into the state narrative was it considered legitimate. One can state that this dual structure, with the confined memory of the state, on the one hand, and the plethora of memories of various families, on the other hand, constituted the formation of history in antiquity.

The modern understanding of the Kiki thus merely captures the homogenous and compounded memory prescribed by the state. As the ancient court lost political power, the Kiki texts were no longer required in order to determine the social status of court officials in relation to clan transmissions and familial records. Instead, the Kiki came to represent the comprehensive memory of a nation that ruled over society. One can surmise that in antiquity, those whose origins did not directly intersect with the Kiki, or regional authorities whose memories were excluded from the Six National Histories, would have possessed dissimilar histories founded on private traditions.

One final point must be made regarding the position of the Kiki in antiquity. In the past, a number of scholars within the field of religious studies have sought to discover the origins of myths within rituals, based on the understanding that the two forms of expression/practice are closely related. In this regard, in Japan, the Kiki narratives are understood to be myths, but the *Engishiki* (a text from the mid-Heian period) is understood to be a ritual text. In contrast to this perspective, what becomes important to understand is the different function the two texts served within the ancient Yamato dynasty, rather than a theory tracing their respective origins. While the divine names and tales recorded in the *Engishiki* are partially distinct from the Kiki, both texts represent a commonly held worldview or *Weltanschauung*. On the one hand, as already noted, the Kiki were recognized as historical texts that regulated the clan traditions within ancient society. The *Engishiki*, on the other hand, contained prayers that the emperor, as the descendant of heavenly deities, would need to recite while facing the spectrum of gods inhabiting Japan, so as to instill peace in the land, ensure a bountiful harvest, and request one's own (the emperor's) spiritual wellbeing. In other words, strictly speaking, the Kiki were texts that declared historical origins and as such were expected to perform the function of regulating clan histories. In turn, the *Engishiki* was a religious text recording human practices directed towards the deities, including the performances conducted by the emperor, the ritual celebrant who approached the deities, and the immortal spirits of emperors manifesting in person.

The Medieval Discursive Space

How did the medieval period bridge the ancient and modern discursive spaces? The pioneering works of Itō Masayoshi and Abe Yasurō provide important clues to understanding the medieval appropriations of the *Nihon shoki*. First, it can be noted that the shift from the ancient to the medieval discursive space is most apparent via the terminology *Nihongi* (Japanese Chronicles, which is very similar to the term *Nihon shoki*) that was to replace *kokushi* (state histories). In describing the corpus referred to as the "Japanese Chronicles," Abe makes the following observation:

> What is most often found are explanations of meanings or origins of individual tales that are utterly unrelated to the main text of the *Nihon shoki*. At first glance, these tales are simulated in the form of a citation from a text called the *Nihongi*, and appear to belong to the scholarly genre of commentaries on ancient sources.[23]

A fixed representation of state history, as in the official histories of antiquity, can no longer be found within *Nihongi*. Instead, the content of the *Nihon shoki* is re-read and rendered fluid by a multiplicity of voices. For example, in the section on Emperor Keikō[24] in *Yamatohime no mikoto seiki* (Life of Yamatohime), the spiritual power of the Kusanagi sword (one component of the imperial regalia) and how it came to be enshrined in the Atsuta shrine of Aichi prefecture[25] is explained in the light of Yamatotakeru's eastern conquest, in the following manner:

> (1) In Winter, on the second day of the tenth month, Yamatotakeru departed on his journey. On the seventh day, he altered his route and prayed at the shrine of Ise. Taking his leave of Yamatohime, he said, "Under the order of the Emperor, I now go east to punish those who resist our rule. I take leave of you." Then Yamatohime took the Kusanagi sword and gave it to Yamatotakeru, saying "Be reverent and do not be neglectful." Yamatotakeru reached Suruga

for the first time that year, entered the wilderness, and unhappily met with a forest fire.

(2) The prince's sword drew itself of its own accord and cut down the grass around the prince. Because of this, the prince was saved. He named his sword Kusanagi [grass-mower].

(3) Yamatotakeru, having pacified the enemies of the east, reached the land of Owari on his journey home. There he stayed for a while with his lover, Miyazuhime. He untied his sword and left it at her house as he walked alone to climb Mount Ibuki. He died there, overcome by poisonous air. The Kusanagi sword is now at the shrine of Atsuta in the country of Owari.[26]

Section (1) quotes the main text of the *Nihon shoki*, the section describing the forest fire in Suruga. Section (2) comes from a variant of the *Nihon shoki*, and Section (3), relating the death of Yamatotakeru, is taken from the *Kogoshūi*.[27]

Unlike the *Kojiki*, the *Nihon shoki* contains variants in the commentary to the main text. Through the Heian period, these variants were cited only as references to the main text and were clearly differentiated by their font size. In *Yamatohime no mikoto seiki*, however, the alternative account describing the Kusanagi sword moving of its own will to save Yamatotakeru is woven into the main text, so as to create a tale demonstrating the spiritual power of the sword. The belief in the power of the sword directly correlated with the authority possessed by the Ise shrine (its source and the home of Yamatohime). This form of interpretation ensured that people acted in accordance with the wishes of the shrine and the creators of the text. Furthermore, the fact that Yamatohime's words are prefaced with "said" (*iwaku*) in the *Nihon shoki*, as compared to "declared" (*notamau*) in *Yamatohime no mikoto seiki*, signifies the desire to elevate Yamatohime's status.[28]

In the medieval period, liberal alteration of the *Nihon shoki* ensued, which resulted in a proliferation of tales and served to promote the interests of the producers. Multiple texts emerged with regard to the legend exalting the spiritual power inherent in the Kusanagi sword, including *Owari no kuni Atsuta taijingū engi* (an account of the origin of the Atsuta shrine which is thought to have been compiled by affiliates), *Jinnō seitōki* (a chronicle of deities and emperors by Kitabatake Chikafusa, a central figure in the Southern Court), *Kanetomo senkenbon Nihon shoki jindaikanshō* (a Yoshida Shintō digest regarding the Divine Age section of the *Nihon shoki*), and the *Tsurugi no maki* (A Tale of the Sword) in military chronicles such as the *Tale of Heike* and *Taiheiki*.[29] For example, in the *Kakuichi* version of the *Tale of Heike*, the tale begins with Susanowo praising the Kusanagi sword upon defeating the Orochi dragon. The sword is then enshrined in the Atsuta shrine following Yamatotakeru's eastern conquest. Later, after the monk Dōgyō's failed attempt to steal the sword at the time of the Tenji court (661–71) and Emperor Yōzei's (r. 876–84) fury, leading to his unsheathing the sword, the Kusanagi is lost at sea when the young Emperor Antoku (r. 1180–85) drowns. Thereafter, the tale concludes as follows:

> A scholar among them offered this explanation: "The great snake killed at Hi River in Izumo by Susanowo longed for the spiritual sword, deep in his head. As foretold by his eight heads and eight tails, he regained the sword after eighty generations of human rulers in the form of an eight-year-old emperor sinking with the sword to the depths of the sea." Having thus become the treasure of a divine dragon in the unfathomable depths of the sea, it will never return to human hands again.[30]

An examination of the *Tale of Heike* variants depicting the loss of the treasured sword reveals three distinct motifs: (1) texts that claim a replica was forged during Emperor Sūjin's reign,[31] which was then lost in the sea (*Engyō* version, *Yashiro* version [extracts], *Genpei jōsuiki*, *Shibu* version); (2) texts that claim a replica was forged, but that the real sword was lost (*Kakuichi* variant quoted above); and (3) texts that mention no replica and depict the real sword being lost at sea (*Yashiro* version [main text], *Hyakunijjuku* version).[32] Takagi Makoto, in explaining the proliferation of these texts, observes that "each variant text refracts the other variants and denies a movement towards the creation of a single 'meaning.'" He sees "the totality of the relations [between the texts] as a corpus."[33] Within this corpus, the historical accuracy of the texts is not a primary concern. Rather, perspectives corresponding to varied positions exist side by side, mutually allowing for contradictions within their narratives.

During this era, debates over whether or not texts were authentic rarely arose with any degree of seriousness. Rather, by overlapping multiple narratives new texts were produced. This is true of the *Tale of Heike* and more so of the medieval Japanese Chronicles as a whole. In the medieval period, the warriors (*bushi*) assumed real political power, while the court lost authority. At the same time, the *Nihon shoki*, which was compiled in order to legitimate the court's influence, could no longer maintain its position as a fixed referent. As a result, the various texts that had been subordinate to the *Nihon shoki*, such as the familial documents (*kachō*) submitted to the imperial court and clan records (*ujibumi*), were replaced by new genres with freer narrative content, such as Shintōist texts (*Shintōsho*), texts on temple and shrine origins (*engi*), and military tales (*gunki*). As already noted, the familial documents and clan records were premised upon the political power of the court, and were designed to be submitted to the court. At that time, the state histories, notably the *Nihon shoki*, functioned as the standard against which the content of the records and transmissions were authenticated.

However, with the weakening of the court during the medieval period, the state histories ceased to have any political function, and the dual structure marked by "fixed authority/fluid familial records" crumbled.

The commentaries on the *Nihon shoki* were situated at the center of the corpus referred to as the Medieval Japanese Chronicles. These were produced by priests of the Yoshida house and esoteric Buddhist monks in the environs of the court. Beginning in the Heian period, commentary on the *Nihon shoki* took place periodically, referred to in a ritualized form as "the lectures on the reading of the *Nihon shoki*" (*Nihongi kōsho*). While private records of official lectures have survived, such presentations were conducted under the jurisdiction of the court and took the form of phonetic instruction with an added discussion on etymology.

In the medieval period, as opposed to the ancient court, the text was no longer literally interpreted as a record of actual events. Rather, by focusing on the *Kamiyo no maki* (Scrolls of the Divine Age), allegorical interpretations based on Buddhist metaphysics were used to re-read the texts.[34] The locus of commentary, while moving away from the court's control, involved various aristocratic houses and schools. The divergence between ancient and medieval commentaries becomes apparent when the following two passages are compared:

> *Nihon shoki shiki* (*teihon*) [a private record of the official commentary on the *Nihon shoki* at the court]: Kuni-Tokotachi-no-mikoto. Query: Who first called this deity by this name? The teacher answers: the *Kana Nihongi*, *Jyōgūki*, and the various ancient texts all contain this name. However, I have never seen the first instance of its use. There is no way to determine its origins in early antiquity.[35]

> *Kanetomo Nihon shoki shindaikanmyō* [a Yoshida Shintō commentary on the *Nihon shoki*]: Kuni-Tokotachi-no-mikoto—this deity is the one spirit of all the people's hearts. The heart of this deity is very clear, like a polished mirror reflecting light on its base. Because it contains no artifice and shines upon all things, it begat Amanokagami-no-mikoto (deity of the heavenly mirror). To contain no artifice in the heart and to remain in nothingness is the essence of Shintō.[36]

The first commentary on the *Nihon shoki* raises the question as to who first named the deity Kuni-Tokotachi-no-mikoto. Since the matter is not recorded in the sources, however, the inquiry is abandoned. In contrast, Yoshida Kanetomo (1435–1511), the medieval Shintōist, begins his commentary with the deity's name, but then goes on to develop a metaphysical argument regarding the essence of the human heart.

Shintōist texts (*Shintōsho*) were written along the lines of this new form of commentary, whereby Buddhist metaphysics provided the means of constructing a discourse which combined an interior "Way" with the historical ontology of Japan.[37] During this era, the *Nihon shoki*—and in some cases the *Kojiki* and the *Sendai kuji hongi* as well—was no longer treated as "state history." Rather, it was considered a scripture,[38] namely, a "divine text" that "narrates the tales of the *kami*."[39] In Ryōbu Shintō's[40] *Reikiki*, for example, Amaterasu Ōmikami's grandson Ho-no-Ninigi[41] states that his name is "imperial descendant Kotokukimi [Buddhist diamond sword]" and claims to have descended from heaven (rather than being the manifestation of the spirit of rice, as described in the Kiki) as the manifestation of the Buddhist diamond sword (*Kongōshō*)[42] in order to spread the true word (*shingon*) of Amaterasu Ōmikami's Buddhist noumenon, Bontennō (Brahma in the Hindu pantheon), throughout the land.[43] The *Kamiyo no maki* (Scroll of the Divine Age) was thus read as a text declaring the salvation of all people by the Buddha. Its narrative form no longer strictly follows a historical chronology, but instead takes the form of topical sequences, such as a discussion on the Three Sacred Treasures, or the Imperial Regalia. In this manner, with commentary layered upon commentary and one provenance placed atop another, the discourse surrounding the *Nihongi* (Japanese Chronicles) proliferated.

 These divine texts (*shinsho*) and commentaries on the *Nihon shoki* were transmitted like an esoteric tradition and were controlled by the houses and schools affiliated to the surviving court. At the same time, it appears that the military tales (*gunki*) and temple and shrine histories (*jisha engi*) that incorporated the chronicles were disseminated through society via regional lords and prominent temples and shrines. Both channels of textual transmission were located within the sphere of influence marked by the political authority based in western Japan, with the court at its apex. In contrast, while recognized to a degree, the discourse of medieval *Nihongi* was either rejected or fundamentally reinterpreted in eastern Japan.

 Moreover, while the divine texts and commentaries gained intellectual authority by virtue of being esoterically controlled, the tales about origins and the military chronicles circulated widely. For this reason, the reception of the Kiki during the medieval period appears to have followed two different trajectories. On the one hand, the Kiki texts were hidden in an obscure form within court circles that were being undermined, with an ever-shrinking audience. On the other hand, the texts attained relevance centrifugally by moving beyond the higher strata into broader segments of society.

 In summary, in the course of the medieval period, the Six National Histories, especially the *Nihon shoki*, lost their focal power as classical sources. Consequently, a distinct corpus called the Medieval Japanese Chronicles (*Chūsei Nihongi*) took shape in light of the emerging Shintō texts, military chronicles, and temple and shrine histories that sought to deconstruct the ancient worldview. While seeking to present a reading beyond the meaning inscribed in the classical texts, the *Honji Suijaku* doctrine (theorizing how the

Buddha became *kami* in the land that is Japan) functioned within this corpus to ground the universal thought of Buddhism in the particular locus called Japan.[44]

At the same time, however, to the extent that such medieval texts continued to claim a formal connection to the Divine Age in the Kiki, delegated groups of people sought to ground their legitimacy in the historical tradition that was embodied through the emperor. Through this process, we can envision the nature of the medieval state in western Japan as being mirrored in the corpus itself.[45] The illustrious families and powerful Buddhist temples, along with regional lords, increased their level of autonomy while at the same time seeking the possibility of uniting all political forces under the emperor. Herein, while still lacking a true center, Buddhist metaphysics emerged as a discursive space propelling the creation of texts grouped together as *Nihongi* (Japanese Chronicles).

With the demise of the Ritsuryō state, the divine rituals (*jingi saishi*), which possessed a different function from the national histories and familial records in antiquity, ceased to be performed. With the exception of private renditions of the divine rituals, such as the Nakatomi purification rite (*harai*), most court ceremonies were discontinued in the late medieval period. In these circumstances, the distinctions between the concept of *kami* in the Kiki as compared to its significance in rituals and ritual texts grew ambiguous. Such inconsistencies were eventually unified via the foundation set forth by the Kiki. By this time, though, the *Kojiki* and the *Nihon shoki* had been fundamentally reinterpreted in relation to the discourses on Buddhist metaphysics and the medieval social structure, which were markedly different from antiquity.

The Kiki as National Memory

In conclusion, having examined the discursive spaces surrounding the Kiki in the ancient and medieval periods, let us now turn to the modern period. Following the work of Yoshimi Yoshikazu (the Shintō scholar of Confucianism) in the latter part of the early-modern period, texts with uncertain origins (as per their date of composition) were declared to be inauthentic, distinguished from ancient texts such as the state histories and official records. Furthermore, Motoori Norinaga's "Nativism" (*kokugaku*) identified the Kiki for the first time as texts containing the memory of the ethnic nation (*minzoku*) as a whole. While texts depicting the emperor did still exist in the early-modern period, as with Chikamatsu Monzaemon's kabuki play,[46] such works dealt with the emperor solely as fiction. In other words, they did not engage with the Kiki to ascertain the description of historical events, as was done in the medieval period. In contrast, through works by scholars such as Yoshimi and Motoori, the status of the Kiki, which had become ambiguous, was once again elevated as being distinct from unofficial records like the *Chūsei Nihongi* (Medieval Japanese Chronicles). Certainly, in the modern period, the *Kojiki* and the *Nihon shoki* achieved canonical status as repositories of national memory. At the same time, the texts referred to as *Nihongi*, such as the Shintō texts and works on temple and shrine origins which had once subsumed the Kiki, were rejected as fabrications.

During the ancient period, the Kiki played a central role in providing evidence to support the social positions occupied by various clans, based on their origins. The status of the Kiki grew ambiguous during the medieval period, while the freedom witnessed through the prevalence of Shintō texts and works relating temple/shrine origins was noteworthy. Yet, even for those parties who were represented by such new texts, the Kiki provided the basis for claims to historical origin, however perfunctory they may have been. However, the discursive space within which the Kiki attained significance, from the ancient through the medieval period, did not comprehensively include all of the inhabitants of the Japanese islands, in terms of class and region. Beginning in the latter part of the early-modern period this began to change. No longer tied to specific groups, the Kiki texts came to be held as the repositories of shared communal memory in association with the emerging nation-state, namely, the developing form of political rule. Needless to say, the homogeneity implied in such a discursive space functioned to elide social differences that still continued to exist.

Ancient clan records that survived into the early-modern period ceased to connect the Kiki to specific groups. Instead, they came to be treated as mere variants capable of filling gaps in the communal memory that the Kiki came to represent. By the early-modern period, *Shintōsho* could no longer exist independently, as texts that could encompass and challenge the Kiki. Instead, they were relegated and ascribed the status of secondary texts that interpreted the canonical statements in the Kiki. The term "Shintō" itself came to be shunned by Nativism. Although Shintō was once again ideologically placed at the center of the *kokutai* (national body) in the modern period, new texts bearing the title *Shintōsho* were never again produced.

During the modern period, the Ministry of Education's history curriculum and the Shintō shrines that came to utilize deities from the Kiki (for teaching and worship) under the directives of State Shintō, authorized by the government, served as the two primary conduits through which the Kiki texts were propagated to the nation.[47] Thus, public schools and shrines formed a part of the foundation of the modern state's newly created administration and were expected to play a critical role in national indoctrination. History education was designed to "shape national thought," while "the rites of the state" were to be handled by the shrines. The identification and preservation of imperial tombs and palace sites mentioned in the Kiki, which had begun in the early-modern period, expanded as well.[48]

In addition to such government vehicles, other books dealing with the Kiki sought to re-read the state's official history in terms of liberalism or nationalism (*kokusuishugi*). Such works spread through the nation via printed media and the intellectual class. As early as the Tokugawa period, woodblock printed versions of the Kiki and other classics saw wide circulation. In response to the growing influence of Yoshida Shintō, during this period many shrines altered the names of their enshrined deities to conform to the descriptions in the Kiki.

Relatively large shrines possessed their own histories or legends dating back to the medieval period. However, when confronted with the Yoshida house governmental mandate to license priests and with the modern state's shrine policies, such histories and traditions were too weak to resist the measures demanding alteration or outright erasure. Small shrines that were devoid of clear histories or distinctive deities were completely subsumed by the doctrinal system of Yoshida Shintō and the modern imperial system. This process was not limited to shrines alone. In the case of newly formed branch families, which rarely dated back more than a couple of generations, the state's narrative, with the Kiki at its core, supplemented the historical void.

While the Kiki's social positionality was fixed, as one constituting national memory centrally, a liberal reading in the form of an "academic essay" that was premised on the texts emerged and came to replace the "commentary." In the commentaries of the early-modern period, it was presumed in all the interpretations that the Kiki texts denoted historical facts as truths, so that each commentator strove to understand its content by locating himself within the texts. In contrast, rather than projecting themselves into the texts, the writers of academic essays strove to grasp the "history" that now existed independent of the descriptions in the Kiki while at the same time including the texts as a part of that "history." Whereas commentaries before the modern period were written under the restrictions of the text itself, the academic essay incorporated the Kiki texts within the scholar's personal narrative, in which he visibly developed his own thoughts.[49]

Commentaries were sparsely produced in the modern era and were thought merely to provide etymological interpretations, which were no longer considered essential to understanding the underlying history. Kazamaki Keijirō, a scholar of Japanese literature, points to the Taishō era (1912–26) as a time when commentaries were supplanted by academic essays. He notes this shift in reference to studies of the *Kojiki*:

Looking at commentaries alone, there were twenty-six during the Meiji period...but only four commentaries on the *Kojiki* during the Taishō era. By contrast, there were twenty titles in the category of scholarly research in the Taishō era. Just as the backgrounds of the scholars changed between the Meiji and Taishō periods, the nature of their research also changed.[50]

Eventually, the commentaries themselves were incorporated into the essay form. The main body of the essay was treated as a main text in its own right, while former commentaries were turned into footnotes or endnotes that supported the author's thoughts. This is clearly different from the medieval commentaries, which were perceived to be on a par with the metaphysical narratives of the Shintō texts.

During both the ancient and modern periods, the Kiki texts continued to occupy a canonical position, although the familial records and clan transmissions were absent from the modern edition. Nevertheless, the ancient and modern periods were fundamentally different in terms of the question as to whether the Kiki texts were to be understood as true histories in themselves or merely as material enabling historical understanding. For example, in the ancient lectures on readings of the Japanese Chronicles (*Nihongi kōshō*), when an undecipherable section in the text was arrived at, all attempts at judgment were suspended: "The way of the deities is unfathomable; the truth of this remains unknown. [There are so many descriptions in the Kiki whereby] what is heard differs and its explanations fail to concur."[51] As a result, commentators could not go beyond the description of the text because the text itself was considered to be history as fact, without any hint of a modern rational perspective. The capacity for the Kiki to maintain a sacred character before the modern era was the result of it being identified as history. Even Motoori proclaimed that the Kiki was the direct record of chronological events: "The ancient records are simply whole truths recording what has been transmitted from the age of the deities."[52]

In contrast, modern scholars distinguished history from the Kiki texts, and hence could freely cut and weave them into their own narratives. In some cases, they integrated clan transmissions and ancient texts in order to engage with new dimensions of history.

While the term "Kiki" was broadly used for the first time in the Meiji period[53] (1868–1912), it did not simply reflect the *Nihon shoki* and the *Kojiki*. Rather, it referred to the discursive space of history that situated and manipulated the two texts. The argument on dating the *Nihon shoki*, put forward by Naka Michiyo (the Meiji scholar of oriental history, 1851–1908) in the 1880s, is a clear example that distinguishes the concept of history from the Kiki. By taking the Christian era into consideration, the measurement of time within the *Nihon shoki* and the *Kojiki*, which was denoted with the imperial reigns and the sixty-year cycle (etc.), was rendered relative. Instead, a different temporal axis, based on the Christian eras, that was shared by both the Western and Eastern worlds was constructed irrespective of the Kiki texts.[54] In the process, however, the age of the deities, which lacked a calendar, posed a conundrum.

During the transition to modernity, Motoori Norinaga's interpretation of the Divine Age was based on his declaration that all the content concerning the age was literally historical. Like Christian fundamentalists in the West, Motoori forbade all allegorical interpretation of ancient texts. By the 1890s, however, Takagi Toshio and Anesaki Masaharu had absorbed the Western concept of "mythology." As a result, the descriptions of the Divine Age came to be understood in terms of a psychological veracity.[55] The term "Kiki myths," broadly employed today, originated during this era. Gradually, the sections of the Kiki concerning the Divine Age achieved a stable position as a kind of "national history" which was related to the worldview of the past, rather than as literal facts of history.

By the Taishō period, this perspective of treating the Kiki texts as historical products was applied not only to the Divine Age but also to the human age, especially in works by Tsuda Sōkichi.[56] Consequently, the Kiki texts in their entirety came to be understood as reflecting the historical perspective of a distinct class of people belonging to a specific time period. Not only was the concept of "history" detached from the Kiki, but simultaneously Japanese literary studies sought to reposition the texts within the axis of historical time.

Within the discursive space called "history," various debates regarding the Kiki intersected. These debates illustrated diverse and competing approaches, including: (1) relocating the Kiki within a given historical context (sakuhinron) or still extracting historical events from the texts (seiritsuron); (2) the conflict over Western and imperial calendars in determining dates (kinenron); and (3) the acceptance of the depiction of the Divine Age as historical fact or as a product of psychological reality. In this manner, the discursive space that came to be generally called "history" allowed one to engage with a variety of positions and perspectives. By emphasizing the unique canonical status of the Kiki texts, the modern approach treated the myths as the shared memory of the nation. "Japanese mythology" was a discourse produced in the light of such developments.

In conclusion, we have traced the transformations of the discursive space circumscribing the Kiki through the ancient, medieval, and modern periods. The ancient age, in the sense employed here, begins with the reign of Tenmu (late seventh century) and ends in the early Heian period (mid-tenth century). The medieval era stretches from the Kamakura period (late twelfth century) through the Muromachi period (late sixteenth century). Finally, the modern era begins in the late Edo period (late eighteenth century). The late

Heian period, which produced the Japanese Chronicles during the cloister governments of retired emperors *(insei-ki)*, corresponds to the transition from the ancient to the medieval period. Likewise, the early Edo period, with the strong influence of Confucian Shintō, corresponds to the transitional phase from the medieval to the modern period. Certainly, this periodization is based on the practices of textual analysis and does not strictly correspond to the conventions employed by historians in general.

Today, historical intentionality, or even historicity, is widely discussed in the light of modernity. Whether or not current historical research can maintain its critical power depends upon whether we can render our own horizon of understanding as an object of analysis. To do so does not imply that one should construct another representation and call it the "true myths of the Japanese ethnic nation," working to resist the authority of the imperial system and the Kiki. We can no longer delve into texts to ascertain literally their trans-historical meaning. Furthermore, it becomes futile to project directly onto the past such modern and Western religious concepts as the sacred and the profane (or the secular) developed by Euro-American religious studies, as is apparent within scholarship on the Medieval Japanese Chronicles and ancient kingship.[57] Rather, we must learn to be aware of the past in order to clarify how the structure of discursive spaces organizes our subjectivity and to understand what forces of integration and opposition bring about our view of the past and present. As part of this process, the significations contained within the concept of "Japanese mythology" would have to be historically examined, in terms of its emergence as a discourse produced by native elites, buffeted by waves of modern Westernization.

We have to acknowledge the fact that the discursive space that we choose to make an object of historical research is only a small, yet privileged, part of the memory that once existed within society as a whole. At the same time, we need to ask ourselves: why is it that the distinct and limited memory of the Kiki became the fountainhead of history? In other words, why did the Kiki entrance those enmeshed within the discourse on history? The field of research on the interpretation of the Kiki must now take up the task of analyzing such historical inclinations, which have to date been rendered as pre-discursive and housed deep inside ourselves.

2 The Canon and Variants: An Examination of the Mythology of Susanowo

An "Authentic Account" of a Wavering Faith

The fact that the Kiki myths have many variants is well known; Kiki here primarily refers to the generic name of the myths and legends authorized by the ancient imperial court to be constituted of the *Kojiki* (Record of Ancient Matters) and the *Nihon shoki* (Chronicles of Japan). This can be observed from the differences between the main text of the *Nihon shoki* and the variant (*Issho*), which takes the form of a commentary pertaining to each paragraph within the main text, as well as within the various versions of myths in the *Nihon shoki* and the *Kojiki*, the *fudoki* (records of the geography and culture of the provinces), and the *Senmyō* (record of oral directives by the emperor). Studies of the Kiki myths up to now have not tried to view differences among accounts as a quandary resulting from various accounts existing concomitantly. Rather, such studies have been attempting to treat the differences as merely derivations that have deviated from the unified and orthodox form of myth over the passage of time.

The Kiki research of Tsuda Sōkichi (1873–1961), for instance, which has had a profound influence on research today, aimed not to elucidate the Kiki itself but to reconstruct the *teiki* (imperial records) and *kuji* (ancient myths), the genealogical records and folklore that were the main material for the compilation of the Kiki, thought to have been established in the sixth century. Tsuda considered the variants of the Kiki myths in terms of their origination, not in terms of the primary form but as offshoots—stating that "the *teiki* and *kuji* that became the basis of the *Jindaishi* [record of the Divine Age in Japan before Emperor Jinmu, said to have been ruled by gods] were originally single [documents], but a number of varying versions sprang up as time passed."[1] For this reason, differences in the Kiki accounts were construed as "the concomitance of disharmonious fables and conflicting ideologies…after embellishments and alterations."[2] Through this form of conjecturing, it was assumed that the "genuine spirit of the entire history of the Divine Age and its structure"[3]—the one and only *teiki* and *kuji*—would be discovered.

In a similar vein, in terms of the theory about the formation of the Kiki that informed the main stream of understanding following World War II, the comparative mythologist Mishina Shōei (1902–71) states:

> Among the variants, there are also ones close to archaic fundamental forms, as well as miscellaneous accounts of later periods that had gone through significant developments. By aligning them according to format and considering their age, we can establish the myths' processes of maturation and stages of development.[4]

In other words, by arranging the various different accounts in a unitary sequence in accordance with their alteration over time and by seeking the archaic form of the Kiki myths, Mishina resolves the problem of concomitance, premising an understanding of variants that is analogous to Tsuda's.

In presuming, unconditionally, an original form of the Kiki that existed prior to its derivations, and without considering the underlying meaning of the co-existing variables, Tsuda, the democratist in the modern period, can be conceived of as standing on the same ground as the fundamentalist Motoori Norinaga (1730–1801) of the early-modern period, who maintained that "the ancient legend of our Empire is the real true account, whereby anything comparable did not exist among foreign nations."[5] Within Nativist studies in early-modern Japan, it was supposed that the variants of the Kiki myths arose due to the nature of the Kiki itself, including "old accounts" and "false accounts" that were "actual legends of earlier ages."[6] For this reason, it was presumed that through diligent commentary-based work, one could "ferret through and pick out the sand and pebbles"[7] and thereby recover the real ancient account.

Such a stance is prevalent through ancient times and the middle ages—as represented by the *Nihon shoki sanso* (commentary on the *Nihon shoki* written in the Muromachi period) of Ichijō Kanera and the "Nihongi kōsho" (lectures of commentaries on the *Nihon shoki*) conducted in the Heian period—and reaches as far back as the reign of Emperor Tenmu, which was the period when the compilation of the *Nihon shoki* and the *Kojiki* commenced. In the preface to the *Kojiki*, Emperor Tenmu mentions:

> I am told, "The *teiki* and *kuji* in the custody of various clans' keeping are already inaccurate and contain many fallacies." One way or another, I wish the *teiki* and *kuji* to be selectively examined, and falsehood deleted, truth determined, and them to be passed on to posterity.[8]

His words reflect the intention of distinguishing the accurate from the inaccurate, and from them determining the true myth as opposed to the myth variants which already existed at that time.

It would be useful to organize the mythological interpretations of the Kiki based on the criteria of arguments and methods determined according to the period and social stratum to which each subject-making interpretation belonged, including that of Tsuda Sōkichi, as well as those from the period of composition down to Emperor Tenmu's edict to compile the texts. For instance, Motoori considered the ancient accounts of the Kiki as the unwavering archaic truth, whereas Tsuda maintained that they were psychological facts established in the sixth century. Both of them, nevertheless, tried to avoid the problem of similarity by acknowledging the differences among variants while making value judgments as to whether accounts were either real or forged or by appropriating them to signify transformations over time. These approaches, although differing in their argument and method, correspond with each other in that they disregard the co-existence of variants in the same period and incline toward supposing a single mythological conception as its origin.

Certainly, research which touched upon the relationship between the *Kojiki* and the *Nihon shoki* ought to have existed. There have been studies which link the *Nihon shoki* to bureaucracy, on the one hand, and the *Kojiki* to the clans, on the other hand, as the dualism characterizing the Ritsuryō state (statutory system) at that time, as well as to opportunities arising from foreign relations. These works, however, ventured no further than merely extending research results in the light of political history, and were not founded upon an in-depth investigation of the Kiki itself. As Sakamoto Tarō, the scholar of ancient history, has pointed out, even "the feeling that the dissatisfaction with the simplicity of the *Kojiki* gave the impetus for the compilation of the *Nihon shoki* has become the common contemporary opinion."[9] This implies an unspoken assumption of a unitarian point of view. Myths with chronologically old and new layers were considered as merely having separated out on the basis of the specificity dictated by the Ritsuryō state, reflecting old and new political strata simultaneously.

In recent years there have been analyses by Kōnoshi Takamitsu that treat the *Kojiki* and the *Nihon shoki* separately, as independent works, because of the differences in their form. Such theorists point out that the *Kojiki* and the *Nihon shoki* are works with differing contexts in spite of the fact that their formulation coincides historically. Taking such circumstances into account, I do not merely compare and contrast the *Kojiki* and the *Nihon shoki* along the dimension of idiosyncrasies within the texts. Rather, as elaborated below, I acknowledge the common foundation from which these very idiosyncrasies developed, and elucidate the points of convergence, thereby recognizing the structural characteristics of the Kiki myths.

The narratives in the Kiki myths, like other kinds of texts, consist of various independent stories, the contexts that fuse them together, and words (place names, names of gods, and so on) which concretize the relevant context. These narratives consist of portions that are common to the *Kojiki* and the *Nihon shoki* as well as segments unique to each text. The portions in common are composed of two dimensions, one of which is the ideological element in the form of writings justifying the rule of the Yamato kingdom. This specifically appears as the main theme consistently present in the works, namely, the origins of the emperor's domination over the earth. The other dimension is the mythological motifs that define various stories which actually constitute the Kiki, namely, the story about the eight-headed and eight-tailed dragon, the story of the pledge between Amaterasu and Susanowo to judge his purity, the story of Amaterasu hiding in the rock cave, etc., to be discussed henceforth.

Although the ideological element and mythological motifs are shared in common by the *Kojiki* and the *Nihon shoki*, each text distinctly characterizes the form of this pledge between Amaterasu and Susanowo. While the ideological element is restricted to the Yamato kingdom, each mythological motif displays a capacity to influence the world from the perspective of comparative mythology. The miscellaneous mythological motifs which comprise the actual works display considerable similarities among the *Kojiki* and the *Nihon shoki*, although they are not completely the same. A number of differences can be seen; for example, the story about the strife between Izanagi and Izanami or the story about Nenokatasu-kuni (the netherworld) do not appear in the *Nihon shoki*. This is because there are differences as to what is considered necessary for the logical structure of the story within each text. In other words, while both are constrained by the ideology of rule, the specificity of the *Kojiki* and the *Nihon shoki* is maintained via the manner that they select mythological motifs to define their commonality.

As an example, we can consider how both the Kiki texts depict the advent of the emperor's ancestor from heaven following the act of creation of the Japanese archipelago by the creator-gods—the couple Izanagi and Izanami. In the *Kojiki*, on the one hand, the creation of the Japanese archipelago is held up by strife between Izanagi and Izanami. The ruling goddess of the heavens (Takamahara), Amaterasu (the daughter of the creator-gods), appears in this story after her parents' break-up. In turn, she fulfills the role of maintaining order in the everyday world, obeying her father Izanagi's command. Her younger brother Susanowo, in contrast, is distraught at his parents' separation and, longing for his mother, acts childishly and insists upon going to Nenokatasu-kuni, his mother's land. He subsequently has trouble with his father Izanagi and also with his elder sister Amaterasu. As a consequence of the pledge between Amaterasu and Susanowo, Amaterasu gives birth to Ameno-oshihomimi, who later becomes the father of Hononinigi. Susanowo, who is thereafter banished from heaven (Takama-no-Hara), slays the eight-headed and eight-tailed dragon and overcomes his own childishness, and then visits his mother's land of his own will. By this act, the two disassociated worlds, the father Izanagi's heaven (Takama-no-Hara) and the mother Izanami's land (Nenokatasu-kuni), while still keeping their independence, no longer remain completely cut off from each other. The suspended process of the creation of the Japanese archipelago, while receiving help from Susanowo, is subsequently completed by his sixth-generation descendant, Ōnamuchi. Finally, the grandchild of Amaterasu, Hononinigi, emerges as the dominant figure of the earth and as the first ancestor of the imperial family.

In the *Nihon shoki*, on the other hand, the creation of the Japanese archipelago is completed prior to the birth of Susanowo, and his parents, the two gods Izanagi and Izanami, do not break up. As a result the story does not proceed with the theme of repairing the disunion but rather elaborates on the selection of the ruler of the world. In this context, Susanowo is born as an evil god not suitable to be the ruler of the world. In sharp contrast to Amaterasu's giving birth, the story unfolds with an episode instigated by the evil deity Susanowo that leads to the birth of Amanooshihomimi. Then the banished Susanowo kills the eight-headed and eight-tailed dragon and, in Izumo province, has a child called Ōnamuchi. In turn, he is deposed from being the ruler of the earth by Ōnamuchi, and Hononinigi, the grandson of Amaterasu, becomes the ruler of the world. The journey of Susanowo to Neno-kuni (the netherworld), unlike the journey to Nenokatasu-kuni in the *Kojiki*, does not bear any strong significance, nor is Susanowo vested with any positive value in the *Nihon shoki*. The differences between the *Kojiki* and the *Nihon shoki* here are differences in how each version depicts the common theme of the origins of the emperor's rule upon earth, which can be deemed as differences in worldview.

It becomes apparent through such myths that sovereignty in the eighth century existed pluralistically. In light of this fact, a unitary interpretation of the texts cannot be presumed to be self-evident. Looking back, the bases for such unitary viewpoints are surprisingly shallow. In referring to the similarities among variants, the contention of Tsuda that "the stories observed in the Kiki resemble each other so much that one would think their source was the same"[10] merely points to the existence of similarities at the time of the Kiki's production. This statement, asserting the basis for similarities among variants, can only be considered as a great leap in logical thinking—namely, the understanding that "in the final analysis, they are but various contrasting theories springing forth from a single *teiki* and *kuji*"[11] and that thereby the sixth-century *teiki* and *kuji*, purported to have played roles in forming the Kiki, were originally unified.

In conclusion, the similarities among the Kiki variants do not indicate a unified source but rather point to the fact that variants coexisted. For the time being, we shall depart from the argument that their formation was from a unitary source. Rather, we begin our discussion with the sober understanding that points to the co-existence of *teiki* and *kuji* variants during the reign of Emperor Tenmu, during the Yamato kingdom of the latter part of the seventh century, when the compilation of the *Kojiki* and the *Nihon shoki* commenced. The debate over the composition of the Kiki has sparingly pointed to differences that existed in the eighth century. Yet, this does not answer the crucial question as to why the Kiki, with their mutually distinct characteristics, were formulated in practically the same period.

In this chapter, I consider the form as well as the significance of variants in co-existing myths found in the Yamato kingdom. Subsequently, I ask why their mutual existence did not become an issue during the long history of Kiki interpretation and in turn I question the grounds upon which the unitary composition of myths was assumed. These considerations will no doubt compel us also to consider the essential character of interpretation with regard to myths in general.

Demarcating Myths

One can infer from the imperial edict recorded in the preface of the *Kojiki*, stating that "the *teiki* and *honji* [*kuji*] in the various clans' keeping are already inaccurate and contain many fallacies," that the clans maintained *teiki* and *kuji* at that time and that their content covered numerous items. In the following section, I will shed light on the characteristics of variants that existed prior to the Kiki, by examining the *teiki* and *kuji* during Emperor Tenmu's reign.

The *Kojiki* has only the main text but no variants, as becomes apparent from the preface, which states, "The *teiki* [is] to be documented and the *kuji* elucidated, [and thereby] deleting falsehood and determining truth." This point of relevance is also evident from the imperial edict of 681 which states, "Inscribe and define the various matters in the *teiki* and remote antiquity."[12] With the adoption of the authorized text as "the Kiki," it cannot be determined whether just one of the various versions in the *teiki* and *kuji* was selected or whether several were combined, compiled, and thereafter inscribed. Therefore, it is not possible to say that the *teiki* and *kuji* directly correlate with the Kiki. They are the only concrete examples approximating the group of variants called "Alleged books' records" in the *Nihon shoki*, recorded as inscriptions beside the main text. Unlike the main text of the *Nihon shoki* and the *Kojiki*, these were not unified into one definitive version, but variant portions are fragmentarily listed alongside each paragraph.[13]

The title "Alleged books' records" itself signifies that the portions were each originally part of independent documents.

The autonomy, plurality, and lack of the uniformity of the "Alleged books' records" in the *Nihon shoki* indeed appear to correspond with Emperor Tenmu's edict, namely, that "The *teiki* and *honji* [*kuji*] in the various clans' keeping are already inaccurate and contain many fallacies." From its characteristics we can infer that "Alleged books' records" corresponds to the *teiki* and *kuji* kept by each clan. Henceforth, we shall consider the co-existence of the *teiki* and *kuji* by examining them in relationship to "Alleged books' records." This amounts to an analysis of the *teiki* and *kuji* during Emperor Tenmu's reign prior to the compilation of the Kiki.

As long as the *teiki* and *kuji* were the material for the Kiki, and considering that they were comprised of the imperial genealogy and stories which also included historical records and legends,[14] we can surmise that genealogies were authenticated according to the reality contained in the content of the stories. It is evident that the *teiki* and *kuji* were documents concerning the kingship, since, if they were not, it would be inconceivable that they would be included in the *Nihon shoki* as "Alleged books' records" comprising the commentary to the main text and as documentation justifying its authority. Without the existence of historical materials that would enable us to distinguish between the *teiki* and *kuji*, however, we have to give up the prospect of trying to define them individually for the time being.

One can infer from the characteristics of family trees of each clan and records of family names, such as *Takahashi ujibumi* (Record of the Takahashi clan) and *Kogoshūi* (Gleanings from Ancient Stories), that each clan's genealogy of sovereignty and stories of justification buttressed its own social status. As Mizoguchi Mutsuko,[15] among others, has clearly shown through research, each clan's genealogy and story did not conclude within the respective clan. Rather, by premising their central orientation on the imperial genealogy and stories that constitute the Kiki, the records specific to the clans were interconnected in a derivative form of relationship leading up to the kingship. In other words, the origins of intimate relations or the forms of services that were offered to the authority established the basis for each clan's role in the imperial court, which designated their social status. Therefore, the imperial genealogy and stories not only pointed to the vital source of order of the imperial family, but revealed the position of each clan under the rule of the kingdom. This formulation was a crucial matter from the clans' standpoint, providing for each one a basis for its existence. In light of the genealogies and the record of family names of the clans in existence since ancient times, this relationship was essential.

From the perspective of political history as well, with the composition of each record, a given clan was able to assure its own existence by presupposing the existence of the imperial reign. Furthermore, the "Alleged books' records," constituted of the *teiki* and *kuji* of a given clan, unanimously manifested the premise which substantiated the ideology of the justification of rule as maintained by each clan. In other words, these variants could exist only under authoritative regulation. An analysis of the "Alleged books' records" in terms of variants centering on the story of the pledge between Amaterasu and Susanowo is outlined below.

The story of the pledge between Amaterasu and Susanowo can be seen in six records: the *Kojiki*, the main text of *Shoki*, "Alleged books' records" 6.1–6.3, and record 7.3.[16] The pledge between Amaterasu and Susanowo (Ukei) is analogous to the following observation made by Tsuchihashi Hiroshi:

> A practice of verbal incantation that is either a method of augury to know… the "truth" about the past, present or future or a method for making a matter pledged … into "truth," and its formulation of "If A, then A will happen" is one form of a spell based on faith in the spirit of language (Kotodama) by which "If it is said, it then will come true."[17]

This practice is found not only in Japan but throughout the world, including India, China, Korea, Vietnam, and various regions of Asia, as well as Europe.[18] Certainly, from a global perspective, a shared dimension of mythological motifs is not limited to the pledge between Amaterasu and Susanowo, as becomes apparent through comparative mythological studies which reveal a geography for the distribution of motifs. Such miscellaneous records support the theory of the commonality of mythological motifs.

Mythological motifs are subject to variations introduced by the region and the person delivering the story; as Lévi-Strauss has elucidated, this includes specific names of the characters who appear, or words referring to places (etc.), as well as the context unfolding in the story.[19] In the case of the pledge between Amaterasu and Susanowo, in all the records the older sister, Amaterasu, and her younger brother, Susanowo, appear as main characters. The content of the "truth" in question, as a result of the pledge between Amaterasu and Susanowo, among both entities, is considered to hinge upon whether Susanowo is pure-hearted toward Amaterasu; in other words, whether Susanowo is trying to take over the heavens that are under Amaterasu's dominion. The truth or fallacy is determined by the creation of gods by the two gods, Amaterasu and Susanowo. Variants of records are generated on the premise founded on the commonality of these words and contexts. A fundamental framework of variants consists of two alternatives: namely, due to the pledge between Amaterasu and Susanowo, whether the gender of each of the gods produced by Amaterasu and Susanowo is male or female, and whether the gender of the children whom Susanowo fathers is consequently a sign of his pure-heartedness towards Amaterasu. By criss-crossing these two alternatives, the fundamental framework of the story results in four types of variant (Fig. 1).

These are: Type One, in which Amaterasu bears all the male gods, Susanowo fathers all the female gods, and the sign of his pure-heartedness turns out to be male; Type Two, in which the genders of the children of both Amaterasu and Susanowo are the same as in Type One but the sign of his pure-heartedness turns out to be female; Type Three, in which the genders of the children born are reversed (female for Amaterasu and male for Susanowo), while the sign of his pure-heartedness is male; and Type Four, in which the genders of the children born are the same as in Type Three, but the sign of Susanowo's pure-heartedness is female. Types One and Two are found in three records: the *Kojiki*, the main text of the *Nihon shoki*, and "Alleged books' records" 6.2, wherein as a result of Susanowo biting Amaterasu's ornamental jewel or sword male gods are born, and as a result of Amaterasu biting Susanowo's ornamental jewel or sword female gods are born. Out of these, the ones mentioned in the *Kojiki* and the main text of the *Nihon shoki* are as follows: "The five gods of male children are born of my [Amaterasu's] sword. They are therefore my children" (*Kojiki*).[20] Amaterasu declared, "If asked about the original owner of the ornamental jewel, it is mine. And the five male gods are one and all already mine" (main text of the *Nihon shoki*).[21]

		The standard/criterion of pure-heartedness		Parent "giving birth" to Oshihomimi
		Male	Female	
Entity to whom children belong	**With exchange of properties** Susanowo: female gods Amaterasu: male gods	Type 1 Susanowo = evil (*Nihon shoki* main text, "Alleged books' records" 6.2)	Type 2 Susanowo = pure-hearted (*Kojiki*)	Amaterasu
	Without exchange of properties Susanowo: male deity Amaterasu: female gods	Type 3 Susanowo = pure-hearted ("Alleged books' records" 6.1, 6.3, 7.3)	Type 4 Susanowo = evil	Susanowo

Figure 1 Basic variants of the story with respect to the pledge between Amaterasu and Susanowo

This suggests that the children's affiliation was determined according to the owner of the objects they were made from, and thus the female gods that were born became Susanowo's children and the male gods became Amaterasu's children.[22] However, in "Alleged books' records" 6.2, the story is fragmented, so that the criteria for belonging are not clarified, nor can the children's affiliations be determined. For these reasons, it has been deleted from the concerns of this chapter.

Furthermore, in the main text of the *Nihon shoki* corresponding to Type One, the story unfolds in the following manner: "If I [Susanowo], in giving birth to a person, have a girl, then assume my heart as evil"[23] and subsequently the evil heart of Susanowo is revealed to Amaterasu. Conversely, in the *Kojiki* corresponding to Type Two, the story unfolds in the following manner: "I [Susanowo] have a pure and clean heart. The children I bore are maidens,"[24] thereby proving Susanowo's pure-heartedness. The male god Oshihomimi, who was born through the pledge between Amaterasu and Susanowo, however, has no bearing on whether Susanowo is pure-hearted, and according to both parts of the Kiki the following deities were born from Amaterasu: "Amaterasu's apparent heir to the throne, the Great Victor Oshihomimi" (*Kojiki*),[25] and "Amaterasu's son, the Great Victor Oshihomimi" (main text of the *Nihon shoki*).[26]

In the three records from "Alleged books' records" 6.1, 6.3, and 7.3, however, which correspond to Types Three and Four, there is no mention of the two gods exchanging their properties and thus the affiliation of children is straightforward. In other words, it is thought that male gods are produced by Amaterasu biting her own sword and a female deity is produced by Susanowo biting his own ornamental jewel. All three existing records make the sign of Susanowo's pure-heartedness male gods and consequently they correspond to Type Three; furthermore, there are no records mentioning female gods that correspond to Type Four.

> Susanowo named the child born to him as Great Victor Oshihomimi. And all five gods born are male gods...Thus it becomes clear to Amaterasu that Susanowo veritably does not have ill intentions (*Nihon shoki*, "Alleged books' records" 6.1).[27]
>
> From Susanowo a male is born... named the Great Victor Oshihomimi... Therefore it becomes clear to Amaterasu that Susanowo veritably from the beginning had a pure heart. (*Nihon shoki*, "Alleged books' records" 6.3)[28]
>
> If he has a pure heart then males will be born without fail...Susanowo...the children born to him...Great Victor Oshihomimi...thus all his six children are male gods. (*Nihon shoki*, "Alleged books' records" 7.3)[29]

Thus, in all accounts, Susanowo is proven to be pure-hearted toward Amaterasu, and the male god Oshihomimi, ancestor of the imperial family, is born as his child.

As discussed above, in the main text of the *Nihon shoki*, Susanowo's wickedness is exposed, whereas in other records he is proven to be pure-hearted. In the *Kojiki* and "Alleged books' records," as well, Susanowo is portrayed as being pure-hearted in a comparable number of instances. Yet, whether the sign of his pure-heartedness is male or female, or whether there is an exchange of properties, or even whether the children of Susanowo and Amaterasu are male or female gods, varies according to the process of proving Susanowo's pure-heartedness, i.e., the story's context.

The Kiki are documents which maintain that Oshihomimi was born from Amaterasu, regardless of Susanowo showing his pure-heartedness to Amaterasu, and other records, namely, "Alleged books' records" 6.1, 6.3, and 7.3 state that Oshihomimi is Susanowo's child. Even "Alleged books' records" 6.3 and 7.3 say, "The child I [Susanowo] begot with a pure heart I will also offer to my elder sister" (*Nihon shoki*, "Alleged books' records" 7.3),[30] and "Then, the six male gods were adopted as the children of Amaterasu to rule over the celestial heavens" (*Nihon shoki*, "Alleged books' records" 6.3),[31] and thus Oshihomimi is adopted by Amaterasu. The fact that such records exist implies that the genealogy of the emperor as directly related by blood with Amaterasu was not a big concern for the members of the imperial court at the time.

As there are no traces left among actual records of Type Four, in which the children born to Susanowo are male gods and the female gods are considered to possess the sign of his pure-heartedness to Amaterasu, which establishes the fact that Oshihomimi is related by blood to Susanowo, we can infer that it was assumed that Susanowo does not harbor evil intentions toward Amaterasu. The reason presumably is to avoid the contradiction of having Oshihomimi, who is the ancestor of the imperial family, represent a being that takes after an evil Susanowo who schemed to rebel against Amaterasu, the one who represents the order of Heaven.

Having reviewed in the above discussion the different forms and contexts that fall within the same mythological motif of the pledge between Amaterasu and Susanowo, we can see that this portion of the story not only generates variants from within but also connects with other mythological motifs. "Alleged books' records" 7.3 is a section that includes the motif of the pledge between Amaterasu and Susanowo, which differs from the fragmented portions of other records, because it includes the section of Susanowo's evil deed in Heaven and the section of Amaterasu's seclusion in the Rock Cave and thereby makes possible a comparison with the *Kojiki* and the main text of the *Nihon shoki*. In this section as well, Susanowo's evil deed in Heaven leads to Amaterasu secluding herself in the Rock Cave of Heaven, for which the direct reason is surmised as being Susanowo's "jealousy" toward the fertile rice paddies belonging to Amaterasu. After the incident of seclusion in the Rock Cave of Heaven, Susanowo is banished by the other gods of Heaven (*Nihon shoki*, "Alleged books' records" 7.3).[32] Yet, instead of heading for Nenokuni (the netherworld), as in the *Kojiki* and the main text of the *Nihon shoki*, he goes to visit his elder sister. Subsequently, the act of making a pledge is performed to determine the real intentions of Susanowo's visit—whether or not it is "for usurping my [Amaterasu's] land."[33] In turn, Susanowo's pure-heartedness is proven and the story abruptly ends at that point.

In the Kiki, as pointed out earlier, there is a basic opposition between Susanowo portrayed as an evil god in the main text of the *Nihon shoki* and as an infantile god in the *Kojiki*. Yet the *Kojiki* and the main text of the *Nihon shoki* concur in portraying Susanowo, after the pledge, inflicting havoc in Heaven, which then triggers the incident in the Rock Cave, for which he is banished from Heaven. In "Alleged books' records" 7.3, the sequence of the story involving the pledge and the Rock Cave is reversed as compared to the *Kojiki* and the main text of the *Nihon shoki*, and the events that occur in connection with the pledge between Amaterasu and Susanowo do not result in Amaterasu's seclusion in the Rock Cave. As Motoori Norinaga states, "this record is indeed what seems appropriate, and [we need] to conjecture that the other records of the *Kojiki* and the *Nihon shoki* have the order of events in disarray,"[34] since, depending on the way it is read, the account seems to have more consistency than the *Kojiki* and the main text of the *Nihon shoki*.

As discussed thus far, various records have mythological motifs in common, while the actual stories have their own distinct contexts. Additionally, the records do not all necessarily have the same mythological motif and we can observe that selections are made according to the needs of the context. "Alleged books' records" 8.4, for instance, has a tree-planting motif in addition to the slaying of the eight-headed and eight-tailed dragon. Here, tree-planting is set as the meritorious deed of Itakeru who descended with Susanowo.[35] On the contrary, the *Kojiki* and the main text of the *Nihon shoki* have no tree-planting motif nor any appearance of Itakeru. However, we see in "Alleged books' records" 8.5 the tree-planting motif also emerging, although the main character switches from Itakeru to Susanowo. In this case, Susanowo heads for Nenokuni (the netherworld) without slaying the eight-headed and eight-tailed dragon. Since "Alleged books' records" 8.5 is fragmentary, we cannot judge whether this is because the mythological motif is missing. Yet, just as the *Kojiki* and the main text of the *Nihon shoki* are missing the tree-planting motif, we cannot deny the possibility of the existence of a variant which does not include the slaying of the eight-headed and eight-tailed dragon. We can consider this to imply that there ensued the selection of mythological motifs with regard to stories about Susanowo upon earth.

Variants are created only out of the context, and in some cases at the level of words that are incorporated. In miscellaneous records concerning the pledged augury motif, we can see differences at the level of words—with the names of gods, the number of gods, the form of the performance of the pledge, the gods that appear in between, etc. In all the miscellaneous records the number of female gods born is three while the number of male gods varies, either six gods (in "Alleged books' records" 6.3 and 7.3) or five gods (in various other records). There are also variations in the names that appear and in the Japanese characters used to denote the names of the male and female gods. Additionally, in "Alleged books' records" 6.2, the god named Hakarutama handed Susanowo the ornamental jewel used in the pledge, and in "Alleged books' records" 7.3 Amanōzume informs Amaterasu that Susanowo is visiting Heaven. There are other subtle differences in the number of swords and ornamental jewels (etc.) used in the pledge between Amaterasu and Susanowo, and at the level of words the differences appear in the details of miscellaneous records, akin to the differences also emerging among various records such as "Alleged books' records" 6.1, 6.3, and 7.3 that have the same context.

"Alleged books' records" 5.11 is an example of alterations in words that produce conspicuous changes in the context of the record. This is a record in which Tsukiyomi and Amaterasu get into a quarrel as a result of Tsukiyomi having killed Ukemochi, a goddess of agriculture. Related stories exist in the *Kojiki*, where Susanowo is described as killing the god of cereal grains Oogetsu-hime, but neither Tsukiyomi nor Amaterasu appears in the story. It can be inferred that the main character who murders the god of cereal grains, namely, Susanowo and Tsukiyomi, are one and the same. In this regard, however, the main character in "Alleged books' records" 5.11 can be surmised to be Tsukiyomi. This is because the story relates the origins of cereal grains and explains the origins of the division of night and day: "Amaterasu then got terribly upset and cried out, 'You are an evil god, indeed. I never want to see you again.' Thus she came to live apart, as day is to night, from Tsukiyomi."[36] Here too, as in the *Kojiki*, Susanowo is said to "be the ruler of the deep blue sea,"[37] but under such a turn of events, there is no possibility that Susanowo as the ruler of the sea would be able to intervene in the main theme of the story.

As discussed above, the various records of the *Kojiki* and the main text of the *Nihon shoki*, as well as the "Alleged books' records," are comprised of three elements: mythological motifs, contexts, and words. Additionally, each record may be considered to be a variant with its respective distinctness, namely, taking the group of mythological motifs that are the common story material, and selecting and fusing them according to its own context, and in addition altering the words that constitute the story. Thus, myths may be regarded as having an inherent potential for producing numerous variants, which works through the alteration of contexts and words.

The preceding examination lends support to the notion of each variant having its own logical soundness. The notes inserted in the article of the Third Month of 533 in the *Nihon shoki* indicate that each variant was considered as reliable for actually compiling the Kiki. The phrases inscribed in the genealogy of the imperial family are as follows: "Concerning *Teiōhongi* [the chronicle of emperors]...examining the past and present we will thus restore authenticity. If [it is] hard to understand in general, then select a reliable one and annotate the differences. Do the same for the other cases."[38] This is a clear statement of the standard for selecting records from "Alleged books' records" in the *Nihon shoki* as and when readers were not able to discern the level of reliability among records. The authenticity of each variant, at issue here, is verifiable only if the text is credible in terms of both context and words.

Viewed from these standpoints, one can value the *Kojiki* and the main text of the *Nihon shoki* as a part of variants that existed, and realize how questionable it is to consider miscellaneous reports as false for merely differing from the Kiki. This, of course, is not to assert that the *Kojiki* and the main text of the *Nihon shoki* and "Alleged books' records" were compiled at the same time. The "Alleged books' records" inserted into the *Nihon shoki* are thought to date to around the time of the reign of Emperor Tenmu. The *Kojiki* and the main text of the *Nihon shoki* can be regarded as being compiled from "Alleged books' records" and therefore they have the possibility of being products of a later period with regards to their content. Myths generate variants according to the circumstances of the given period and according to variables that one could presume were neither set in that given time nor came to co-exist when each myth was generated. We should recognize that myths intrinsically have the structure for generating variants and that numerous variants existed generally in the form of the *teiki* and *kuji* of clans at the time of Emperor Tenmu's reign. While their period of establishment may differ, the variants basically have as much credibility, in terms of depicting historical truth, as the *Kojiki* and the main text of the *Nihon shoki*.

Clan records which existed around the time of Emperor Tenmu's reign, sharing in common the mythological motifs that underwent widespread distribution, contain their specific variants in terms of the selection and construction of contexts and words. In other words, the context and words dually constitute portions specific to certain records as well as those shared in common with other records. A case in point is the story concerning the pledge between Amaterasu and Susanowo, for instance, whereby the birth of Oshihomimi constitutes the common portion among miscellaneous records. Whether the parent by birth is Susanowo or Amaterasu, Oshihomimi is regarded as suited for becoming the ruler of Heaven. One can tell the significance of Oshihomimi in terms of his son, Hononinigi, who in every record subsequently descends into this world and becomes the ancestor of the emperor ruling over the Japanese archipelago.

In terms of representing the history of the Divine Age, various records have factors in common which ultimately explain the historical origins of the imperial family (as the offspring of Amaterasu via Oshihomimi and Hononinigi) and its rule over this world, namely, accounts of the world being created by the gods, the creation of the Japanese archipelago, and the advent of a world leader suitable for Japan as a country. On the one hand, such common factors involve portions intricately connecting the legitimacy of rule by the emperor, which are strongly enveloped in the restrictions propounded by the dominant ideology. On the other hand, the remaining portions of the various records can be divided into those shared in common among a number of records, and those that are unique to each of the records. Despite the range of differences, depending on the disposition of the various clans, such sections are generally not under strong restrictions. Commonality and uniqueness are ideational distinctions, of course, that in reality indicate gradations.

The fundamental structure of the *teiki* and *kuji* is situated between the expansiveness of mythological motifs and the constriction of the ideology of kingship, and maintains the originality of the actual records in a form that includes each clan's disposition. By understanding matters in these terms, we can for the first time correctly position the uniqueness of the *Kojiki* and the *Nihon shoki*. As a result of research in the contemporary period, debate has arisen as to why the *Kojiki* and the main text of the *Nihon shoki*, as well as the other numerous records, came to exist via the sovereignty of the eighth century. Myths are fundamentally not singular by nature, but can be said to have an intrinsically flexible structure to generate many variants at the level of context and words. Therefore, the question that needs to be addressed is how myths such as the *Kojiki* and the *Nihon shoki* were reduced and fixed as two texts. In other words, why was there not a move toward the diversification rather than the attenuation of myths? The *Kojiki* and the main text of the *Nihon shoki*, from such a perspective, are merely two formulations among numerous records that existed. In this light, I wish to examine what propelled the Yamato kingdom of the eighth century to attempt limiting the myths to those recorded in the two predominant texts.

The Formation of the Canon

I seek first of all to examine how the co-existence of various *teiki* and *kuji*, around the time of Emperor Tenmu's reign, unified to result in only two documents, the *Kojiki* and the *Nihon shoki*. The imperial edict of Emperor Tenmu, mentioned in the *Kojiki's* foreword, explicitly states the intention for the selection of records in the *Kojiki*. This is based on their evaluation for establishing a history that was suited for the sovereignty: "At this time, unless the shortcomings [of the co-existing variants] are corrected, the authority of its truth will be lost in the years to come. This indeed is the history of the state, the foundation of imperial influence." In rejecting the concomitant records of the clans because "the *teiki* and *honji* [*kuji*] in the various clans' keeping are already inaccurate and contain many fallacies," and by "eliminating falsehood, determining truth, and passing [the records prescribed by Emperor Tenmu] on to posterity," the intention was to create an authentic rendition from the records prescribed by Emperor Tenmu as the standard suitable for later generations. In other words, the *Kojiki* was an attempt to reject the situation of co-existing myths and to centralize the accounts under the ruling kingdom. Therefore, this amounted to rejecting the validity and autonomy of the records in the custody of the various clans. From a specific standpoint, in a parallel sense to research on the Bible, we can consider this state of affairs, of limiting myths, as signifying "canonization."[39]

The situation is presumably no different with the *Nihon shoki*. The imperial edict of 683, thought to be the turning point for compiling the *Nihon shoki*, prescribes selection activities for "defining and inscribing the various matters of *teiki* and remote antiquity." While there are contexts and wordings which are limited to the *Nihon shoki*, spanning the period from the "Creation of the World" to the reign of Empress Jitō, we can likewise surmise the intention to canonize this document as being akin to the *Kojiki*. However, the *Nihon shoki* includes the alternative records of the clans. This compels us to question the status and significance of the "Alleged books' records" within the *Nihon shoki*.

The "Alleged books' records" was primarily inscribed as a commentary in relation to the main text, in the form of small letters which correspond to a given line in the main text. Basically following the words and phrases of the main text, "Alleged books' records" can be considered to comply with the main text in terms of its format. In addition, all of its passages are inscribed merely as fragmented paragraphs, with the preceding and following portions cut off, in such a way that it is impossible to read it as a whole story like the main text, from beginning to end, or even to read several paragraphs in succession.

The Canon and Variants

The "Alleged books' records," clause 511, states the standard for the adoption of the alleged records within the *Nihon shoki*. The authenticity of some records at the time was difficult to judge, and the alleged records served to supplement the process of identifying truth in the form of explanatory notes set in relation to the main text, as indicated in the following statement: "If [the text is] hard to understand in general, then select a reliable text and annotate the differences." However, unification was persistently implemented in the selection process, as implied in the following words: "Examining the past and present, we will thus restore authenticity." There is nothing strange about this objective attitude. One can also witness the same position throughout the *Nihon shoki*'s commentary on citing other historical documents, beginning with the section on the first Emperor Jinmu. Herewith, in order to elaborate on a means of assessing the canon and its variants, I present the example of the fifth paragraph on the Divine Age from the *Nihon shoki*, which includes the highest number of inscriptions (eleven from the "Alleged books' records") alongside the main text; this comprises the most complex form of alignment (Figure 2).

The main text of the fifth paragraph recounts how the two gods Izanagi and Izanami in turn created the four gods, Amaterasu, Tsukiyomi, and Susanowo, as well as Hiruko (the disabled god), and the Japanese archipelago and its landscape of mountains and rivers, among other things. Here, as we already know, Susanowo is described as an evil god banished to Nenokuni (the netherworld). "Alleged books' records" 5.1 is a variant of the

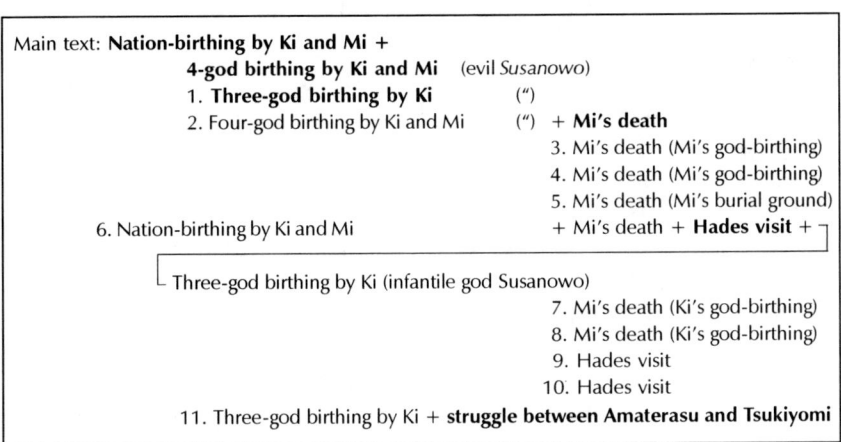

Figure 2 "Alleged books' record" alignment according to the fifth paragraph. Numbers indicate order listed in the record within this paragraph and words in **bold** are parts of records appearing in the *Nihon shoki* for the first time.
(Ki: Izanagi; Mi: Izanami; Hades: Yominokuni)

main text on the birth of these four gods. In this version, Izanagi alone is said to give birth to the three gods, Amaterasu, Tsukiyomi, and Susanowo. Here, similarly to the description in the *Kojiki*, Izanagi and Izanami are considered to have already separated. Like the main text of the *Nihon shoki*, however, it states that, given the episodes of the evil god Susanowo being banished, the one "who enjoys harming everything," and who is "thus sent down to reign over Nenokuni," in terms of context, is a mixture of the *Kojiki* and the main text of the *Nihon shoki*.

"Alleged books' records" 5.2 is also a variant on the main text of the *Nihon shoki*. The first half consists of the creation of the four gods and the banishment of the evil god Susanowo, which is akin to the main text, but the latter half is similar to the *Kojiki*'s description, in which the birth of Kagutsuchi (the fire god) ensues. As a result Izanami suffers burns, and on her deathbed she gives birth to various other gods. Yet, the context of the gods Izanagi and Izanami giving birth to the gods Amaterasu and Susanowo, among others, prior to their separation, is nevertheless original. Further, the records 5.3 to 5.5 are variants of 5.2 rather than of the main text, in terms of the portion recounting the death of Izanami. Records 5.3 and 5.4 concern the gods whom Izanami, nearing death, gives birth to and record 5.5 clearly gives information missing in the other records, including the fact that the burial place of Izanami is "Kumanonoarima village in Ki province."[40]

"Alleged books' records" 5.6 is again a variant of the main text, in which the two gods Izanagi and Izanami create gods, such as the Japanese archipelago, as well as nature, like the mountains and rivers, among other things. In turn, as a result of giving birth to Kagutsuchi, Izanami dies. Subsequent to stories narrating the visit by Izanagi to the Land of the Dead, Izanagi alone creates gods, namely, the three children, Amaterasu, Tsukiyomi, and Susanowo. Susanowo is not described as an evil god here, but rather ends up being banished when he is affected by the separation of the gods Izanagi and Izanami and, out of a longing for his mother, states, "I wish to follow my mother into Nenokuni."[41] This record generally is similar to the *Kojiki* but draws parallels with the main text of the *Nihon shoki*; namely, when Susanowo is ordered to rule over the "earth," the focus lies on the ruler of this world. The next records 5.7 through 5.10 are variants of record 5.6. Records 5.7 and 5.8 are variants concerning the gods born as a result of Izanagi killing his child, Kagutsuchi, and records 5.9 and 5.10 are variants concerning the story of Izanagi visiting Yominokuni (Land of the Dead). All of these sections have no relation to the main text. Record 5.11, at the end of the fifth paragraph, is again a variant of the main text. As already mentioned, it recounts the creation of cereal grains and the origins of the separation of the sun and the moon, as in the stories of younger brother Tsukiyomi and elder sister

Amaterasu, with an originality not found in other records within the *Nihon shoki*.

In this manner, the alignment of "Alleged books' records" comprises a two-layered structure: one layer of variants to the main text, such as records 5.1, 5.2, 5.6, and 5.11, and another layer of variants to the preceding records, as in the case of records 5.3 to 5.5 and 5.7 to 5.10. The records are restricted in format and do not possess any coherency beyond the limits of a given paragraph, they are all but fragmentary without the existence of the main text. The first layer, as a result, directly reverts to the main text and the latter layer is subject to the first, and ultimately reverts to the main text. That is to say, while the main text of the *Nihon shoki* is coherent as a story, the text as a whole has diversity in its descriptions, unlike the *Kojiki*. By inserting the excerpts from "Alleged books' records," the *Nihon shoki* supplements the content of the main text along with an attempt at meticulous fact-finding, which then amounts to forming its "objective description."

Certainly, the supplementation of descriptive authenticity is secured in two dimensions, in terms of the context and the wording, which comprise the constructive elements of the record. In the case of direct variants to the main text, one finds many comparatively lengthy records with a certain degree of clarity regarding the context, and in the case of variants to preceding records, the writings are short and differ only at the level of wording. In either case, as earlier records are edited with abridgment in their respective ways, the *Kojiki* and the *Nihon shoki* can be identified as the canon of the eighth-century Yamato kingdom.

Now, as mentioned in a previous section, the *teiki* and *kuji* during the reign of Emperor Tenmu consisted of various records—specifically, contexts and wordings—that had parts in common and parts that were unique to particular records. On the one hand, common factors appeared most emphatically in parts substantiating the advent of power, such as the context and names of central figures who appear in sections concerning the creation of the Japanese archipelago and the advent of the ancestor of the imperial family. On the other hand, unique elements were vividly expressed in other sections. The existence of commonalities in various records indicates the common consciousness with regards to the kingship which the clans fell under; in turn, the distinctness conveys the fact that the main characters of the myths were in actuality each clan.

The co-existence of both commonality and distinctness in the records portrays the manner in which the structure of rule was then managed. At the time, the sphere of influence was enabled via a vertically oriented organization that assumed a strong sense of political independence, which each clan upheld. As long as the kingdom was constituted by a composite of clans with their distinct characteristics, disparate interpretations had to be avoided. In a territorial society comprised of various clans, by bringing awareness to legal blood relationships, particularly in the period preceding and under the Ritsuryō social system, the comprehension of the myths was necessarily differentiated according to the clans.

While the clans did not exist completely independently, pursuing their own respective interests required a political mechanism that surpassed the particular interests of the ruling authority. In other words, the clans needed to secure an advantageous position by belonging to the political system, namely, by standing up to opposing groups, including domestic forces and foreign powers, as well as the masses within acquired territories. As long as kingship justified their existence, the centripetal desire to uphold a common story regarding its authority was indispensable for each of the clans. Clans became incorporated into the ruling structure, what might be called their superordinate mechanism, which then tightly knit their mutual relations in both political and ideological terms. Commonality as opposed to distinctness in the myths of each clan can be understood as a means to manifest a sense of belonging, thereby reflecting a particular social structure. The co-existence of commonality and distinctness of the *teiki* and *kuji* can thus be considered as responses to the political circumstances of the time, namely, a means of accepting the prevailing authority while expressing each clan's autonomy.

However, as times moved into the reign of Emperors Tenchi and Tenmu, in light of the defeat of the Japanese forces by the Chinese and Silla allied forces in the Battle of Hakusonkō (663), and with the destabilization of the system of domination by territorial chieftains, given the emergence of the patriarchal system (among other developments), a crisis in both international frontiers and the domestic arena threatened the continuation of the clan system and the Yamato kingdom that embraced it.[42] The result was the demise of the clan structure and the rise of a state system strongly bearing the characteristics of a bureaucracy. The various Ritsuryō system reforms that represented the bureaucracy and dictated the ideology that the land and people belonged to the monarch were implemented. At the same time, a Ritsuryō system-based state was established by reorganizing the clan system.[43] In particular, one can surmise that from the reign of Emperor Tenmu to the early Nara period, the Ritsuryō system became well established. The *Kojiki* and the *Nihon shoki* produced during this period strongly reflected the prevailing tendencies to negate the traditional clan system.

As is apparent from the discussion thus far, on the one hand the *Kojiki* and the *Nihon shoki* were a set of documents forming a canon which denied the autonomy of distinct clan records. In the words of Emperor Tenmu, with respect to the compilation of the Kiki, "This indeed is the procession of events of the state, the foundation of imperial influence...[See to it that] falsehood [is] eliminated [and] truth determined." The statement "Inscribe and define the various matters of *teiki* and remote antiquity" expresses the captivating force of the sovereignty and the state that was strengthening. On the other hand, the inclusion of clan records into the *Nihon shoki*, even if in a subordinate form with respect to the main text, does not merely indicate an objective means of certifying facts. It rather suggests that a certain amount of respect existed toward clan records. This characterizes the establishment of the Ritsuryō state system with the clan system as its foundation.

By enhancing the bureaucratic side, the imperial court also increased its controlling power over the clans, which inevitably brought about a sense of cohesion among diverse clans. The close-knit ties developing among the clans enabled a process of comparison of their respective mythological perspectives and brought out the contradictions in interpretations. As friction and disorder arose over interpretations, the imperial court worked to integrate them and instill order. This is also conceivably the reason for the creation of the canon during the period from Emperor Tenmu's reign to the beginning of the Nara period.

The correspondence between the Ritsuryō system and formation of the *Kojiki* and the *Nihon shoki* becomes clear through comparing the various policies of the system and the progress made in the compilation process. The compilation of the *Kojiki* and the *Nihon shoki* was pursued in parallel with the compilation of laws, the formation of the family register, the reorganization of the court rank and clanship system, and the establishment of the castle town system, among other developments. In this perspective, the *Kojiki* and the *Nihon shoki* became products of the modern Ritsuryō state and not relics of the past. The question becomes: what was the relationship between the *Kojiki* and the *Nihon shoki* concerning their canonical status in the early Nara period? I will be addressing this issue next. In any event, it is evident that, as the Ritsuryō system established itself from the reign of Emperor Tenmu to the early Nara period, the question of the *teiki* and *kuji* existing autonomously (among clans that maintained their commonality with the imperial line) was nevertheless ignored. This consequently led to the canonization of the *Kojiki* and the *Nihon shoki* by the early Nara period.

The formation of the canon, moreover, amounted to the rejection of other records.[44] This is clear from Emperor Tenmu's words which signify the compilation policy of the *Kojiki*: "The *teiki* and *honji* [*kuji*] in the various clans' keeping are already inaccurate and contain many fallacies." In a similar vein, in the "Alleged books' records," the article of the Third Month of 533 which signifies the compilation policy of the *Nihon shoki* states: "Examining the past and present we will thus restore authenticity." This statement indicates that such historical records were in some cases judged as false, and in such instances were not used in the *Kojiki* and the *Nihon shoki* or even as a part of the "Alleged books' records."

Records that were not used, left alone as they were, had a meager possibility of being transmitted to later generations. The *Suishu* (Book of the Sui Dynasty; article on the country of Japan, in the section on "Eastern Barbarians") suggests, however, that records which differed from the content of the *Kojiki* and the *Nihon shoki* existed during the Yamato reign under Empress Suiko, from the late sixth century to the early seventh century. In the alleged words of the Yamato kingdom's delegate to the Sui dynasty: "The ruler of Yamato has Heaven for an elder brother and Sun for a younger brother."[45] This relates the belief that the Sun deity, who was male, and the God of Heaven were brothers, and the emperor or empress was their middle brother or sister. The records in the *Suishu* are, of course, historical material from a period older than the *Kojiki* and the *Nihon shoki* and in fact were written from a Chinese point of view. As such they cannot be compared so easily with the Kiki. However, from an elementary perspective, the various records of the *Kojiki* and the *Nihon shoki* describe the sibling relationship corresponding to the *Suishu* as one between the "female goddess Amaterasu," "the male god Tsukiyomi," and "the male god Susanowo," and designate either the eldest sister Amaterasu or the youngest brother Susanowo as the ancestor of the emperor; they therefore differ from the records in the *Suishu*. Given that the *Suishu* represents just one fraction of records that differ from the *Kojiki* and the *Nihon shoki*, we can surmise that the variants on imperial mythology had a broader scope at a given point in history than the existing "Alleged books' records" that we have analyzed.

The Renewal of Myth

Canonization was not a singular event, solely attempted during the reign of Emperor Tenmu. The tension between the independence of each clan's myth, in terms of the kingship, and the move toward canonization to unify such myths could already be witnessed in the *Tennōki* (Record of the Emperor) and the *Kokki* (Records of the Country) during the reign of Empress Suiko, and following the reign of Emperor Tenmu, as well as in the movement concerning the *Nihongi kōsho* (lectures of commentaries on the *Nihon shoki*) of the early Heian period. In ancient times, there had been a dispute over the naming of clans and their designated name-titles, which represented political or social standing, in the imperial court in the chronicle of Emperor Ingyō in the *Nihon shoki*. The following statement can be surmised as being a transmission from the fifth century:

As a result of fights between the high and low classes, there is unrest among people. In some cases a person loses his *kabane* (name representing political or social standing) due to his mistake. In other cases, a person intentionally insists on acquiring a higher *uji* (clan name) than that which is original.

The imperial court, judging by means of *kugatachi* (a way of testing truth or falsehood by swearing before the gods and plunging one's hands into boiling water, with the presence or absence of wounds as the determining factor), is said to have established integration with regard to such controversies, "after which, the clan names and their social standings were naturally fixed so that no person falsifies them."[46]

In these circumstances, all the clans explained the validity of their clan names and their respective social standing by stating their historic origins: "Regarding aristocrats and officials as well as the hereditary regional officials, and others, each and all claim to be offspring of emperors or to have otherwise descended from heaven."[47] As mentioned above, the fact that the problem of determining the social standing of clan names was closely tied to the story of the imperial family is evident in the accounts presented by *Takahashi ujibumi* (Document of the Takahashi clan) and *Kogoshūi* (Gleanings from Ancient Stories), among others. Given the way the *Kojiki* and the *Nihon shoki* are constituted, we can see that stories were crucial in giving credibility to a lineage or clan name and its social standing. From these considerations, it is conceivable that there had been disagreements among clans concerning the myth of kingship, in addition to the issue involving the social standing of clan names at the time of the chronicle of Emperor Ingyō. If we presume that the notion of a social standing (*kabane*) was created from the end of the fifth century to the sixth century, the account from the chronicle of Emperor Ingyō probably dates back to that time as well.

To continue our discussion, *Tennōki* (Imperial Lineage Record) and *Kokki* (Records of the Country) were inscribed during the reign of Empress Suiko in the period from the end of the sixth century to the beginning of the seventh century.[48] This is thought to have been the age in which the imperial court reorganized the clan system through its new policies of Kenpō Junanajyō (The Admonition with Article 17), namely, in terms of Kan'i Jūnikai (the twelve ranks signified by court headwear) and the bureaucratic system. As with *Tennōki* and *Kokki*, these developments can be viewed as part of "the clan system reorganization policies" undertaken during the reign of Empress Suiko. We consider this to be, in other words, the presentation of the authority's integrated opinion on its own history in relation to the *teiki* and *kuji*, which presumably had already been in existence. From the above documents, we understand that canonization did not occur just once but had been attempted before the *Kojiki* and the *Nihon shoki*.

Tennōki and a large part of the *Kokki*, however, were burned during the rebellion within the imperial court in 645 (Isshi no Hen). Eventually, the *Kojiki* and the *Nihon shoki*, which were compiled later, became the most authoritative documents—the canon—with political power that was enabled via the establishment of the Ritsuryō system as its backdrop. This stabilized the myth of kingship that had existed in a segregated form, and thereafter interpretation was conducted on the basis of the *Kojiki* and the *Nihon shoki*. As subsequent history shows, beginning in this period, the interpretation of the Kiki myths was constricted.

By no later than the early Heian period, of the two documents comprising the Kiki, the *Nihon shoki* became the canon of the state. This is demonstrated through various developments. The interpretation of the text within books was primarily based on the *Nihon shoki*, rather than the *Kojiki*. At the time, *Nihon shoki*-based writings were the main axis in all of the documents officially submitted, one after another, including *Takahashi ujibumi* (compiled approximately 789), *Kogoshūi* (compiled 807), *Sendai kuji hongi* (Chronicle of Ancient Matters, compiled in the early tenth century) and related clan records, as well as *Shinsen shōjiroku* (New Selection of Clans' Names and Standings, compiled 815), which included records directly related to the clans and involved content that was not included in the *Nihon shoki*. Accounts from the *Nihon shoki* were employed as the basis of judgment in litigation cases in the imperial court, stemming from disputes among clans concerning official duties and falsified names. The *Nihon shoki* was the very first book to be enumerated among the Rikkokushi (Canonical Japanese History, constituted of six books). In contrast, as mentioned in the foreword to *Kōninshiki* (written as the private memorandum for imperial lectures on the *Nihon shoki* during the ninth century) and the lecture on the *Nihon shoki* in the Sōhei period (931–38), the *Kojiki* was placed on a par with the *Kuji hongi* (Chronicles of Ancient Matters), and *Shinbetsuki* (Genealogy of Gods), and thereby perceived to be private writing that was one rank below the *Nihon shoki*.[49]

The establishment of the canon, though, did not make the act of interpretation completely standardized. Differences in the *Kojiki*, the main text of the *Nihon shoki*, and the "Alleged books' records," in terms of both context and wording, hampered a unified understanding for future generations of interpreters. This brought about the formation of a new horizon for interpretation that introduced a subjective mode for selecting and compiling the various records, with a concern to make adjustments for contradictions.[50] The lecture on the commentary of the *Nihon shoki* that commenced in 814 in the imperial court was the result of the sovereignty itself attempting a contemporary interpretation of the sovereign myth centering on the *Nihon shoki*.[51]

The quotation that follows has the same characteristics as the edict of Emperor Tenmu, in terms of the act of compiling the *Kojiki* and the *Nihon shoki* during his reign, and displays a strong intent to adopt the role of the canon representing the state:

> There are so many texts with omissions still ubiquitously present among the people. They are full of falsehood and contain little truth. Printing falsehood without reason, this is the case of not reading the old history books [the *Nihon shoki*, *Kojiki*, and so on]...[and] from grave concern that such falsehood is annihilating this authentic history, we amend their errors ... and inaugurate the lecture on the *Nihon shoki* in the imperial court.[52]

During the early Heian period, struggles erupted among clans over their official roles, such as those between the Takahashi and Azumi clans or the Inbe and Nakatomi clans, and clan records were in turn submitted to the imperial court, such as the *Takahashi ujibumi* and *Kogoshūi*. Among the general population there were a lot of cases involving applications for the use of pseudonyms or the claim to inheritance assuming a different identity, or even with regard to the reconsideration of social status. One can conjecture that these applicants were trying to use the system of clan names, denoting social status, to assert their own rights at a time when the Ritsuryō system was being transformed and society was going through upheaval. An official document issued during the Enryaku period (728–806) stated:

> There are numerous people and clans, who have the same origin but separate into different lines, or otherwise do not share origins yet have the same family name, desiring to be based on lineage records, yet many go through historical changes. In examining family register records it is difficult to distinguish between the main line and the branches...These names have in many cases deviated from the original name. This should be corrected. We cannot permit the false use of names.[53]

Furthermore,

> Many people in recent years are changing their names. They amount to a significant number of people avoiding the imposition of tax. The people try to move their belongings to become holders of court rank [elevating in status] from having had none. Such dishonest people are numerous.[54]

Such words describe a given milieu, as well as imply that there was confusion arising over clan names and their status. The imperial court regarded clan names and their social standing as "the most important affair concerning moral principles. [Namely] the state's foundation."[55] It repeatedly burned books of genealogical tables as well as holy books, and prohibited the false use of family names in official documents issued by the cabinet to ministries or regions during the Ritsuryō period. Then in 815 the imperial court completed the *Shinsen shōjiroku* to rectify the social order, with respect to clan names and their social standing, as a means of substantiating its own legitimacy.

During the Heian period, the process of lecturing on the commentary of the *Nihon shoki* commenced in 814, the year before the selection of *Shinsen shōjiroku*. As mentioned in the foreword of *Kōnin shiki*, it was implemented in this intensified social situation and amidst the succession of policies. That is to say, the lecture on the *Nihon shoki* was thought to serve as a means for establishing a general agreement on a unified perspective on the history of kingship, including the issue of clan names and their social status. By this time, since it was established that the *Nihon shoki* was the canon of the ruling authority, a new text was not being produced. Rather, the connotation of the *Nihon shoki* was being transformed by way of commentary, through lectures on the commentary of the *Nihon shoki*. The lecture was based on the premise that the main text of the *Nihon shoki* had utmost authority, and yet it attempted to create a new understanding that was not bound by it. In a broad sense, this process can be considered to have renewed the canonization process.

One can thus surmise that canonization was not a singular event but occurred repeatedly, counterbalancing the structure of interpretation with the propensity for autonomy. The compilation of the *Kojiki* and the *Nihon shoki* during the reign of Emperor Tenmu was merely one example of this process. The interpretation of the canon functioned effectively as long as it conveyed the social situation accurately, when the kingship had political power. The monarchy was an organ overarching individual clans and also reflected the relationships among the clans constituting the imperial court. Furthermore, it possessed the capacity for being influenced by the interests of prominent clans. For this reason, the content of the canon was also predisposed to the power-ridden landscape of the clans. For example, the *Kojiki* was considered to reflect the disposition of Emperor Tenmu, while the lecture on the *Nihon shoki* was said to take into consideration the Fujiwara and other powerful clans. As time passed, however, the canon, as an inscribed and fixed document, became divorced from the social situation that was transient and required remolding as the clans' positions were transformed.

The everlasting struggle between canonization and independent interpretation has as its background the relationship between the kingship and its constituent groups. This form of social structure dates back not only to the pre-Ritsuryō State period and the Heian period, but even further back to the time of agricultural collectives (in minor provinces), as apparent during instances of water control in the Yayoi period (fourth century BCE to third century CE). The formation of a class-based society occurred through the merging and expansion of various groups, a process accompanied by the spirited relationship between canonization and independent interpretation. Therefore, we can regard the competitive relationship of interpretations as having existed from earlier times; namely, such a milieu was not limited to the period corresponding to the Kiki, *Tennōki*, and *Kokki*, although the names of gods and contexts might have differed with the evolving *Kojiki* and *Nihon shoki*. For instance, even if the *teiki* and *kuji* were organized into one entity in the sixth century, as Tsuda Sōkichi has pointed out, this was merely an instance of canonization rather than signifying the dismissal of the pluralizing structure of interpretations which co-existed in the Kiki. We must recognize that canonization and autonomy comprised a dynamic structure which accompanied interpretation. It is therefore possible to conclude that one answer to the theoretical problem of the origination of the Kiki has been presented here—in a form differing from what Tsuda presupposed.

Under such circumstances, when we consider matters objectively, myth essentially has the structural characteristic of pluralizing. This is recognized in various ways, depending on the point of view of the interpreter. Emperor Tenmu considered the splitting dynamic with respect to the *teiki* and *kuji* as "already inaccurate" and as containing "many fallacies." In his words, "This indeed is the history of the state, the foundation of Imperial influence...[and there is need for] eliminating falsehood, determining truth." He thereby justified his authority over the abridgment activities which signified the restoration of an authentic past. This concept regarding the state of affairs as being flawed had also been expressed in the compilation of the *Kojiki*, during the reign of Emperor Genjō in the sixth century, in the following manner: "Deploring the errors in *kuji*, we rectify the mistakes that had been entered in the past chronicle."[56] Similarly, during the lectures on the *Nihon shoki* at the beginning of the Heian period, it is stated, "writings, such as old false legends, are fascinating for the eye...[and] are still ever present among the people, beyond our control. Falsehood abounds while truth is sparse."[57] Finally, in a similar vein, with the compilation of the *Shinsen shōjiroku*, it is stated, "many clan records submitted newly to the kingship reveal a contradiction in the old authoritative history."[58]

This conviction had been supported by the passage in the chronicle of Emperor Ingyō in the *Nihon shoki*, thought to be transmitted in the fifth century, which presupposes that orderliness was maintained in ancient times: "In the ideal governance of ancient times, because there was no confusion with regard to family names, people were assigned their proper social status."[59] Although this historical material directly relates to clan names and their status, the concern to preserve authentic legends from ancient times is also apparent in the words of Emperor Tenmu (reigning from 673 to 686), on the occasion of the compilation of the *Kojiki*: "At this time, unless the shortcomings [of concomitant variants] are corrected, the authority of its truth will be lost in the years to come." Similarly, the words of Emperor Saga (reigning from 809 to 823) on the occasion of the lecture on the *Nihon shoki* point to the "grave concern that such a falsehood is annihilating this authentic history."[60]

The notes of the *Nihon shoki* explain the reason for variant accounts deriving from what was originally a single record, in the following manner:

> In the chronicle of the Emperor, there are numerous old characters, and the people that select them change from time to time. When people of later times study and read them, they abbreviate and revise them according to their personal judgment. There are many errors and discrepancies as they get transcribed.[61]

This mode of reasoning points to the countless old characters and the difficulty of transcription as being an inherent problem with historical material. The words in the foreword of the *Shinsen shōjiroku*, etc., although not as detailed, point to the same dilemma, stating:

> As is well-known, in researching ancient records and looking broadly through old histories, the transliteration of words by characters in accordance with their sounds has produced confusion. All the more, such treatment creates incongruities and, by conflating them together, winds up causing contradictions.[62]

This implies that the myths would have retained their unitary state had these elements not existed.

With canonization, interpreters had presupposed a single authentic record in the past and consequently denied the state of "pluralizing interpretations" that were contemporaneous. The perpetual unitary state presupposed in the past had sparse historical material and existed as an obscure antiquity, far removed from the interpreters. Therefore, they could let their imaginations wander.[63] Believing that the recovery of the unitary state could be achieved by their efforts at elucidation, the interpreters self-referentially attested to the authenticity of their own interpretations.

When we consider the relationship between the *Kojiki* and the *Nihon shoki* with respect to the canon, at the time when they were compiled, we can surmise the belief in one canonical formation restoring the authenticity of the lost ancient legend. As described earlier, canonization resulted from a process of selecting among a large number of variants. In fact, pluralizing interpretations and canonization were two distinct currents that flowed side by side. In their midst emerged a movement calling for unification and propelling the multiple variants into forming one canon. From this we can naturally infer that the process of reduction selected one variant of the *Kojiki* and the *Nihon shoki*, rather than conceive them as two texts fitting together. The conventional view has been that the *Kojiki* and the *Nihon shoki* were made contemporaneously but for different purposes (one for foreign use and the other for domestic use, etc.). Yet, these differences were not merely a matter of literary style, but extended to basic worldviews. Therefore, one can assume that the imperial court would have had difficulty in simultaneously having faith in two worldviews and so would use them for specific situations. One would then conclude that clusters of variant *teiki* and *kuji*, each with its distinctive characteristics, had to have existed before the Kiki because documents reveal that within a short eight-year span the *Kojiki* and the *Nihon shoki*, with varying worldviews, were established in succession.

Ritsuryō were also created over and over as canonic laws, such as Asukakiyomihara-rei (established 689), Taihō-ritsuryō (implemented in 701), Yōrō-ritsuryō (established 718, implemented in 752), and finally Santei-ritsuryō (established 769, implemented in 791) during the reign of Emperor Kanmu; in particular Taihō-ritsuryō and Yōrō-ritsuryō were compiled within a period of seventeen years. As canonic laws emerged from the new authoritative perspective on each occasion, the canonization of the *Kojiki*, the *Nihon shoki*, and the lectures on the *Nihon shoki* was repeatedly initiated in order to be integrated on the basis of the new perspective. Following this train of thought, at the time of establishing the *Nihon shoki*, there is a high probability that the canonic laws of the state identified with it. This also coincides with the fact that people of ancient times considered the *Nihon shoki* as the paramount history of Japan and did not place much importance on the *Kojiki*.

Construing the past as a justification for the authenticity of one's own interpretation was not limited to the canonization process. A comparable orientation is recognizable even within individual interpretations that were in fact criticized by the canon. These circumstances were explicated in the chronicle of Emperor Ingyō in the following manner: "Regarding aristocrats and officials as well as the hereditary regional officials, and others, each and all claim to be offspring of emperors or otherwise descended from heaven." Similarly, in the edict of the Second Month of 809, the following is stated:

> [In] *Wakan sōreki teifuzu* (The Comprehensive Imperial Genealogical Chart of Japanese and Chinese Emperors), with Amenominakanushi-no-kami as the progenitor, Chinese kings and Korean kings including the founder of the Han dynasty and others came forth, thereafter leading to descendants. Japanese and Chinese are mixed together, daring to blemish the dignity of the Emperor.[64]

Also, the *Kōninshiki* maintained, "This book [The Comprehensive Imperial Genealogical Chart] insists on the existence of the person who proclaims himself as the emperor among the common people."[65]

As communicated in a straightforward manner via the phrase, "the history of the state, the foundation of imperial influence," in ancient times canonization was related to political power and its consequences. From the middle ages, as the sovereignty lost political clout, it became difficult to envelop society with one interpretation. Regardless of the level of political effectiveness *per se*, in light of establishing the canon, the belief that a single interpretation would in itself explain the past was on a par with Motoori Norinaga and Tsuda Sōkichi's endeavors. Research to date on the *Kojiki* and the *Nihon shoki*, as exemplified by Tsuda Sōkichi's theory that the *teiki* and *kuji* were established in the sixth century, focuses solely on the canonical aspects and hardly ever reflects on the pluralizing structure of interpretations. This also applies to Motoori Norinaga, who attempted to demonstrate what he considered "genuine" ancient records by eliminating elements resembling the Chinese classics.

As far as one can tell from viewing historical documents, in no given period has interpretation actually ever been unified in spite of the constant assertion that myths are originally unitary. Pluralizing interpretations which projected themselves onto the external world, whereby a plethora of interpretations existed alongside each other, often resulted in friction and developed into disputes over the question of validity. Miscellaneous interpretations had co-existed, which amounted to the *teiki* and *kuji* of each clan during the period of the compilation of the *Kojiki* and the *Nihon shoki*, and subsequently included the *kuji hongi*, *Kogoshūi*, *Takahashi ujibumi*, *Tensho*, etc. during the period marked by the lectures on the *Nihon shoki*. Although limited to clan names and their status, and to the genealogical records, the chronicle of Emperor Ingyō alludes to the disparate interpretations of individual clans. Even thereafter, leading up to modern times, conflicts over interpretations are prevalent and far too many to enumerate here—between medieval Shintō and Suika Shintō, Confucianism and the study of Japanese classical literature, schoolbooks compiled by the state and the leftist view of history, among other examples.

Finally, we can surmise that the assumption of the unitary state of myths is like a motionless picture that human beings generate out of the past, stemming from the fact that they live in a world marked by the autonomy of interpretations; in turn they unconsciously criticize the interpretations of others so as to assert the validity of their own position. To identify one's own interpretation with what is supposedly the "actual past" simultaneously authenticates one's perception of the external world. What is presumed to be common among various records helps incorporate similar features within various interpretations, building up the conviction that each interpreter is working on the basis of a common historical tradition. As long as myth structurally tends to splinter, interpretation oriented toward a unitary view which ignores this very structure is necessarily committed to abridging "new" mythological canons. If we are to head toward an objective clarification of the world of the past through the interpretation of the Kiki texts, we need to overcome the insistence on a single understanding by first and foremost recognizing the structural character of myths.[66]

In contrast, by freeing one's own interpretation from an essentialist understanding of the past, and by creating one's own foundation with dissimilar interpretations, one is able to construe a new interpretation. Every interpretation reflects distinct subjects and is an expression of a worldview comprised of periods, classes, and individual characteristics varying in accordance with each interpreter. As there has always been a multitude of interpretations in any given period that are based on the integration of earlier perspectives, surely interpretations do potentially co-exist in a parallel sense and mutual differences are the catalyst for elucidations in successive periods. In other words, the act of interpretation, while dialectically repeating the splitting and integration process, opens new vistas for comprehending historicity.

In this milieu, the evaluation of a text in light of its authenticity would virtually not matter, and the *Kojiki* and the *Nihon shoki* would merely be one formation of a worldview denoting a distinct subjective configuration that is relevant to a given era. Thus, different interpretations would be valid in their own right, and each interpretation would potentially stand on equal footing, capable of attaining relevance through various periods and for different classes. Each interpretation would not assert itself as being absolute but rather maintain a relative standing with an awareness of the differences that persist. In addition, by engaging in dialogue, interpretations will continually be capable of producing a renewed understanding. In practice, this would not amount to the proclivity to return to a unitary past but rather signify a chance to constitute a multifarious past as it signifies the present and future. By achieving this, the history of the interpretation of myth will reflect the dynamic movement of the human spirit.

3 Myth in Metamorphosis: Ancient and Medieval Versions of the Yamatotakeru Legend

In the first quarter of the eighth century, the compilation of the *Nihon shoki* (Chronicles of Japan) in 720 was an epoch-making event. Together with the *Kojiki* (Record of Ancient Matters), compiled in 712, it was composed to sort out and consolidate the various legends and historical accounts relating to the Yamato imperial rule which had been fragmentarily preserved by individual clans associated with the Yamato court. The *Nihon shoki* eventually acquired a pre-eminent position as the first official national history. As a consequence, its account of the legends relating to the Yamato court significantly influenced the versions in texts written thereafter, such as the *Kogoshūi* (Gleanings from Ancient Stories, compiled by the Inbe clan in 807) and the *Sendai kuji hongi* (Chronicle of Old Things, including the oral tradition of the Mononobe clan, compiled in the early tenth century; also known as *Kujiki*). This chapter focuses on one of these legends, that of the ill-fated hero Yamatotakeru (Valiant Prince of Yamato), who was the son of the twelfth emperor according to the traditional chronology used in the work. By examining the development of the Yamatotakeru legend, we can explore the ways in which subsequent compilers of texts, while simultaneously developing their distinctive points of view, negotiated with the authority of the *Nihon shoki*.

The vivid accounts in the Kiki of Yamatotakeru's pacification of regions not yet under the Yamato rule and the powers of his sword, Kusanagi, enabled the legend to gain and uphold its popularity. It is thus an excellent vehicle for tracing the history of the interpretation of Kiki myths. While today we tend to view these myths from a perspective shaped by interpretations developed in the early-modern period by Kokugaku (Nativist) scholars such as Motoori Norinaga (1730–1801), a substantial gap separates such interpretations from ancient and medieval positions.

Henceforth, in revealing such distinctions and their implications, I will consider the metamorphosis of the Yamatotakeru legend in three parts: 1) the forms found in the *Nihon shoki*, the *Kojiki*, and the *fudoki* (provincial gazetteers ordered to be compiled by the Yamato court in 713); 2) the interpretations developed in the Heian period (794–1185); and 3) the interpretations that took shape in the medieval period, namely, in the Kamakura (1192–1333) and Muromachi periods (1338–1573).

Early Versions of the Yamatotakeru Legend: the *Kojiki*, *Nihon shoki*, and *Fudoki*

The oldest versions of the Yamatotakeru legend available to us today are those included in the *Kojiki*, the *Nihon shoki*, and the *fudoki*, all of which were compiled in the span of time extending from the reigns of Emperor Tenmu (672–87) and Emperor Jitō (687–97) to those of Emperor Genmei (707–15) and Emperor Genshō (715–24), the period in which the Ritsuryō state was fully established. The versions of the Yamatotakeru legend found in Kiki (in both the *Kojiki* and the *Nihon shoki*) describe the pacification of outlying areas and record incidents that demonstrate the powers of the Kusanagi sword.

According to the Kiki, Yamatotakeru, because of his unusual strength, is twice ordered by his father, Emperor Keikō, to undertake pacification expeditions. His first expedition is directed to the west in order to pacify the Kumaso in southern Kyushu.[1] In the second expedition, he is bound for the northeast to quell the Emishi in eastern Japan and other recalcitrant elements. Although he encounters various obstacles in both expeditions, he manages to carry out his mission. According to the Kiki, as a result of Yamatotakeru's efforts, the authority of the Yamato court became more firmly established by geographically extending over these regions. Subsequently, members of the ruling lineage were dispatched to the distant regions, and the boundaries of provinces and districts were demarcated during the reign of Emperor Keikō's successor, Emperor Seimu. Two reigns later, an expedition to Korea was undertaken by the female ruler Empress Jingū. In effect, the Kiki depicts Yamatotakeru's pacification of the east and west as bringing about a unification, whereby most of the Japanese islands are brought under the influence of the Yamato court. As a result, his accomplishments mark a key turning-point in the narrative embellishing the history of the nation.

The Kusanagi sword plays an important part in the story of Yamatotakeru's pacification of the east. As related in the Kiki, Susanowo had extracted the sword from the body of the eight-headed and eight-tailed dragon, after having slain the beast. Due to its fearsome potency, the sword is later transferred from the ruler's palace to the Ise shrine, where Yamatotakeru receives it from his aunt Yamatohime, the Ise vestal. Ultimately, however, without the sword in hand, Yamatotakeru confronts the hostile local deity of Mt. Ibuki and as a consequence is wounded and dies.

While the powers of the Kusanagi sword are described in the Kiki versions of the Yamatotakeru legend, as compared to medieval versions, this is not of major concern within the texts. The *Kojiki* and a variant account included in the *Nihon shoki* both relate that an enemy attempted to trap Yamatotakeru by setting a grass fire at Yaizu, and that Yamatotakeru escaped by using the sword to cut the grass (which is the source of the name Kusanagi, meaning "grass-mower"). This story does not appear, however, in the main text of the *Nihon shoki*. Rather, the main text only describes how the Kusanagi sword was left behind by Yamatotakeru in a fatal moment and came to be enshrined at Atsuta shrine in Owari province. At the time of the compilation of the Kiki, it has been argued that the regalia, consisting of the mirror (Yata no Kagami), the sword (Kusanagi), and the jewel (Yasakani no Magatama), were not yet regarded as the quintessential markers of royal succession. Rather, it was in the medieval period that such objects acquired regal implications.[2] We need to keep this in mind when considering the stories about Kusanagi in the Kiki texts, being careful not to inadvertently ascribe assumptions that actually arose in subsequent periods.

The *Kojiki* and the *Nihon shoki* formulated their own distinctive versions of the Yamatotakeru legend by adding different components to shared elements, in accordance with their own narrative strategies. Let me briefly distinguish the two texts.

Today, the *Kojiki* version of the legend is principally well known. While in the *Nihon shoki* Yamatotakeru is identified as the crown prince, in the *Kojiki*, as indicated by the phrase "the three princes ... bore the title of heir apparent," he is presented as one potential successor to the throne. His behavior in the *Kojiki* is that of a trickster, and his inability to control his extraordinary strength is a source of disturbance. A prime example is the murder of his elder brother Ōusu. Commanded by Emperor Keikō, his father, to teach and admonish (*negioshie satose*) Ōusu for failing to come to the morning and evening meals, Yamatotakeru misinterprets his father's words and kills Ōusu, tearing him limb from limb. While Emperor Keikō merely seeks to request Ōusu's presence in stating "*negioshie satose*," Yamatotakeru takes it to imply that Ōusu has to be literally crushed (following the implicit meaning of "*negioshie satose*").[3]

Consequently, terrified by Yamatotakeru's fearless and wild disposition, Emperor Keikō decides to dispose of him by sending him on a campaign against the Kumaso in southern Japan. Yamatotakeru nevertheless remains devoted to his father. Even after he recognizes the emperor's true intention, he harbors no grudge and simply laments. Being perturbed by the situation, in which Yamatotakeru suspects the emperor wishes him dead, his aunt Yamatohime comes to his aid.

In the *Kojiki*, Yamatohime appears in both the western and eastern expeditions to pacify the land. At the start of the western expedition, she gives Yamatotakeru female garments, while for the eastern expedition she offers him the Kusanagi sword and a bag containing flints. In his campaign against the Kumaso, Yamatotakeru makes use of the garments by disguising himself as a young girl and infiltrating the enemy camp. In the second expedition, he utilizes the flints, together with the Kusanagi sword, when his opponent attempts to trap him by setting fire to the plain at Yaizu. After mowing the grass with the sword, Yamatotakeru sets off a counteracting fire with the flints, and defeats the enemy by burning them to death. Yet, despite its apparent power, perhaps out of despair that his father Emperor Keikō hates him, Yamatotakeru forgets to carry the Kusanagi sword when he confronts the deity of Mt. Ibuki, which fatally ends his life. The legend of Yamatotakeru as presented in the *Kojiki* is thus the tale of a son sent to death by his father.[4]

In the *Kojiki*, the greater part of the account of the reign of Emperor Keikō expounds the feats of Yamatotakeru. In contrast, in the *Nihon shoki*, episodes concerning him appear intermittently as a part of the annals of Emperor Keikō's reign. Yamatotakeru's birth is noted under the events marking the second year of the reign. His expedition to the west is recorded under the twenty-seventh and twenty-eighth years. His expedition to the east is described as occurring in the fortieth to forty-third years. The *Nihon shoki* also reports that Emperor Keikō himself undertakes a campaign to Kyushu in southern Japan to fight against the Kumaso and other rebellious groups in the twelfth year of his reign, prior to Yamatotakeru's western expedition. It further records Emperor Keikō initiating a tour of inspection around the eastern provinces in the fifty-third year, after Yamatotakeru's death. The legend of Yamatotakeru thus constitutes only one part of the annals.

In the *Nihon shoki*, the pictographic characters (*kanji*) used to form Yamatotakeru's name, through the words "mikoto" attached to his name, signify that he is indeed the "emperor prince." The text refers to his mother, Harima no Tarōhime, as empress, thereby indicating that he is to be regarded as the crown prince, whereas the *Kojiki* transcribes "mikoto" to mean just one of the princes in the kingdom. Attesting to his status, in the *Nihon shoki*, Emperor Keikō declares to him, "This empire is thy empire, and this dignity is thy dignity." Yamatotakeru proudly identifies himself as the child of Emperor Keikō, while at the same time the emperor is described as having commended his good service and as having bestowed extraordinary affection on him. In this manner, Yamatotakeru's expeditions in the *Nihon shoki* are represented as missions properly undertaken by the heir to the throne, rather than, as in the *Kojiki*, a means of expelling him from the court.

The *Nihon shoki* further represents the mutual trust of Yamatotakeru and Emperor Keikō as one founded on the hierarchical relationship between lord and vassal. Yamatotakeru consistently terms himself the vassal of the emperor, his father. This usage is true with regard to the particular features of the position of heir apparent in the formative period of the Ritsuryō state (statutory system) in the eighth century[5] and indicates that the narrative principally informing the *Nihon shoki* version of the Yamatotakeru legend dated back to this period. By contrast, the narrative structure of the legend in the *Kojiki* reflects earlier patterns of succession.

While the *Nihon shoki* emphasizes the relationship between father and son, it portrays Yamatotakeru's relationship with Yamatohime in much fainter colors, as compared to the *Kojiki*. On the one hand, Yamatohime makes no appearance in the campaign heading west. On the other hand, on the occasion of the eastern expedition, she simply hands over to him the Kusanagi sword. The main text does not depict the sword as being quintessential to the eastern expedition; at Yaizu, when Yamatotakeru sets the counter-fire with a flint that he produces on his own, he does not use Kusanagi to mow down the grass. Yamatohime warns Yamatotakeru of his overconfidence, stating, "Be cautious, and yet not remiss." He disregards her advice. Certainly, in contrast to the *Kojiki*, where Yamatotakeru laments being dispatched on an impossible mission, the *Nihon shoki* describes him as taking the initiative in the eastern expedition. "Thy servant," he declares to his father, notwithstanding that it is a heavy task to speedily quell the disturbance. Hastily, leaving the Kusanagi sword behind, he goes off unarmed to fight the deity of Mt. Ibuki and receives a fatal injury. In both versions, failure to take the Kusanagi sword leads Yamatotakeru to his death. While in the *Kojiki*, being distracted, he forgets the sword, in the *Nihon shoki*, Yamatotakeru invites his own defeat by being overconfident of his own strength.

Apart from the versions found in the Kiki, the Yamatotakeru legend is also taken up in various *fudoki*. In the *Fudoki of Hitachi Province* in eastern Japan, references to Yamatotakeru appear in the preface and the sections on the Shida, Namekata, Kashima, Kuji, and Taka districts, while in the *Fudoki of Hizen Province* in southern Japan, references are found in the sections on the Saka, Oki, and Fujitsu districts. In terms of fragments of *fudoki* from other provinces held to be authentic, Yamatotakeru is mentioned in the gazetteers of the provinces of Owari, Mutsu, and Awa. These works describe him as bringing rebels under the sway of the court and opening up land for cultivation, as he progresses throughout the country. They also frequently include episodes not found in the *Kojiki* or the *Nihon shoki*. In the extant fragment of the *Fudoki of Owari Province*, for instance, Yamatotakeru, while staying in the dwelling of the local maiden Miyazuhime, one night at midnight happens to see the Kusanagi sword shine with an unearthly light. He tells the maiden, "This sword exhibits the signs of a deity; enshrine it and hold it as a token of me." This is explained as the origin of the enshrinement of the Kusanagi sword at Atsuta.[6]

Rather than being regarded as conflicting with the Kiki, such episodes from the *fudoki* should be thought of as complementary, providing a different yet valuable perspective. The order to compile the *fudoki* called on provincial officials to do the following: 1) choose auspicious pictographs for the names of the districts and villages in the provinces throughout the capital region and the seven circuits; 2) record in detail the locatable sources of silver, copper, and mineral pigments, and the native plants, trees, birds, animals, fish, and insects within the districts; 3) record and submit information about the condition of the soil, and the reasons for the names of mountains, rivers, and fields; and 4) report stories about notable matters and events passed down by the elders of the area.[7]

While the Kiki traced the process of expansion and consolidation of the Yamato rule through a chronological account centered on the imperial lineage, the *fudoki* looked at the same set of concerns from a spatial perspective. In other words, the *fudoki* surveyed the geographic component that signified the imperial reign, inspecting and elaborating on its involvement in the development of the land acquired through the various expeditions. While serving different purposes, both the Kiki and the *fudoki* complemented each other. The *fudoki* offered a spatial orientation and geographic comprehensiveness, while they did not inherently have a coherent chronological framework. Instead, the temporal dimension was substantiated by the Kiki, which focused on the process through which the Yamato rulers extended their authority over the archipelago.

Since different people were said to have composed the *fudoki* during the period following the compilation order in 713, they contain substantial inconsistencies in the content and transcriptions of names. Those for the Kyushu region exist in two forms: the complete version of texts, which corresponds in information and terminology to the *Nihon shoki*; and another version constituted of scattered fragments that do not match.[8] References to the Yamatotakeru legend found in the complete version of the *Fudoki of Hizen Province* closely parallel the account of Emperor Keikō's pacification of the west contained in the *Nihon shoki*, and in a number of instances they adopt the same wording.[9] The fragmented version of the *Fudoki of Hizen Province* does not include passages concerning Yamatotakeru. Yet, fragments of the *fudoki* from other provinces that incorporate episodes about Yamatotakeru reveal the divergence prevalent within different versions of the *Hizen Fudoki*. The account found in the fragmentary *Fudoki of Owari Province*, for instance in examining Miyazuhime and Yamatotakeru, does not correspond with either the *Kojiki* or the *Nihon shoki*. The same is true of the *Fudoki of Hitachi Province* and the fragments of the *Fudoki of Awa Province*.

In particular, the last two documents both speak of Emperor Yamatotakeru.[10] The *Fudoki of Hitachi Province* is believed to have been written before 715, on the basis of the terms employed in it. One can interpret its reference to Yamatotakeru as emperor (*tennō*) as suggesting that, prior to the compilation of the Kiki, he was regarded as such. While scholars have utilized this material in an attempt to recover a single original version of the myths, it would be more accurate to infer that multiple variants of the Yamatotakeru legend continued to exist even after the compilation of the Kiki, which consolidated divergent versions of the myths. Other evidence is apparent from an entry in the *Shoku Nihongi* (an imperially commissioned historical chronicle dating to the Heian period)[11] which notes reports of the ground rumbling in the vicinity of Yamatotakeru's grave. Although the entry is included as the sequel to the *Nihon shoki*, it does not adopt its pictographic signification but rather follows the *Kojiki* in transcribing Yamatotakeru's full name.

In conclusion, the versions of the Yamatotakeru legend contained in the *Kojiki* and the *Nihon shoki*, while incorporating various differences, were both built around the personality of Yamatotakeru and his relationship with his father. The *fudoki* preserved this perspective within their distinctive framework of the gazetteer format. However, subsequently, from the Heian period into the medieval period, such orientations began to be transformed.

The Yamatotakeru Legend in the Heian Period

The versions of the Yamatotakeru legend dating from the Heian period were formulated out of excerpts from the *Nihon shoki*. There were two types of passage that were recreated: one centering around the eastern and western expeditions, and the other focusing on miraculous events that were associated with the Kusanagi sword. An example of the former type may be found in the *Sendai kuji hongi*, said to have been compiled around the Engi period (901–23) by someone associated with the Mononobe clan.[12]

The *Sendai kuji hongi* (Chronicle of Old Things), which in its overall orientation follows the *Nihon shoki*, simply sums up the results of the eastern and western campaigns, incorporating this information at different points in the annals of the reign of Emperor Keikō. Regarding the western expedition, for instance, it adopts from the *Nihon shoki* the phrase "Yamatotakeru was sent to attack the Kumaso. He was at this time sixteen years of age."[13] In the *Nihon shoki* this is the opening sentence of a passage that goes on to relate various details of Yamatotakeru's campaign against the Kumaso and other rebellious elements. The *Sendai kuji hongi*, however, omits such details. Furthermore, given that the *Nihon shoki* does not offer a summation of the eastern expedition, it can be surmised that the compilers of the *Sendai kuji hongi* devised one on their own: "Although Yamatotakeru-no-mikoto subdued the eastern barbarians, he did not succeed in returning to the court; he passed away in the province of Owari."[14] Again the compilers did not include any details about the eastern expedition or refer to episodes involving the Kusanagi sword.

From the way that the compilers of the *Sendai kuji hongi* excerpted material from the *Nihon shoki*, one can surmise that they were not interested in replicating the character of human relationships found in the *Nihon shoki*. Rather, they were focused solely on the process and consequences of unifying the Japanese archipelago. To illustrate Yamatotakeru's bravery, the *Sendai kuji hongi* quotes the following description from the *Nihon shoki*: "Whilst a child he had a manly spirit; when he arrived at manhood his beauty was extraordinary. He was a rod in height, and his strength was such that he could lift a tripod."[15] However, this depiction does not include Yamatohime admonishing Yamatotakeru, nor does it mention the episode in which Yamatotakeru leaves the Kusanagi sword behind and fights unarmed with the deity of Mt. Ibuki. As a result, the character of Yamatotakeru in the *Sendai kuji hongi* is not attractive to readers. He has no hint of carelessness and is simply a figure with strength, carrying out the eastern and western expeditions.

The *Sendai kuji hongi* also reports that Yamatotakeru had offspring, implying that Tarashi-Nakatsu-Hiko-no-mikoto, who becomes Emperor Chūai, is his son. Likewise, the clear statement that Yamatotakeru "passed away in the province of Owari," was presumably included to account for the subsequent enthroning of Wakatarashihiko (later known as Emperor Seimu) as crown prince. Both passages essentially served to trace the evolution of the imperial lineage. While deriving its account of Yamatotakeru from the *Nihon shoki* (as apparent by the characters used to denote his name), the *Sendai kuji hongi* was narrowly focused.

In addition to historical works like the *Sendai kuji hongi*, Heian-period references to Yamatotakeru's expeditions are also found in *waka* poetry compositions celebrating the *Nihon shoki*. During the Heian period, lectures on the reading of *Nihon shoki* (*Nihongi kōsho*) became an established court custom. Following such presentations, participants would compose poetry based on themes associated with the characters who were introduced and discussed.[16] On one such occasion after the lecture held in 906, the councilor Fujiwara Arizane wrote the following poem for Yamatotakeru:

> Yamatotakeru smote the rebels
> in the provinces of the west and east,
> and brought them to submit to the monarch;
> how inspiring his example![17]

At the time, Fujiwara Arizane was the chief of the imperial guards,[18] and his poetry suggests how he identified his own position as one entrusted to guard the palace, by relating it to the acclaimed Yamatotakeru.

During the Heian period, in contrast to the aforementioned works that focus on Yamatotakeru as the pacifier of the land, the *Kogoshūi* (Gleanings from Ancient Stories) exemplifies a second form of expression which emphasizes the miraculous events associated with the Kusanagi sword. References to Yamatotakeru occur in three passages of the *Kogoshūi*. The first involves Susanowo presenting the sword to Amaterasu, having pulled it from the eight-headed and eight-tailed dragon's body. As an explanation as to why the sword, originally known as Ame-no-Murakumo (Gathering Clouds of Heaven) came to be called the Kusanagi sword, the passage states: "The year he pacified the eastern provinces, in Sagami province, Yamatotakeru met with danger from a plains fire. He escaped by mowing the grass down with this sword. Therefore it was renamed Grass Mower."[19]

As noted above, the Kusanagi sword does not figure in the grass-fire episode as described in the main text of the *Nihon shoki*, nor does the main text mention its former name, Ame-no-Murakumo. This passage from the *Kogoshūi* thus appears to have combined elements from the *Kojiki* and a variant of the *Nihon shoki*.[20] As an account of the miraculous powers of the Kusanagi sword, it is more comprehensive and focused than any of the versions found in the *Kojiki* and the *Nihon shoki*. The *Kogoshūi* evinces little interest in Yamatotakeru, as a character, or the circumstances of his expedition, and does not discuss the events leading up to his escape from the plains fire or what ensued thereafter. The focus of attention is rather on the Kusanagi sword. Certainly, the *Kogoshūi* played an influential part in medieval renditions of stories about the sword.

The second reference to Yamatotakeru occurs in a passage concerning Emperor Keikō's reign. While based on the account in the main text of the *Nihon shoki*, this passage makes no reference to Emperor Keikō's activities (which occupy a considerable portion in the original text). Instead, it only records Yamatotakeru's eastern expedition. Furthermore, it relates very few details about the expedition as such. In noting Yamatohime's bestowal of the Kusanagi sword upon Yamatotakeru, it quotes from the *Nihon shoki* with regard to her reprimand, "Be cautious, and yet not remiss." In turn, it sums up Yamatotakeru's accomplishments with the brief phrase: "Having pacified the eastern rebels, he returned." In the *Kogoshūi*, the primary focus of interest continues to be the Kusanagi sword, noting that Yamatotakeru, on his way back, broke his journey to stay with Miyazuhime in Owari province. This passage goes on to relate how, by "taking off the sword, he left it at her house ... encountered poisonous vapors and died."[21] As is apparent from the concluding sentence, "The sword Kusanagi is now at Atsuta shrine in the province of Owari," the author's main purpose seems to be to clarify how Kusanagi was moved from Ise to Atsuta. Yamatotakeru appears simply as an instrument for explaining this transference.

The third reference to Yamatotakeru comes in the addendum following the narrative section of the text, which states: "The divine sword Kusanagi is one of the imperial regalia. In the year when Yamatotakeru was returning from battle, he stopped at Owari, and the sword is there at Atsuta shrine."[22] The thrust of this note (its wording being original to *Kogoshūi*) is the same as that of the second passage.

The author's interest thus lies in the history of the Kusanagi sword rather than in Yamatotakeru as a figure. Each passage serves to support a resonant assertion, as apparent in the conclusion of the third passage:

> The miraculous powers of the divine object are thus apparent. It is only proper that on the ceremonial days when the court sends offerings to major shrines, it should be given the same reverence as the greatest of shrines. Yet, [the fact] that this has been long omitted and its rites left incomplete is a lamentable oversight.[23]

By 807, when Inbe Hironari submitted the *Kogoshūi* to the court, the Inbe clan's role in the ritual functions of the court had been largely taken over by the Nakatomi clan. Therefore, Hironari's major motive in composing this work was to call for the restoration of his clan's status as ritual specialists, appealing for their participation in various ceremonial activities.[24] One of the ritual functions of the Inbe clan was to present a duplicate of the Kusanagi sword on the enthronement of a new emperor. Such considerations underlie Hironari's emphasis on the history of the Kusanagi sword, offering reverence to the original sword.

Documents from the Heian period concerning Yamatotakeru are largely faithful to the wording in the main text of the *Nihon shoki*. One can surmise that when the compilers of such works were unable to fulfill their goals via the main text, they cited a variant of the *Nihon shoki* or the *Kojiki*. Yet, for the most part, they did not deviate from the framework of the story as narrated in the main text. The *Nihon shoki*'s influence over them attests to its significance in the Heian period, as the first account of state history. At the same time, Heian authors emphasized different aspects of the myths found in the *Nihon shoki* and the *Kojiki*, thereby composing distinct articulations of the Yamatotakeru legend.[25]

The Six National Histories reveal that in the early Heian period there were numerous petitions and appeals involving clans and their official claims to status. Through these appeals, people sought to affiliate themselves with the influential sectors of the aristocracy and to elevate their status in order to obtain more advantageous positions and reductions in tax obligations. While the parties initiating such appeals were asked to supply supporting evidence, most cases reveal that family histories which commenced with passages from the *Nihon shoki* were submitted to the court. The desire to use the official history of the ruling house to legitimate one's claims motivated people to literally copy the phrasing from the *Nihon shoki*. Yet, such writers also combined excerpts from the text in a way that would advance their own agendas. Through this process of excerpting, on the one hand, and recompiling, on the other, petitioners surrounded themselves with an aura of historical antiquity and carved out a space for launching their own perspectives. The *Nihon shoki*'s function, as the first state history, had an important social dimension, which at the same time may have contributed to an intellectual antiquarianism.

In conclusion, by reconstituting the narrative focus on particular figures found in the Kiki, Heian versions of the Yamatotakeru legend reveal a tendency to emphasize discrete elements, such as the expeditions to pacify the east and west (as in the *kuji hongi*), or the powers of the Kusanagi sword (as in the *Kogoshūi*). As indicated by the statement in *The Tale of Genji*, the Heian literary masterpiece by Murasaki Shikibu, works such as the *Nihon shoki* transmitted "a mere fragment of the truth."[26] During the Heian period (ninth to twelfth centuries), the portrayal of the activities of individuals entered the world of literary tales, which were praised for their capacity to capture the inner life of characters. Similarly, conceptions of deities became absorbed within the framework of esoteric Buddhism, and myths about kingship in its original form ceased to have an influence over people.[27]

The Yamatotakeru Legend in the Medieval Period

The Ritsuryō state balanced the monarchical authority, on the one hand, and the power of an office-holding aristocracy, on the other hand. In the latter part of the Heian period, the disintegration of this structure gave rise to the so-called power-bloc state (*kenmon taisei*), in which the influential elements of the aristocracy and the major religious institutions were in competition. As the centripetal force which held the state together weakened, people no longer looked to the *Nihon shoki* as an instrument for shaping social order, and by and large they ceased to compile collections of excerpts or commentaries on the text. In the medieval period, however, a heightened interest in the imperial regalia (and its three symbolic components) drew renewed attention to the Yamatotakeru legend, as one among a plethora of tales elaborating miracles associated with the Kusanagi sword.

A typical example of this phenomenon from the Kamakura period is the Ise Shintō work, *Yamatohime no mikoto seiki* (Life of Yamatohime). References to Yamatotakeru appear in sections elaborating on events during the reigns of Emperor Keikō and his predecessor, Emperor Suinin. The section concerning the reign of Keikō takes up the pacification of the east, and notes the miraculous powers of the Kusanagi sword while providing the background for its enshrinement at Atsuta. The description of Yamatohime's bestowal of the sword on Yamatotakeru is taken from the main *Nihon shoki* text and the passage on his escape from the grass fire is adopted from the *Nihon shoki* variant, while the account of his death derives from the *Kogoshūi*.[28] The combination of these elements makes it possible to tell the story of how the Kusanagi sword, while manifesting its divine powers during the plains fire, came to be enshrined at Atsuta.

Written in smaller letters in a glossed manner so as to differentiate them from the main text, the variants traditionally had been regarded as of secondary importance. In contrast, a notable feature of the new composite story was its inclination toward the *Nihon shoki* variant, which was regarded as being valid and as significant as the main text. For the compiler of *Yamatohime no mikoto seiki*, the reason for being attracted to the variant over the main text was its account of the Kusanagi sword, which acted on its own volition to rescue Yamatotakeru. As stated in the text: "The sword Murakumo, which the prince wore, wielded itself, and mowed away the herbage near the prince, thus enabling him to escape. Therefore that sword was called Kusanagi." By adopting this version, *Yamatohime no mikoto seiki* was able to go beyond the *Kogoshūi* in fashioning an evocative account of the powers of the Kusanagi sword. The compiler's close association with the Ise shrines gave him a good reason to try to enhance the powers of the sword. This in turn served to elevate the authority of both Yamatohime, who had presented the sword to Yamatotakeru, and the Ise shrines, where the sword had originally been located. In quoting Yamatohime's admonishment of Yamatotakeru as found in the main text, the compiler heightened her stature by changing the original status-neutral phrase "she stated" (*iwaku*) to the honorific expression, "she proclaimed" (*notamawaku*).

For the description of Yamatotakeru's death, *Yamatohime no mikoto seiki* chose the account in the *Kogoshūi* rather than the one in the *Nihon shoki*, presumably because the former includes the statement: "The sword Kusanagi is now at Atsuta shrine in the province of Owari." The *Kogoshūi* goes on to add: "It has yet to receive appropriate offerings from the court." For Inbe Hironari this statement reflected a key concern. In contrast, the compiler of *Yamatohime no mikoto seiki* omitted the sentence. In quoting the passage about the grass fire from the *Nihon shoki*, the compiler similarly left out the phrase which offered an etymology for the name of the area, namely, an understanding that "therefore that place was called Yaizu (Burning Harbor)." These omissions attest that for the compiler of *Yamatohime no mikoto seiki*, only Ise was of importance.

In the passage on the reign of Emperor Suinin, *Yamatohime no mikoto seiki* relates the history of the "eight-span weaving hall" in the Ise shrines. It declares that Yamatotakeru had bestowed on the shrines an "eight-span pike made of holly," which Yamatohime then enshrined in the eight-span weaving hall.²⁹ While this pike is not mentioned in the *Nihon shoki*, the *Kogoshūi*, or the *Sendai kuji hongi*, this passage appears to be based on the statement in the *Kojiki* about Emperor Keikō having given Yamatotakeru a pike of this sort during his send-off to the eastern expedition. The fact that this passage uses the same character as the *Kojiki* for "takeru" (as in Yamatotakeru) lends support to this supposition. However, the *Kojiki* does not mention anything about the pike being given to the Ise shrines. This element seems to have been derived from the *Shoku Nihongi* (an imperially commissioned historical chronicle dating to the Heian period), where the entry for April 702 states that the court presented a spear made of holly to the shrines.

The version of the Yamatotakeru legend found in *Yamatohime no mikoto seiki* thus incorporates phrases from the *Kogoshūi* and the *Kojiki*, as well as from the *Nihon shoki*. Given the fact that the *Kogoshūi* was based largely on excerpts from the *Nihon shoki*, *Yamatohime no mikoto seiki* can generally be perceived as being under its influence. Yet, it is apparent that the compiler did not find it necessary to cite the *Nihon shoki* directly, and furthermore that he blurred the distinction between the main text and its variants. As compared to the Heian period, this reflects the decline of authority accorded to the main text. Greater freedom for citation facilitated the elaboration of the story of Kusanagi to the point that it came to overshadow its bearer. Likewise, there continued to be little interest in Yamatotakeru as an individual personality.

Watarai Yukitada incorporated both these sections from *Yamatohime no mikoto seiki* in another work, *Ise nisho kōtai jingū shinmei hisho* (Secret Book of the Names of Deities of the Two Great Shrines of Ise), compiled in 1285. This work records the deities worshiped in the various shrines under the jurisdiction of the Ise shrines, and includes the legends of the Kusanagi sword and the eight-span pike in the section on *Saigu* (the vestal for the Ise shrine). In this section, Watarai also included a passage from the *Kojiki*, which is not cited in *Yamatohime no mikoto seiki*, that describes Yamatohime giving Yamatotakeru a bag containing a flint, along with the Kusanagi sword.³⁰ The point here is that the bag was presumably attractive, which provides further evidence of the spiritual powers of Yamatohime and the Ise shrines.

The tendency to re-read the Yamatotakeru legend as an account of the powers of the Kusanagi sword can also be witnessed in the commentaries on the *Nihon shoki* dating back to this period in general. In *Shaku Nihongi* (edited in the early fourteenth century), Urabe Kanekata cites the passage from the *Kojiki* involving Yamatotakeru's escape from the grass fire and adds a commentary to the phrase cited from the main text of the *Nihon shoki*, "Yamatohime-no-mikoto took the sword, Kusanagi, and gave it to Yamatotakeru-no-mikoto." In his commentary on the Kusanagi sword, he similarly cites the account of the origins of Atsuta shrine from the *Fudoki of*

Owari Province.³¹ Urabe is also involved with the *Kojiki uragaki*, a set of brief notes that constitutes the oldest extant commentary on the *Kojiki* to elaborate on various details in the text. One of the items taken up in the *Kojiki uragaki* is "the matter of the Kusanagi sword." Here again, it is the sword rather than the Yamatotakeru legend as such that attracts the compiler's interest, as compared to the prevalent orientation in the Heian period. Furthermore, one can infer that the renewed interest in the *Kojiki* indicates a greater openness to works other than the *Nihon shoki*.³²

Out of this textual activity revolving around the Kusanagi sword, new images of Yamatotakeru began to emerge. One was that of a romantic hero. This perspective is exemplified by *Owari no kuni Atsuta daijingū engi* (The Historical Origin of Atsuta Shrine in Owari Province, thought to have been composed by the end of the Kamakura period, hereafter cited as *Atsuta engi*), which offers an account of how the Kusanagi sword came to be worshiped as the divine treasure of Atsuta shrine.³³ This work describes Yamatotakeru's eastern expedition, paying particular attention to his escape from the grass fire and his relationship with Miyazuhime. In its utilization of phrases from the main and variant texts of the *Nihon shoki* to depict the grass-fire episode, *Atsuta engi* resembles *Yamatohime no mikoto seiki*. But, unlike the latter work, by drawing from the *Kojiki*, it also emphasizes the role of the bag received from Yamatohime. It thus reports:

> The sword he wore at his waist removed itself of its own accord from the sheath and mowed down the grass in all directions. And when he opened the bag he had been given, he found a flint. Amazed and delighted, he struck it, and lighting a counter-fire, escaped.³⁴

In *Ise nisho kōtai jingū shinmei hisho* there is only the citation from the *Kojiki* concerning the bag, as a supplement to the information found in the *Nihon shoki*, while in the *Atsuta engi* one sees that the two versions are joined in a single composite account.

By combining elements from the Owari province *fudoki* and the *Kojiki* to tell the story of Miyazuhime, the *Atsuta engi* presents her relationship with Yamatotakeru in a more powerful manner than either the *Nihon shoki* or the *Kojiki*. The *Atsuta engi* adopts the transcription used by the *fudoki* for Miyazuhime's name in relating the account of Yamatotakeru witnessing the sword shining at night, when he realizes it is invested with divine powers. It goes on to depict him as overriding the advice of his followers and deliberately leaving the Kusanagi sword with Miyazuhime as a sign of his love: "'After I return to the capital I will be sure to summon you to join me,' he declared. 'Cherish this sword as the guardian of your bed.' Removing the sword, he gave it to her."³⁵ (The parallel section of the *Fudoki of Owari Province* is unfortunately missing.) Given that this passage is not found in any of the other sources, one can conjecture that it was added by the compilers of the *Atsuta engi*. In comparison, in the *Kojiki* and the *Nihon shoki*, the Kusanagi sword remains at Atsuta simply as a result of Yamatotakeru's unexpected death.

Furthermore, in the *Atsuta engi*, the immediate cause of Yamatotakeru's death cannot be traced to overconfidence, as in the *Nihon shoki*. Rather, although he dies as a consequence of being unarmed while confronting the deity of Mt. Ibuki, it is related that he in fact leaves the Kusanagi sword behind as proof of his love for Miyazuhime. In a parallel manner, while in the *Nihon shoki* Yamatohime alludes to an imminent danger and warns Yamatotakeru as he sets off to pacify the east ("Be cautious, and yet not remiss"), in the *Atsuta engi*, she simply cautions him by stating, "Be sure never to let go of this Kusanagi sword from your side."[36]

The *Atsuta engi* emphasizes Yamatotakeru's love for Miyazuhime in other ways as well. In the *Kojiki* the two characters mutually exchange a poem (amounting to two poems) and in the *Nihon shoki* no poems are mentioned, but in the *Atsuta engi* they reciprocally exchange two poems (amounting to four poems). In the poems in the *Kojiki*, Yamatotakeru expresses regret for not being able to sleep with Miyazuhime because she is in the midst of her menstrual period. One of the poems by Yamatotakeru in the *Atsuta engi*, which is not found in any of the other texts, declares his expectation that "the sweet girl Hikami [Miyazuhime]" still awaits him:

Does the sweet girl Hikami,
of the Ayuchi inlet,
no longer set out her bed,
waiting for me to come?
Ah! the sweet girl! [37]

While the *Atsuta engi* was written as an account of the origins and history of the Atsuta shrine, it effortlessly awards Miyazuhime greater prominence than do other works and even introduces her brother, Inatane-no-Kimi. Yet, there appear to be other factors as well behind its detailed depiction of the relationship between Yamatotakeru and Miyazuhime. While works of this nature that date back to the Heian period were likely to simply note Yamatotakeru's conjugal relations with Miyazuhime, a distinct means of authenticating the text underlay *Atsuta engi*'s effort to portray the ties of love binding the two figures. This implication is relevant with regard to its depictions of other relationships in the story as well. In its description of Emperor Keikō's relationship with Yamatotakeru when he was undertaking the pacification of the east, and his grief upon receiving the news of his son's death, the *Atsuta engi* further emphasizes their mutual trust as compared to the *Nihon shoki*. In the same vein, it draws attention to Yamatotakeru's bravery by noting his elder brother Ōusu's cowardice.

The *Atsuta engi*'s account adopted the basic framework of the *Nihon shoki* with regard to the relationship between the focal characters. At the same time, by reworking excerpts from the *fudoki* and the *Kojiki* to relate the history of the Kusanagi sword and the Atsuta shrine, it developed a new image of Yamatotakeru—as a brave, yet romantic, hero. This contrasts with the Heian and earlier medieval works that emphasize the expeditions of pacification and the Kusanagi sword and have only a limited interest in his character.

A similar phenomenon may be seen in the *Jinnō shōtōki* (A Chronicle of Gods and Sovereigns), written by Kitabatake Chikafusa (1293–1354) in 1339. Here, however, Yamatotakeru is depicted as a paragon of bravery rather than as a romantic hero. While Chikafusa was influenced by the ideas of Ise Shintō, unlike other medieval works, *Jinnō shōtōki* elaborates on the western expedition in addition to the eastern mission that is traditionally associated with Ise Shintō. Although its content and phrasing basically follow the *Nihon shoki*, it notes that the *Kogoshūi* represents Yamatotakeru's escape from the grass fire as having occurred in Sagami.[38] The influence of *Atsuta engi* may also be witnessed from its reference to Miyazuhime's brother as "Inatane-no-Sukune [Inatane-no-Kimi] of Owari."[39]

Despite its general adherence to the storyline found in the *Nihon shoki*, *Jinnō shōtōki* omits elements that signify Yamatotakeru's craftiness or arrogance, such as when he adopts the disguise of a young girl in his expedition against the Kumaso, or when he belittles the deity of Mt. Ibuki. As a result, his cunning and pride, as characterized in the *Kojiki* and the *Nihon shoki*, grow fainter in the face of his stalwart valor. As in the *Nihon shoki*, his relationship with his father, Emperor Keikō, is described as being founded on a strong bond of trust. In short, *Jinnō shōtōki* goes beyond the *Nihon shoki* in depicting Yamatotakeru as a faultless hero.

Similarly, the founder of Yoshida Shintō, Yoshida Kanetomo (1435–1511), adopts a glorified view of Yamatotakeru in his commentary on the *Nihon shoki*. In his remarks on the Kusanagi sword, which reveal the influence of *Jinnō shōtōki*, Kanetomo takes up Yamatotakeru's eastern expedition. In doing so, he omits several descriptions included by Chikafusa, such as the confrontation with the deity of Mt. Ibuki and the failure to retain the Kusanagi sword. There is no hint that Yamatotakeru's death results from overconfidence or from being defeated by a deity. Rather, with regard to his death, Kanetomo simply writes: "He passed away at Atsuta in Owari as a consequence of his valiant efforts in battle."[40] Kanetomo's version, far beyond *Jinnō shōtōki*, elevates Yamatotakeru as an impeccable and brilliant human being. Consequently, due to this virtue, Yamatotakeru becomes a guardian deity in the Buddhist mountains of Reishuzan and Tendaizan.[41] This significantly differs from the Kiki's depictions, in which, upon his death, Yamatotakeru becomes a swan and flies away.

Additionally, the glorification of Yamatotakeru served to further elevate the stature of the Kusanagi sword. In describing Yamatohime bestowing the sword upon Yamatotakeru, Kanetomo states: "This commenced the practice of awarding [the commander of a pacifying force] an insignium of authority."[42] Here, Yamatohime's gesture does not signify her empathy for Yamatotakeru, but rather is incorporated as an official order. In the *Nihon shoki*, when Emperor Keikō grants Yamatotakeru a battle-axe on the occasion of the eastern expedition, this implies that he is being officially commissioned as the commander of an expeditionary force.[43] It can be conjectured that the reference to a battle-axe was derived from the regulations for military affairs in the ancient Chinese Tang code, which specify that "when dispatching a general on an expedition, this should be proclaimed at court and he should be granted a battle-axe." In Kanetomo's commentary, it is the Kusanagi sword that serves this function, as an insignium of authority.

As becomes evident from the discussion thus far, the Yamatotakeru legend is intricately entangled in the midst of various sources that span the Heian and medieval periods, including the *Kogoshūi*, the medieval *Jinnō shōtōki* and *Atsuta engi*, etc. In addition to such citations, references to the legend also appear in *Shintōshō* and *Jinja-engino*, and furthermore in what has come to be known as "the Medieval Nihongi [*Nihon shoki*]" (which includes works of diverse origins), and in military tales such as *The Tale of the Heike* and *Taiheiki*. Rather than the figure of Yamatotakeru, the Kusanagi sword becomes the primary focus of attention in these works. Additionally, the grass-fire episode and the account of how the Kusanagi sword came to be enshrined at Atsuta are joined with other episodes attesting to its miraculous qualities, including the story of its discovery by Susanowo, its transfer to Ise during the reign of Emperor Suinin, and the thwarted attempt of the Silla priest Dōgyo to steal it during the reign of Emperor Tenmu (673–86).

One reason for this interest in the Kusanagi sword revolved around its loss at sea during the battle of Dannoura in 1185, when the sword was held by the emperor as part of the imperial regalia. This event in turn led to a debate regarding the authenticity of the Kusanagi sword enshrined at Atsuta. On the one hand, *The Tale of Heike* (Kakuichi version) and *Taiheiki* take the position that the true Kusanagi had sunk to the bottom of the sea when Emperor Antoku (reigned 1178–85) drowned at Dannoura. On the other hand, *Jinnō shōtōki*, Yoshida Kanetomo in his commentary on *Nihon shoki*, and the Engyō version of *The Tale of the Heike* all assert that the sword which was lost in the sea was only a replica and that the real Kusanagi was preserved at Atsuta. *Yamatohime no mikoto seiki* and *Atsuta engi* do not refer to the drowning of Antoku, but, like *Jinnō shōtōki*, assert that the true Kusanagi sword exists at Atsuta. *Kogoshūi*, originally perceived to be no more than an account of history as seen from the perspective of one particular clan, was important to this debate because it provides a record stating that a replica of the Kusanagi sword was indeed manufactured. As a result, *Kogoshūi*'s stature was enhanced.

For the court, whose authority in the medieval period represented both political power and symbolic tradition, the fate of the Kusanagi sword was a vital issue. The same was true for those associated with the Ise and Atsuta shrines, who were pressed to find a new means of economic sustenance, given the financial decline of the court. For these parties, objects such as the Kusanagi sword were critical in tangibly substantiating the traditional legitimacy of their claim, which in turn helped substantiate their privileged standing.[44] In their worldview, the hierarchy of texts as anchored in the *Nihon shoki*, which was characteristic of the ancient period, no longer had any significance. With the court's loss of political power, *Nihon shoki* likewise lost its capacity to reinforce a court-centered social order. Thereby, adherence to its wording and content ceased to be a criterion for textual validity.

Toward the Early-Modern Period

As revealed in the discussion so far, during the ancient and medieval periods, the mode of engaging with the *Nihon shoki* and the *Kojiki* was transformed. With the formation of the statutory system, the *Nihon shoki* was officially recognized as the canon of state history, while alternative texts with differing content, such as the *Kojiki* and the *fudoki*, maintained a certain level of authority. The authority of the *Nihon shoki*, and more particularly the validity of its main text, which increased in the Heian period, had a noticeable effect on new works taking up the same subject matter. Although such works closely followed the *Nihon shoki*'s lead in transcribing names and phrases, they did not perfectly quote the text as such. Instead, the compilers excerpted the relevant parts from the *Nihon shoki*, as suited their purpose, and supplemented them with information from the *Kojiki* and the *fudoki*. While this process stylistically aligned the new works with the *Nihon shoki*, it also facilitated the modification of content. As a result, the interest in the activities and fate of key characters such as Yamatotakeru, which had until then helped to vividly sustain the accounts of the *Kojiki* and the *Nihon shoki*, faded. Rather, attention was brought to bear on particular episodes, such as the expeditions of pacification and the events surrounding the Kusanagi sword. While the more private genre of literature, the *monogatari*, undertook the exploration of the motivations and behavior of individual characters as a special feature, texts drawing on the *Nihon shoki* primarily functioned to legitimate the social position held or sought by the compilers. This circumstance was closely related to the pre-eminence of the *Nihon shoki* during the

Heian period. Its dominance at the time did not rest on an abstract authority that served as the source of information about a mythological past, but rather on the specific capacity to locate particular entities within a larger sociopolitical structure.

In the medieval period, as the *Nihon shoki*'s capacity to bestow social status weakened alongside the decline of the institutional structure, its regulating influence upon those who examined the Yamatotakeru legend anew diminished. There emerged several texts, including material from a variety of other sources, that boldly introduced significant changes into the wording of phrases derived from the *Nihon shoki*. Certain works, such as *Jinnō shōtōki*, were written in Chinese characters and Japanese syllabary, rather than solely in Chinese as was the *Nihon shoki*. Works that had originally reflected concerns specific to a particular clan or institution came to be regarded as generic sources of information about the past, and thus, akin to the military tales like *The Tale of the Heike*, became relevant to a broader audience. In these circumstances, people showed an increasing interest in Yamatotakeru as a personality, as an exemplar of virtue, or even as a romantic hero.

Such medieval developments heralded the interpretations of the *Nihon shoki* and the *Kojiki* which took shape in the early-modern period. This was a time when various figures challenged the supremacy of the *Nihon shoki*'s authority as the first state history, while Nativist scholars proclaimed the preeminence of the *Kojiki*. Having ceased to carry absolute authority, the *Nihon shoki* simply became one of many sources of information. People grew accustomed to thinking of it in conjunction with the *Kojiki* and began referring to these works as the "Kiki," which represented a single historical space tying together both the *Nihon shoki* and the *Kojiki*. Regarding its linguistic format as well, people began to perceive the hybrid Sino-Japanese language of the *Kojiki* as more authentic than the Chinese of the *Nihon shoki*. Having a greater interest in the characters who appeared in these texts, people claimed to discover ideal types of human feelings therein. A prime example of such developments is the image of Yamatotakeru that Motoori Norinaga drew from his reading of the *Kojiki*, which conformed to his characteristic emphasis on emotional sensitivity as the prime value of human existence.

In the modern period, the tendency to re-read the Kiki in terms of the inner sentiments of its characters grew increasingly strong. While being grounded in an understanding of human nature that is specific to the early-modern and modern periods, such interpretations were driven by a distinct set of interests that differed from those of the ancient and medieval periods. Rather than a concern for the explicit character of the original text, their orientation was derived from reading between the lines. It would certainly be ineffectual, however, to claim that such interpretations were necessarily more "true" or "false" as compared to the original works.

4 Myth and Rationality: Understanding God in the Early-Modern and Modern Periods

The Constellation of Early-Modern Interpretations of Kiki

In the early-modern and modern periods, the interpretation of the Kiki texts was finally being transformed, freed from the constraints of the *Nihon shoki*, and the subjects who engaged in interpretation extended to include those beyond the ruling class. It is conceivable that during the period from the reigns of Emperor Tenmu and Empress Jitō to the early Nara period (i.e., from the latter half of the seventh century to the beginning of the eighth century), when the Kiki was compiled, the *Kojiki* and the *Nihon shoki* were distinct bodies of work maintaining their respective reasons for existing via rhetorical logic. In turn, during the early Heian period (ninth century), the interpretation of the Kiki was unified under immense constraints formulated in light of the *Nihon shoki*. However, in the medieval period (from the end of the twelfth century to the end of the sixteenth century), as such constraints waned with the demise of the social strata that made up the imperial court, the *Kojiki* and the *fudoki*, as well as a number of apocryphal books, began to be included within interpretations which still retained the *Nihon shoki* as the founding framework. This in turn brought about the formation of the so-called medieval *Nihongi* (Japanese Chronicles), which actually was a distinct myth, unlike the *Nihon shoki* or the *Kojiki*.

Consequently, on entering the early-modern period (from the seventeenth century to the nineteenth century), on the one hand, the restrictions of the *Nihon shoki* loosened significantly. At this time, the argument in favor of comparing the *Nihon shoki* and the *Kojiki* (namely, comparative Kiki studies), as well as the argument for criticizing the authority of texts written in Chinese (namely, criticism of writing in the Chinese language) emerged, whereby supporters of the latter view held that the *Kojiki* which was written in both Chinese and Japanese was actually the true account rather than the *Nihon shoki* written only in Chinese. The scholars who upheld the former view were Confucianists such as Arai Hakuseki, Ichikawa Tazumaro, and Yamagata Bantō, and those who typified the latter view included Kamo no Mabuchi and Motoori Norinaga, among other Japanese classical scholars. On the other hand, arguments endorsing the Chinese writing as being the legitimate style that was founded on the medieval mythological interpretation which extolled the standpoint of the *Nihon shoki* were propounded by scholars who followed the teachings of Chushi, who supported the feudal system under the Tokugawa shogunate, as represented by works like the *Honchōtsugan* (Comprehensive Mirror of the Japanese Dynasty) and the *Dainihonshi* (History of Great Japan).

While one can conclude that the three new orientations focused on their respective texts and literary styles, in light of their assessment of the authority of Kiki's descriptions, one finds that "the criticism of the Chinese writing" pursues a non-rationalist line of argument, while "comparative Kiki studies" extol rationalism in criticizing the descriptions found in the texts. Additionally, "works endorsing the Chinese writing," which are not as thorough as comparative Kiki studies, engage with what could be called "a lax form of rationalism." The early-modern configuration of Kiki interpretation can be construed as being dualistic, marked by a rational and a non-rational means of comprehending the texts. In the modern period, constraints from the *Nihon shoki* weakened even further and consequently comparative Kiki studies became pertinent for both a rationalist and non-rationalist mode of thought. However, the rationale pertaining to such developments in the early-modern and modern periods differed in essence.

In this chapter, I shall examine the rationalist interpretations of the Kiki in the early-modern and modern periods, and by elaborating on the methods and orientations prevalent in each period, consider the meaning and significance of rationalism. In what follows, rather than attempting to discuss each type of interpretation comprehensively, I select interpreters who typify the temporal and ideological characteristics of the age, and elaborate on this discourse from the standpoint of interpretations emerging therein.

Rationalism during the Early-Modern Period

Criticism from the standpoint of objective reality
The point of departure for rationalism in the early-modern period involves questions regarding the existence of the gods and oral transmission. For instance, the Confucian scholar Arai Hakuseki (1657–1725), who pioneered the rationalist interpretation of Kiki, pointed to the lack of historical

authenticity in the notion of Jindai (Divine Age). In his work *Koshitsū* (The Understanding of Ancient History), completed in 1712, he stated:

> When closely examining the period called the Divine Age, we should note that it actually corresponds with the end of the Zhou period and the beginning of the Qin period (of China). In the final analysis, in substantiating the imperial lineage, it extinguishes things prior to it by evasively asserting the Divine Age.[1]

Consequently, interpreting the Divine Age metaphorically, he wrote: "Gods are human. The common people of our country generally referred to people of respectable standing as *kami* (god)...This made them sound godlike."[2] This metaphorical interpretation of reading the Divine Age as human events was set forth on the basis that the existence of gods can be denied on a physical level, and was an attempt to rationalize the descriptions in the Kiki through objective interpretation. One can presume that at its foundation there lay the difficulty in acknowledging the existence of gods as a physical phenomenon, and the impossibility of literally believing the descriptions of the Divine Age in the Kiki, as understood in terms of early-modern reasoning. Arai also pointed out the following:

> In very early antiquity, writing itself did not exist. Things that had been passed on by word of mouth from earlier generations would be merely passed on again by later generations. Then, in the autumn of Year 15 of the reign of the 16th Emperor Ōjin, an envoy named Achiki came from the ruler of Kudara...this appears to be the starting point of the dissemination of writing that we now have in our country...in the autumn of Year 4 of the reign of the 18th Emperor Richū, the history of the nation was instituted in the various provinces...and this is viewed as the beginning of the use of writing in our country.[3]

He thus distinguished the period marked by the reigns of Emperor Ōjin and Emperor Richū from earlier periods. The reign of both emperors was considered as having been around the fifth century, a time when writing was supposedly introduced and record-taking began, distinguished from the preceding era of oral tradition. In this context, reference was made to the account in *Kogoshūi* (Gleanings from Ancient Stories): "From what has been said, in truth, 'In remote antiquity when writing did not exist, the noble and lowly, young and old, preserved the statements and deeds of persons past by transmission through word of mouth, so that they are not forgotten.'"[4]

Referring to the existence of numerous variants in books concerning Japan's ancient period that were related through the Kiki, Arai wrote:

> Events of the distant past have already vanished and some of them barely transmitted, namely, some of them have been concealed but some revealed. The authors of ancient historical texts decided which version of the description had to be affirmed or refuted according to their own standpoint, and by

the act of making different selections, their records were not the same. In any event, for both matters denied and those affirmed, they all originate from the ancient past, and what is not authentic is beyond our knowing.[5]

He therefore suggested that the accounts stem from differences which reveal the subjectivity of each historian and the equivocalness of oral tradition as a means of transmission. In another section, he stated that the reason why variants marked by the difference in interpretation arise is because of the nature of recording orally transmitted content through phonetic symbols.

In other words, Arai adopted a critical stance that oral transmission was inferior to the functional transmission of writing. He considered records dating to the period preceding Emperor Chūai's dynasty (including the Divine Age, the period prior to the fifth century) to be weak with regard to their credibility, since this was an age marked by oral tradition. The aforementioned critique of the nature of mythological description and the function of oral tradition, and of the notion that the gods actually exist, emerged from the viewpoint that reliability needs necessarily to have a physical dimension, which may be coined as a form of "objective criticism."

Objective criticism, through which Arai had decried the traces of oral tradition, was also subsequently subscribed to by Yoshimi Yoshikazu of Suika Shintō, a sect of Confucian Shintō which vehemently criticized the orally transmitted world of medieval Shintō. As time passed, this mode of thought became ever more intensified in *Yume no shiro* (In Place of Dreams, completed in 1820), by the Confucian scholar Yamagata Bantō (1748–1821). Yamagata's criticism of the Kiki denied the actual existence of gods in the physical sense and alluded to the factual contradictions in mythological accounts of the beginning of the universe, for instance, the creation of the nation by gods, the creation of the Sun deity Amaterasu, and so forth.[6] Knowledge of the natural sciences originating in the West, particularly from the Netherlands, was the basis of his argument. Yamagata's understanding largely depended upon *Rekishō shinsho*, a full-scale introduction of Newtonian mechanics, which was translated by Shizuki Tadao and published in 1820. Prior to this, in discussions involving Motoori Norinaga (1730–1801) and Ueda Akinari (1734–1809) over an emperor-centric view of Japan, the contradiction emerging through knowledge of world geography as opposed to the mythological worldview was elaborated.[7] Yet, Yamagata was the first to bring up a criticism of mythology that applied a fully fledged knowledge of Western natural sciences, including the heliocentric theory, the notion of the solar system, etc.

As Yamagata stated, "the so-called Divine Age is a vacuous argument to say the least,"[8] in that its descriptions fail to reconstruct historical facts. Yamagata's criticism was based on physical perceptions and adopted a standpoint that was critical of descriptions in the Kiki dating back to the age of oral tradition and elaborated on the so-called "human" emperors said to have reigned after the Divine Age, from the first Emperor Jinmu to the fourteenth Emperor Chūai.[9] On the basis of the theory that writing was introduced during the reign of Emperor Ōjin, supposedly in the fifth century, Yamagata, as with Arai, maintained that the descriptions of the Kiki prior to Emperor Chūai were orally transmitted. In dismissing such content as unreliable, he stated: "The advent of writing in Japan was during the reign of Emperor Ōjin and what happened thereafter is evident. Matters before this time are legends transmitted by way of mouth and lack factuality."[10]

The existence of other theories was summoned to prove the arbitrary characteristics of oral tradition. With respect to the Divine Age mentioned earlier, he offered a critical viewpoint on the nature of oral transmission, stating: "Primarily, at the time of remote antiquity, no one existed to see the beginning of the world. Had there been anyone to see it, that person could not have left a trace of it without writing. That which has been transmitted by mouth does not comprise proof."[11]

Now, as opposed to a metaphorical interpretation in the vein of Arai, who denied that gods actually existed, Yamagata's criticism of oral tradition called into question the accuracy of descriptions in the Kiki while fundamentally affirming the truth of its content. With regard to these perspectives, it can be noted that metaphorical interpretation had more depth as opposed to a straightforward criticism of oral tradition. However, both perspectives can be construed as emerging from a position that questioned the propriety of the descriptions in the Kiki, which was at the root of rationalist arguments based on the physical dimension. Furthermore, by thoroughly criticizing mythological descriptions from the point of view of the natural sciences, and by being overly concerned with "objective criticism," Yamagata refrained from using the Kiki to reconstruct ancient history. In contrast, Arai interpreted the Kiki texts as an exposition redescribing ancient history as having involved human acts, in order to resolve the emerging contradiction in terms of the physical manifestation of the gods. This appears in Arai's *Koshitsū* (The Understanding of Ancient History), which involves the determination of historical facts through the conventional revision of variants, so as to reconstruct Japan's ancient history.

A criticism of oral transmission does not amount to a total negation of the content of the transmission itself. Rather, by acknowledging that oral transmission includes facts in spite of its arbitrary nature, one can view the content as having been relayed in an incorrect and confused state. Therefore, the criticism of oral tradition involves a judgment about the functionality of oral transmission, while at the same time extracting and reconstructing facts from the oral content, which comprises the historical material.

Accordingly, with respect to the irrational character of ancient and medieval interpretations, Arai stated the following: "Concerning ancient matters as explained in the *Nihon shoki* …one should not stop his/her interpretation of Kiki's description for the reason that 'the Divine is incalculable' (which is the common logic of the ancient and medieval period)."[13] He thus attempted to overcome the contradictions in the descriptions of various accounts and unintelligible sentences by rational means, criticizing the notion that "the Divine" was "incalculable."

Furthermore, instead of considering the descriptions of the *Nihon shoki* as being absolute, Arai stated,

> We will make the text of *Koshitsū* (The Understanding of Ancient History) adapt only material that is authentic history and actual records, such as the *Kujiki, Kojiki, Nihon shoki* and *Kogoshūi* as well as the *kokushi* and *fudoki*, etc., by excluding the false records.[14]

He criticized the former treatment of Japan's ancient material, including the Kiki texts. Instead, he used the comparative method to treat all authoritative material equally so as to fully ascertain the historical facts in the descriptions. In other words, Arai had taken up the challenge of uncovering historical facts rather than the authority of the *Nihon shoki*. Thus, while becoming free from the restrictions of the *Nihon shoki*, it can be surmised that he helped formulate comparative Kiki studies. His understanding that actual historical facts are inscribed in the Kiki, and that solitary historical facts can be recovered from among a multitude of variants, was based on the notion that "history is the recording of matters based on fact" in the objective dimension.[15]

Arai, in referring to the chronicles on Japan in Chinese historical documents, stated the following: "Although writings are definitely scarce in ancient Japan, one can gather many historical facts about ancient Japan through the many Chinese writings after the book of the Latter Han dynasty."[16] Moreover, taking into account archeological materials that had by that time been unearthed, Arai observed that there are no declarations corresponding to the archeological relics within the Kiki descriptions of the Divine Age. He opined: "There is no way for anything to be passed on by word of mouth from the Japanese periods before the reign of Emperor Jinmu, namely, from the Divine Age."[17] Such reference to Chinese historical documents and archeological materials served an important role as criteria, pointing to omissions within the descriptions in the Kiki texts or to the selection process of variants. This kind of criticism of historical material was prevalent during the early-modern period, not merely in terms of Arai but also centering around Confucianists such as Tō Teikan (1732–97). The attitude of attaching importance to Chinese historical material not only stemmed from the objectivity inherent in historical material but also the Chinese ideology of

Confucianism. In this manner, rational thought in the early-modern period, although in a premature form, had already developed three methods of historical criticism: the comparison of the *Kojiki* and the *Nihon shoki*; the referencing of Chinese historical documents; and the utilization of archeological material.

Yet, in the case of both Arai, who poured his vigor into historical criticism, and Yamagata, who emphasized objective criticism in the physical dimension, a shared belief resonated – namely, that, "by and large, beginning with the eastern expedition by Emperor Jinmu and thereafter, [events] should be viewed as factual."[18] Thereby, neither thinker raised any doubt about the authenticity of the description within the texts concerning "human" emperors who reigned after the Divine Age, namely, following Emperor Jinmu. In other words, they did not question the objective existence of emperors who were described as being "human." Even the most basic form of early-modern criticism concerning the descriptions of the "human" emperors questioned the continuity of the unbroken line of emperors, beginning with Jinmu and continuing into the contemporary age; this is apparent in the assertion by Tō Teikan in *Shōkōhatsu* (Crucial Statements without Hesitation, completed in 1781) that "[the ancestors of] the offspring of Emperor Jinmu ended with Emperor Chūai."[19] Yet such perspectives never problematized the historical existence of such hypothetical "human" emperors. In this respect, this form of criticism was no different from that of the medieval ages. In other words, it was directed solely toward the inaccuracies within the descriptions of the Kiki while assuming that the texts included historical facts in essence. Given the difficulty in acknowledging the physical existence of the gods in the Divine Age, amounting to a basic criticism founded on "common sense" stemming from the physical realm, the denial of their existence was understandable. However, one can see that, given that the sections on the "human" emperors were descriptions of mortals, objective criticism could not go so far as to deny their existence.

Arai's and Yamagata's interpretations were characteristic of early-modern rationalism, whereby objective criticism of the Kiki was apparent even in documents that retained medieval elements, such as the *Honchōtsugan* (Comprehensive Mirror of the Japanese Dynasty, completed in 1670) and the *Dainihonshi* (History of Great Japan, started in 1657 and completed in 1906).[20] The *Honchōtsugan* and *Dainihonshi*, by adopting a writing format that offered legitimacy to the Chinese writings, basically viewed the *Nihon shoki* as legitimate. They did not particularly dwell on the differences between oral transmission and written record, but rather blindly adopted the descriptions from Emperor Jinmu to Emperor Chūai and Empress Jingū, which even Tō Teikan had criticized.

The *Honchōtsugan* and *Dainihonshi* were historical documents compiled on the basis of Chushi's teachings and ideology, to legitimize the Tokugawa regime; the former was compiled by the Hayashi family under the command of the Tokugawa shogunate, and the latter by the Tokugawa family of Mito province, which was closely related to the shogunate, thereby signifying an official perspective of the establishment. Differing from forms like *Koshitsū* that Arai personally read to the shogun, these documents were little influenced by the new narrative on historiography. The ambiguity seen in the objective criticism of the *Honchōtsugan* and *Dainihonshi* is thought to have been due to the critical positions held by the compilers within the feudal system, situated between the Tokugawa shogunate and feudal lords. The texts therefore propounded the traditional rendition of the "history of the state", namely, that which supported the *Nihon shoki* as having existed from ancient times. According to the teachings of Chushi, who informed the ideology of the feudal system, the *Nihon shoki* has legitimacy because it was based on Chinese literary style. For this reason, both documents were restricted by the framework of the *Nihon shoki* and conceivably could not help but follow the content inscribed therein.

One can conjecture such constraints from the statement made by Asaka Tanpaku (1656–1737), who had participated in compiling the *Dainihonshi* of Mito province: "Our compilation should not examine whether the *Nihon shoki* is truthful in its own descriptions, in order to avoid being reprimanded for our book."[21] A similar vein of objective criticism, which is not scrupulous, can be found in the interpretation of the *Kiki* by Aizawa Seishisai (1782–1863), who is said to have brought to completion the ideology of the Mito School of thought. Critical of the stance on the centrality of the Empire presented by Motoori Norinaga, who literally recognized validity only in Japanese legends, Aizawa took the position of endorsing the relativity of all nations. In accordance with the Mito School of thought, which advocated reverence for the emperor, however, his criticism was not deep enough, since it upheld from the beginning to the end, while affirming the *Kiki*'s content in literal terms, a Motoori-like irrational position on the Divine Age.[22]

However, even in the case of the *Honchōtsugan* and *Dainihonshi*, which approved the Chinese writings, analogous to a description in the *Nihon shoki* of ancient or medieval times, the Divine Age was not accounted for, except for descriptions of the so-called "human" emperors from Emperor Jinmu onward. Both documents, although following a traditional form, could not help but recognize that the Divine Age viewed in objective terms did not match historical evidence. From this orientation, one can observe the proliferation of a substantial form of rationality in the early-modern period.

Ideological and psychological interpretation

As criticism of mythology strengthened, it became difficult to accept the descriptions in the Kiki as literal. Under these circumstances the standpoints discussed thus far arose, such as that of Arai, who replaced accounts of the Divine Age with human acts, or even, along the lines of Yamagata, who completely denied them. In both cases, such formulations judged the descriptions in the Kiki only in terms of the physical or material dimension. While rationality in the form of objective criticism obstructed mythological descriptions, in doing so it also needed to be complemented by an irrational stance, as represented by Motoori Norinaga, which defended the essence of mythology.

Although Motoori opposed rationalists, he was also criticized by fellow Nativists, including Ueda Akinari, Murata Harumi (1746–1811), and Fujitani Mitsue (1768–1823), with regards to the apparent contradiction in his line of reasoning about the physical dimension as related to literal interpretation. From this perspective it can be understood that, even among Nativists, Motoori represented the most thoroughgoing form of irrationality. Of course, Motoori himself was aware of the contradiction posed by a literal mode of understanding the mythological descriptions. In this regard, he wrote: "It is indeed childish of criticizers to marvel at what even children could easily raise doubts over."[23] However, Motoori considered that, for mythological interpretation, the capacity to maintain the worldview projected by mythological descriptions had to take priority over the conformity demanded by the physical dimension. He therefore asserted that the world of the *Kojiki* should not be narrowly judged in terms of rationality but rather needed to be perceived literally, so as to maintain its essence.

Motoori's perspectives formulated an understanding of the physical dimension and the ideological/psychological dimension as being unitary, and in turn they propounded a means of discerning a mythological worldview even in light of the physical dimension. The process of conflating these two dimensions was not limited to Motoori but was related to the development of rational thought. Consequently, an endless dispute whether "authenticity" existed in the same dimension as "physical actuality" arose. This debate was brought about by the inclination to identify knowledge of the natural sciences, which were thought about more along the lines of "common sense" at the time, with the mythological worldview, which ordinarily would have been considered inapplicable to evaluate the physical dimension.

When the substantive understanding of the Kiki reached an impasse, a perspective involving the non-physical dimension (namely, the ideological/psychological dimension) arose, so as to substantiate a renewed understanding of the texts. The ideological and psychological interpretation, without conflicting with "common sense" in the physical realm, was one that acknowledged the existence of the mythological world. Thereby, mythology could co-exist with the basis of early-modern and modern rationality without being construed as illogical. A typical example of this form of interpretation is found in writings by the Confucianist, Ichikawa Tazumaro (1740–95). Ichikawa expounded his theory on the intentional production of the Divine Age and on the primacy of the imperial family in *Maganohire* (An Alcohol to Make People Crazy), said to have been written between the years 1772 and 1780. Ichikawa's orientation becomes apparent in the following statement:

> The gods in the Divine Age are actually human beings...All things that are claimed as passed down orally should be prone to errors, with a lot disappearing, and only the matters that did not occur remain and become the customary truth.[24]

Ichikawa argued against the way that objective criticism denied the gods' existence and questioned oral transmission. As a result, in his words: "The period between Emperor Ōjin and Tenmu, spanning over 300 years, is the period when the records which were the original material for the Kiki were produced."[25] He thus propounds that the original content of the Kiki was composed during the period between the reign of Emperor Ōjin, when writing was introduced from China, and the reign of Emperor Tenmu, when the compilation of the Kiki commenced. Ichikawa maintained that the content of the Kiki was not historical fact. Rather, he stated that "the events of ancient times are the matters successively ordered in secret by the emperors' intentions" and noted that the "secret" implied "matters dictated to be the means of ruling over the realm."[26] This led to the formation of the concept that the Divine Age and descriptions prior to the reign of Emperor Chūai were produced by the imperial family.

The "secret" that Ichikawa mentions is akin to Motoori's perspective on the Kiki. In Motoori's words: "The essence of the section on the Divine Age is that our nation marks the root and the various nations [denote] the branches."[27] Yet, a major discrepancy between the two thinkers revolves around the act of recognition in the psychological dimension or the act of acknowledgment in the physical dimension. By establishing the psychological dimension distinctly, rationalism and non-rationalism, which had once opposed each other in questioning whether the physical dimension actually existed, now could stand back to back, working to identify analogous worldviews in the Kiki. This shows how ideological/psychological criticism, even with a common foundation that substantiated the physical dimension, provided early-modern rationalism with an understanding of the Kiki that differed from the rationalism of Arai, Yamagata, and others – those who had relentlessly delved into the physical dimension alone. The interpretation that

Myth and Rationality

focused on objective criticism merely understood the Kiki as a record accumulating individual events. However, with the establishment of the ideological/psychological dimension, a perspective for understanding the Kiki had developed, not as a set of individual facts put together, but as one unified image of the world, which was not paradoxical in terms of the physical realm.

The scope of early-modern interpretations of the Kiki

The preceding discussion suggests how historical images of Japan's antiquity were commonly held within rational interpretations of the Kiki. Henceforth, by reconsidering the writings of Yamagata Bantō, I will expound on this reflection of the historical image accorded by rationalism. As mentioned above, Yamagata had primarily discarded descriptions of the Divine Age in the Kiki, and did not elaborate on matters during or prior to the time of Chūai. Rather, by depending solely on the essence of the Kiki, while refraining from interpreting the detailed segments, he had managed to vividly manifest the historical perspective of the rationalists as compared to other interpreters.

Japan's ancient times, in Yamagata's conception, reflected a theory on the civilizing influence of wise individuals:

> Generally speaking, the realm came into existence and then people did, and with the existence of people came the sovereign, in this order…This had to be the order of development and not the reverse. Everything in the volumes concerning the Divine Age is in reverse. In the beginning that is of relevance, there was no distinction of high or low. Thus, everyone did as he pleased, with endless strife. It became necessary to put a sovereign in place who would rule. Consequently, a sovereign was established. This is nature's principle. In view of our Japan… Ōyashima (the islands of Japan) were all in a state like Ezo (the unconquered land), without a sovereign, without headmen, [and] the situation [was] out of hand with everyone fighting each other, but there were developments eventually. Then in the time of Nagasunehiko (long-legged man), the villages had leaders, the villages had headmen, and every village competed with each other. At this time, in the land of Hyūga, dwelled the Emperor Jinmu, who by conquest …took over the entire realm.[29]

This passage suggests that the state of barbarism was eventually civilized, and with the emergence of a sagacious leader, a social order that was based on a prototypical Confucian view of history was established, assuaging the discord. In turn, what was considered epochal pointed to the unification of Japan and the transmission of writing during the reign of Emperor Ōjin. Regardless of whether the wise sage had come to Japan from China, a Confucian view of history was commonly held by rationalist interpreters. Even Ichikawa, in presenting an ideological/psychological interpretation, wrote:

> For governing over the realm of people between heaven and earth, nothing can surpass the way of the sagacious person…If the ancestor of the current

emperor was just a person, the people extract the manner for being virtuous from this person.[30]

By this, he construed the Kiki to be a story about the "sagacious person" who, at some point in time, taught the Japanese the way of correct living.

It is generally known that the rationalist interpreters who were representative of the early-modern period, including Arai, Yamagata, and Ichikawa, were all Confucianists. Arai, a scholar of the doctrines of Chushi, was a disciple of Kinoshita Jun'an, while Yamagata was the pupil of Nakai Riken and Nakai Chikuzan of the Kaitokudō School, and Ichikawa was the pupil of Ōuchi Yūji, who in turn was the disciple of Ogyū Sorai. In addition, the rationalistic, detailed compilation in the *Honchōtsugan* and *Dainihonshi* focused on Confucianism as well, which mainly consisted of the doctrines of Chushi. As becomes apparent, the rationalist interpretation of the Kiki was closely tied to Confucianism, and the point at which they converged plausibly involved the Kyūri ideology (the determination of principles and laws concerning the way things come about). The Kyūri ideology was prevalent within various schools of Confucianism, and the notion of Kakubutsuchichi (attaining a perfect knowledge of the laws inherent in nature) can be considered as exemplary in this regard. Kakubutsuchichi was the act of striving to become a well-rounded person in realizing the principles which pervaded *ten-chi-jin* (heaven, earth, and humans) by understanding the principles inherent in the objective universe.[31] The Kyūri ideology presumably was the impetus for Confucianists to read the Kiki in ways that agreed with their principles, particularly in a manner that would not contradict physical phenomena.

In contrast, Motoori, who denied the theory of a sagacious person instilling a civilizing influence, saw Japanese cultural traditions as unadulterated and sought to discover a unique identity which did not include foreign elements.[32] According to Motoori, Japan had been an orderly nation since ancient times and did not need the impetus of sagacious individuals to confer civilization. This amounts to an archetypal theory about the Divine Age, whereby Motoori adopted the model of Japan in its primitive form, prior to the influx of Chinese culture, as exemplified through the *Kojiki*, which had a non-yin/yang dualist foundation and was not influenced by pure Chinese classical literature. However, the ideal world illustrated therein was a Confucian world, in which "conduct was thoroughly courteous and full of loyalty and filial piety, and society was well-governed."[33] This fact indicates that society at that time was premised on Confucian values and that interpretations of the Kiki, whether in a rational or non-rational vein, could not but resort to touching upon objective criticism related to the Kyūri ideology of Confucianism.

Moreover, what made the rationalists and non-rationalists alike take up Kiki interpretation was not directly connected to political motives, but rather involved a desire to discover the origins of Japan and its inhabitants. The individuals involved with early-modern Kiki interpretation shifted to Confucianists and Nativists, and other intellectuals in this vein, who were from the middle stratum of society. When these individuals sought for their own origins, with the exception of the Kiki, no other records which predated the Nara period existed in Japan. In the early-modern period, during which the imperial system did not have real political power, the Kiki did not directly represent political authority. Consequently, the imperial system of Japan itself was not the object of criticism in rationalist interpretations of politics. In the words of Ichikawa, "[the fact that] the imperial line has not been extinguished is not something heard about in foreign countries and is to be celebrated."[34] From this standpoint, the present-day understanding based on the popular view criticizing early-modern Kiki interpretations for not having ventured out of their politically conservative bounds overlooked the shift in social characteristics during the modern and the early-modern periods. As long as the sole record for establishing origins was one that mentioned the formation of the ancient royal authority, the interpreters of the Kiki had no choice but to connect with the imperial system in unearthing their own individual origins. At this juncture, people traced back their individual origins to suit their respective ideological standpoints, whereby rationalism was tied to the theory of sagacious persons and their civilizing influence, and non-rationalism was connected to the archetypal theory of the Divine Age. Early-modern interpretation can thus be characterized as involving a wide-ranging stratum of interpreters who engaged with the search for origins and concurrently addressed the issue of reality in the physical dimension.

By citing examples from Arai, Yamagata, Ichikawa, and Motoori, the above discussion has elucidated the prevalent strains of thought that engaged with rationalism and non-rationalism, as well as objective criticism and ideological/psychological interpretation as connected to rationalism. Such scholarly analyses were representative of the times, and other rationalists, to be discussed below, expanded on such viewpoints or even adopted an intermediary stance. Tō Teikan and Murata Harumi, for instance, accepted Arai's viewpoint because they had retained their commitment to objective criticism while attempting to develop a critical understanding of historical documents.[35] Ise Sadatake (1717–84) and Ueda Akinari, who tried to reconcile the mythological image of the world and objective criticism, can be situated in between Arai and Motoori.[36] In addition, Hirata Atsutane (1776–1843), who claimed to be a pupil of Motoori, and also maintained a Motoori-esque mythological image of the world, attempted to elucidate the fact that his perspective did not contradict the knowledge of physics at the time.[37] His representative work, *Tamanomihashira* (The Whereabouts of Our Soul in the Afterlife), contends that the descriptions of the Divine Age conform with the heliocentric theory and that the existence of the gods has been confirmed by physical evidence. Yet, the advances in Western scientific knowledge did not make Hirata's proposed union feasible, and the longer he struggled, the more pronounced the schism became.

Rationalism during the Modern Period

The Kiki as a symbol of power

As a result of the Meiji Restoration, the imperial system once again became the symbol of state power, and the Kiki that accounted for its origin also became vested with analogous political characteristics. The Kiki texts were represented as being factual in the history textbooks used in the Westernized educational system that catered to Japanese students in modern Japan.[38] From the outset, the accounts from Emperor Jinmu onward were treated as history. Yet, during the period from 1878 to 1888, it was not compulsory to include the Divine Age, and, furthermore, certain textbooks discussed the attributes of primitive society in accordance with archeology. The compilation scheme in textbooks followed the standpoint of the *Dainihonshi* and *Honchōtsugan*. In fact, reference was made to the *Dainihonshi*, besides the Kiki, in school textbooks.

Kiki criticism as expounded by Miyake Setsurei (1860–1945) in the first volume of his *Nihon Bukkyōshi* (The History of Japanese Buddhism), published in 1887, presumably reflected the atmosphere at the time. However, this volume only went about critiquing the physical realm that denied the existence of gods and oral transmission. It did not venture out of the realm of objective criticism of the early-modern period, since it affirmed the historical existence of the human emperors before Emperor Ōjin.[39] Rationalist interpretation of the Kiki, up until the 1870s, had inherited a structure that did not differ significantly from the objective criticism of Arai and Yamagata, and the ambiguous style of objective criticism apparent in the *Dainihonshi* and *Honchōtsugan* of the early-modern period. However, during the modern period, the restrictive pressure of the *Nihon shoki* subsided even further, and school textbooks that reflected the intentions of the establishment combined both the *Nihon shoki* and the *Kojiki*. Yet, on entering the period from 1898 to 1907, national textbooks underwent a third revision and, in place of the exposition on primitive society, it became compulsory to include the Divine Age as part of history. The 1892 incident involving "the slip of the pen" by Kume Kunitake (1839–1931) was a precursor to this ruling. This was an incident of political suppression by conservatives against the historian Kume of the University of Tokyo, who in his interpretation stated, "Shintō is the remnant of ancient ritual practices to worship the heavens." It must be noted that Kume's intention was not to criticize Shintō, but rather, as in the case of early-modern rationalists, to interpret it in terms of rational criteria.[40]

This sort of oppression was applied not only to cases that were related to Shintō, in light of the intention to sanctify the imperial system, but also to interpretations of the Kiki. The novel written in 1912 by Mori Ōgai (1862–1922), entitled Kanoyōni (As If to Exist), realistically depicted the struggle between the establishment that intended to validate the Kiki literally, on the one hand, and the intellectuals who desired to rationalize the Kiki myths, on the other hand. From 1898 onward, the Japanese Empire strengthened its power through its victories in the Sino-Japanese War of 1894–95 and the Russo-Japanese War of 1904–05. As a consequence, even early-modern objective rationalism was considered a danger to an establishment which aimed to sanctify the Kiki as being unchallengeable in an even more deterministic manner. This indicates how unified the imperial system and the political power of the state had become in the modern period. In light of the fact that this situation, with regard to the imperial system, did not exist in the early-modern period, one can begin distinguishing the unique characteristic of Kiki interpretation in the modern period.

However, according to a character in Mori's Kanoyōni, "if I dabble in scholarly learning...it will not permit viewing myth as the truth. It steers one to consider mythology and history as separate and simultaneously brings into question the existence of ancestors and other divine spirits."[41] This passage indicates the tendency, prevalent up until the 1890s, of deleting the Divine Age from textbooks, and at the same time points to the difficulty confronting intellectuals with regards to their capacity to comprehend the Kiki myths literally. This was the new structure of contention within Kiki interpretation during the modern period, between the objective realism prevalent through the interpretations of the early-modern period and the standpoint of the establishment restricting all Kiki interpretations. For this reason, rationalism in the modern period could not help but criticize the movement to substantiate Kiki's descriptions, as well as the mounting power of the state founded on the imperial system. Even objective criticism akin to rationalism in the early-modern period was not tolerated by the state, which affirmed the authenticity of Kiki's descriptions. A breath of fresh air was blown into the stagnating interpretations of the Kiki by Tsuda Sōkichi, a historian of East Asia.

Taishō Democracy-style Interpretation

Shindaishi no atarashii kenkyū (New Studies on the Divine Age of History)[42] of 1913 marked the beginning of Tsuda Sōkichi's writings on the Kiki, in which he developed an ideological/psychological interpretation premised on an objective criticism of the Divine Age. In *Bungaku ni arawaretaru waga kokuminshisō no kenkyū – kizoku bungaku no jidai* (Research on the People's Ideology as Seen in Literature: The Age of Aristocratic Literature) of 1916, he wrote, "the ancient history of the Kiki, at least the section prior to Empress Jingū, cannot be considered to be history in a strict sense,"[43] thereby denying the authenticity of the "human emperor" section, from Emperor Jinmu to the reign of Emperor Chūai. This argument was concretely developed in the *Kojiki oyobi Nihon shoki no atarashii kenkyū* (New Studies on the *Kojiki* and the *Nihon shoki*) of 1919, in which he addressed the issues that arose from the many coincidences of the names of monarchs during and prior to the period of Chūai and Jingū, the names of emperors from the sixth century onwards, and the numerous legendary elements attached to the descriptions, as well as the lack of historical authenticity of the records of the imperial line and the various events described therein. Along this line of reasoning, Tsuda concluded:

> The first *teiki* (Imperial Records) and *kuji* (Ancient Myths) that comprise the basis for the ancient history segment in the Kiki, explained the origins of the imperial family in light of the ideology of the imperial court … of the mid-sixth century…[which were written] from material like the sparse records and legends which began to be gathered at the end of the fourth century.[44]

The denial of the "human emperor" section was difficult to achieve merely via a criticism of the Divine Age in light of the physical realm. Rather, this became feasible for the first time as a result of developments that offered a new means of evaluating historical material, which involved the fields of archeology, Chinese historical texts, and comparative Kiki studies. These modes of criticism of historical material were introduced by Arai and other Confucianists. Yet, unlike the early-modern period, Tsuda was critical of Confucianism's feudalistic morals, which impeded the progress of the populace, and therefore was averse to Chinese historical material. As a result of a thorough engagement with the past enabled via archeology,[45] and from the viewpoints discussed above, the criticism of historical material had become highly objective as compared to the early-modern period.

Another characteristic of Tsuda's interpretation of Kiki is the ideological/psychological dimension that is connected to the theory of the primacy of the imperial family. Tsuda disapproved of early-modern rationality's adherence only to the viability of the physical dimension, and clarified his own perspective, as being rooted in an ideological/psychological understanding, in the following manner:

> Although the content appearing in the Kiki has a lot of stories that seem removed from the truth, in fact, because there is no truth in it, it has special value. This is not truth in terms of actual existence but ideological truth or psychological truth.[46]

In general, Tsuda's orientation in Kiki studies has been perversely interpreted, as one which separates the Kiki from historical facts. Yet, in actuality, by clarifying the historical non-authenticity of the Kiki, Tsuda asserted the importance of transforming the basis of understanding the texts in terms of their ideological and psychological dimensions.

Tsuda, on the basis of an ideological/psychological interpretation, had presented a theme which pervaded the Kiki:

> The history of the Divine Age is a description of how the imperial family, as "Arahitogami (gods that have appeared in this world as people)," had come to comprise the sovereignty of our nation, in terms of the reigns of the ancestors who purportedly were authentic gods; in other words, in the form of the story of the Divine Age.[47]

Furthermore, with regards to the "human emperor" segment from Emperor Jinmu to the reign of Emperor Chūai, he added:

> The order of nation management [by the imperial family] is extremely well-regulated...distant rather than proximate, having an effect from the proximate to distant areas [having been written as fiction]...The purpose of describing the history of the Divine Age in the Kiki and stories of ancient times was primarily to account for the origins of the imperial family.[48]

Tsuda also pointed out that the common people of the time lacked their own political and cultural identity, stating: "The general populace merely existed as a group with specialized skills serving the clans, and were not given recognition as having any political standing."[49] He added: "Our national people in ancient times fundamentally did not have their own legends, etc., taking note of national worth,"[50] and furthermore,

> The history of the Divine Age was the product of the officials of the court, and not the story of the nation... it is not a naturally forming representation of the lives of the people or the crystallization of the national spirit...the history of the Divine Age, therefore...throughout has aristocratic characteristics.[51]

As a consequence, he claimed that the Yamato imperial power was the direct creator of the Kiki. In spite of this, Tsuda did not develop his argument to refute the concept that the Kiki was related to national character. As the Yamato imperial court amassed power, he explained: "It [the history of the

Divine Age] became widespread among the clans throughout the Japanese archipelago… and its authority was gradually internalized."[52]

> To use present-day language, the imperial family is situated among the people and serves as the central point of ethnic unification and the nucleus for ethnic solidarity; it is not something that came from outside the nation, not a power stemming from suppression and subordination, but has developed from the affinity of one family tied together by blood relations. This constitutes the fundamental reason for the imperial family having eternal continuity for the succession of their imperial rule, and because it is the nucleus of national solidarity, it exists eternally with the nation's people and the state. This is the source of the imperial family's true dignity.[53]

By inference, one can say that Tsuda's theory on the primacy of the imperial family was premised on their "affinity"[54] to the nation, whereby the cultural and political identity of the people can be guaranteed.

The scholar of Japanese intellectual history, Ienaga Saburō (1913–2002) once commented on Tsuda's interpretation of the Kiki, stating:

> Tsuda judged that the non-rational mystified theology concerning the beginnings of the imperial family was not necessarily appropriate for maintaining the relationship between the imperial family and citizens in modern-day Japan, and tried to show a scheme for the modern-day rationalization of the imperial system, and at the same time the democratization of politics, releasing the emperor from having to bear responsibility, stressing that he is the "living symbol of the citizens' spirit."[55]

Thereby he argued that the purpose of Tsuda's Kiki interpretation was not to overthrow the imperial system, but in fact was to understand the Kiki in the modern period as having been transformed into the symbol of state power in a Taishō Democracy mode, on the basis of ideological/psychological interpretation. Tsuda therefore criticized the perspective represented by national textbooks, espousing an uncritical acceptance of Kiki descriptions (such as the Divine Age), and the attitude positing the Kiki as the symbol of state power.

Watsuji Tetsurō (1889–1960), the scholar of ethics who published *Nihon kodai bunka* (Japan's Ancient Culture) in 1920, adopts the same standpoint as Tsuda, as is apparent from his interpretation of the Kiki as a "piece of art" from an ideological/psychological perspective, deeming the obedience of the people to the emperor as a spontaneous sentiment based on "harmonious attachment." Watsuji regarded the Kiki as ultimately "the product of the nation's people," and also criticized the view of the emperor taken by the government during the Meiji period.[56] This characterized the scope of Kiki interpretation in the period marked by Taishō Democracy. The ideological/psychological interpretation begun during the early-modern period became commonplace in the modern period, opening new horizons for the age.

Under these circumstances, it was European anthropology and mythology that helped promote the ideological/psychological understanding of the Kiki.[57] Mythology had come to be studied in Japan from 1899 onward. As Tsuda and Watsuji themselves admitted, the descriptions of the Divine Age attained value via a dimension introduced through non-historical facts. In terms of assuming an ideological/psychological position, rationalism in the modern period had inherited early-modern forms of rationalism as its premise, with regard to the aforementioned criticism concerning the physical realm. In addition, by combining with the mythological and archeological perspectives from the West, the ideological/psychological interpretation attained a higher claim to "objectivity." However, such thinkers did not reduce the significance of the Kiki and merely claim it as a remnant of mythology. Their insistence on continuing to identify the Kiki as "the history of the Divine Age" demonstrates a disposition to unravel a historical tradition that was unique to Japan.

The materialist view of historical interpretation

In the beginning of the Shōwa era (1926–89), Japanese capitalism sank into a crisis and the domineering characteristic of the Japanese Empire with the emperor as its symbol became manifest. At the same time, the establishment's endorsement of the Kiki grew stronger, which promoted its authority. The national textbooks incorporated the mythology to a greater degree, even more than before, flamboyantly relating the continuity of the history of the Divine Age. In these circumstances, Marxist historians ventured to criticize the politically dominant characteristics of the Kiki. A typical example of this was the interpretation of Watanabe Yoshimichi (1901–85) as presented in *Kojiki kōwa* (Lectures on the *Kojiki*) published in 1937.

Watanabe characterized the Kiki as the product of the formative stages of the "centralized ancient state," and held that the original myth was primarily maintained by each "clan."[58] Watanabe's interpretive framework subscribed to Tsuda's theory on the primacy of the imperial family. He also incorporated Watsuji's analysis promoting the notion that the materials in the Kiki were at one time independent components of stories from the imperial family, and that the section on human emperors prior to Emperor Chūai did incorporate "historical elements."[59]

Watsuji, in contrast to Tsuda, in reference to each section comprising the Kiki, had stated, "even if they were stories compiled according to a single concept, the material cannot be regarded as wholly the product of fantasy… Each story bears within itself old folk legends and historical legends."[60] He inferred that the account from the reign of Emperor Jinmu to Emperor Chūai included historical facts as part of its elemental structure.[61] While Tsuda focused on the main subjects in the Kiki, as a product conceived by the sixth century that was distinct from communal myths, Watsuji acknowledged Tsuda's theory regarding the main subjects in the Kiki and yet contended that it included old communal myths and historical facts as a part of its material. A Watsuji-inspired perspective was further substantiated by Kurano Kenji's (1902–91) *Kojiki no shinkenkyū* (New Studies on the *Kojiki*),[62] published in 1927. Yet, this perspective was proposed in Watanabe's writings, whose standpoint was completely contrary to the intentions of Watsuji, who praised the imperial system as a symbol of the people's submission to the national totality.

Watanabe reconstituted Tsuda's theory on the primacy of the imperial family and Watsuji's narrative theory on the basis of the formation of a class society according to a Marxist view of history. He argued that the myths of the independent clans were absorbed by the centralized nation, leading to the formation of the Kiki. The purpose of this interpretation, which was not publicly visible because of political suppression during the prewar period, clearly exposed the fact that the Kiki was a symbol of the suppression of the people that was construed as a symbol of the people. In this light, the rationalist interpretation of the Kiki constituted a criticism of the imperial system as the symbol of power. For Watanabe, very likely in a Marxist vein as well, historical origins were not to be sought through the imperial system, but rather from a communal entity that preceded it, namely, something that was liberated from the emperor's overbearing authority.

However, as the socio-political conditions of the period drastically swung to the right, Watanabe's criticism of the Kiki was not tolerated: his book was suppressed. In 1940, Tsuda too was prosecuted and his book, which had a general influence on intellectual society, was also suppressed. Furthermore, around 1944, Watsuji's book became the target of attacks from rightists. In this manner, the rationalist interpretation of the modern period lost its footing in the imminent tug-of-war between the strengthening authority of the Kiki as propounded by the state and the corresponding criticism of state authority. It was eventually smothered as Japan moved forward with the developments that led into the Asian–Pacific War.

After the war, though, the interpretation oriented toward the Marxist view of history became prevalent in Kiki studies. Rationalist Kiki interpretation from before the war resurfaced. Postwar rationalist interpretation traced its roots to Tsuda in terms of its methodological genealogy. With regard to its political purpose, however, Tsuda's orientation seemed much too conservative in supporting the emperor as the cultural symbol of the nation. Rather, it was clearly Watanabe's concept that bore influence, which was in turn adopted as the purpose for interpretation. Herein, the argument on the age of heroes propounded by Ishimoda Shō, the Marxist historian who was representative of the postwar period (as elaborated in Chapter 6), attains its relevance. The interpretation oriented toward the Marxist view of history, however, conflated the outlooks of Tsuda and Watsuji within a single framework, without sufficiently considering their differences. Consequently, this form of interpretation incorporated Tsuda's and Watsuji's unresolved questions as well, namely, the confusion as to how old the myths and traditions included within the Kiki texts were, and whether the material truly bore ethnological characteristics pertaining to all Japanese people. These unresolved issues are apparent in Ishimoda's as well as Watanabe's works. Due to this, the postwar theory on the age of heroes can be surmised to have induced an internal split and breakdown of the leftist historian camp. This situation has not really changed even at present, when such unresolved problems continue to persist.

Grounds for Being Historical

As is clear from the discussion above, while the constrictive imposition of the *Nihon shoki* subsided, Kiki interpretation of the early-modern and modern periods came to question the existence of the gods as well as the historical authenticity of descriptions corresponding to the age marked by oral tradition. In this context, through the restoration of descriptions in the Kiki, in terms of historical relevance, the rational argument of the early-modern period developed by reflecting upon the authenticity of the physical dimension. In reaction to this form of objective criticism, there arose the literal interpretation which tried to preserve the mythological world. In turn, the two standpoints opposed each other with regards to the validity of the physical dimension. The ideological/psychological dimension emerged as being distinct from the physical dimension, attempting to give credence to the mythological world while retaining consistency with the physical dimension. The conflict between criticism stemming from the physical realm and a literal interpretation was sublated with the emergence of the ideological/psychological mode of interpretation.

However, on entering the modern period, rationalism had to contend with issues that were not present in the early-modern period. This was the stand-off between the Kiki and the establishment that positioned the imperial system as the symbol of absolutist state power. In this regard, modern rationalist criticism exposed the contradictions of capitalism. During the transition from the 1920s to the 1930s, it proceeded in an increasingly radical direction that extended to include both the bourgeois standpoint, which tried to link the Kiki to the symbolic imperial system, and the leftist standpoint, which aimed to undermine the imperial system. In terms of rationalist interpretation and its transition from early-modern to modern times, one can surmise that the proportion of middle-class intellectuals engaging in Kiki interpretation (who constituted the bulk of subjects in society) had grown larger. An aspiration toward finding the origins of self, by establishing one's own identity historically, was the driving force behind such interpretations. After all, in these circumstances, the Kiki had thrived as the oldest writings of Japan that revealed origins dating back to the obscure and distant past. In the vicissitudes of history, the Kiki and the imperial system were traditional entities transcending time while bestowing a sense of historical origin. This perspective probably fascinated the newcomer, so to speak, from the main strata of society.

Origins of self sought out from the Kiki were established by tying the ancient world illustrated in the myths with the self situated in a given period, whereby the images of ancient times differed in accordance with one's own position. For instance, early-modern rationalism projected a Confucian theory of sagacious leaders propelling a civilizing influence and non-rationalists projected a theory modeled after the Divine Age that was orientated toward the Japanese classics. Taishō democratists who followed the theory of wise leaders, in one sense, ascribed to the theory of a symbolic emperor, while leftist historians posited family–clan communities existing prior to the establishment of the imperial system. The leftist historians' interpretation, in particular, was one that opened new horizons in the postwar period, by making relative the conventional point of view which sought the origins of the imperial system. Yet, like other interpretations, they shared the characteristic of creating a historical identity premised on a particular standpoint. In other words, one can conjecture that the role played by rationalism within interpretation amounted to reproducing the world of antiquity, as it was understood in terms of a given criterion of rationality, which in itself was changing with the times. This was how rationalism satisfied people's reasoning in a given period and facilitated the individual quest for identity as founded on a viewpoint of the historical past, with a distinct feeling of security. In this light, the history of Kiki interpretation, which has continued ceaselessly from ancient times, reflects the manner that the human inclination to seek for a connection with the historical past is constructed and construed as being fundamental within both rational and non-rational modes of thought.

If one were to say that it is essential for humans to secure a meaning for their own existence in order to thrive, the Kiki have certainly been serving a very important purpose. However, if the act of interpretation justifying our existence is *a priori*, without critical evaluation, dogmatism inevitably results. As is well known, historical research is the reconstruction of the world of the past according to a contemporary frame of reference and is not by any means an act that actually restores the past. In other words, if reconstructing the past only serves to justify the contemporary worldview, then there is no need to analyze the past. It is my contention that historical research with an alienating effect needs to be employed in Kiki studies, situating and stimulating a re-examination of how meaning constitutes one's existence. At present, both the viewpoint criticizing the conventional understanding of the Kiki, which categorizes the *Kojiki* and *Nihon shoki* together as Japanese mythology, and the perspective denying that the existence of Emperors Ōjin and Nintoku is unquestionable, have been presented.[63] By delineating the transformations in the worldview surrounding the Kiki, we must recognize a view of the world that emancipates us from our limited perspective. It is important for us to consider how we, as perceivers and simultaneously as historical subjects, while being aware of the trials and tribulations of rationalism's search for legitimacy, must be cautious not to turn complacent from within our own individual standpoints and perspectives on history.[64]

5 Myth and Nationalism: Motoori Norinaga's Creation Myths

A Distinct Understanding of the Mythological

The Kiki interpretation by Motoori Norinaga (1730–1801), the early-modern scholar of Nativism, lays the foundation for our present-day understanding of Japanese myths. This chapter reveals how Motoori's theories and his preference for the *Kojiki* over the *Nihon shoki*, which reflects his theory of *mono no aware* ("an aesthetic, empathetic feeling toward things"), continue to influence our interpretation and evaluation of the content of the Kiki texts. In many respects, in the late eighteenth century, changes in the interpretation of classic Japanese myths intellectually paved the way for Japan's modernity.

In annotating the passage from the *Kojiki* in which Yamatotakeru laments having understood the real feelings and intention of the father who wishes him dead, Motoori wrote, "because Yamatotakeru's bravery and sincerity never wavered, he entirely fulfilled his father's expectations of victory. Nevertheless, Yamatotakeru resented what was to be resented and, crying, lamented what was to be lamented. This is true human feeling." Through such an interpretation, Motoori extolled the prince's sense of *mono no aware*.[1] At the beginning of the ancient period, the exploits of Yamatotakeru as related in the *Kojiki* and *Nihon shoki* shared many similar motifs, while the tale of Yamatotakeru as a whole was structured differently within each text. In the *Nihon shoki*, a brave Yamatotakeru enjoys his father's deep abiding trust, while in the *Kojiki* he becomes a tragic hero exiled by his father.[2] Motoori chose to emphasize the *Kojiki* version of the tale, reading it as a paean to a tragic hero.

Motoori selected the *Kojiki* because the construction of the text made it possible for him to introduce his own style of emotionality (describing his own emotions and people's emotions as emerging naturally), in order to read into it and affirm his theory of *mono no aware*. This did not mean that the *Kojiki* itself had been created as a tragic tale. Indeed, as Hans Robert Jauss has pointed out, "only with the mediation of the reader does a work… enter into the constantly changing horizon of experience."[3] One must always make a distinction between the text itself and the commentaries that are applied to it. What can be understood from an interpretation is in the end less about the text itself than the worldview of the interpreter.[4] For, at the time of interpreting, the interpreter chooses and compiles a text that makes possible the projection of his or her worldview.

Today people feel an affinity for the *Kojiki* and feel distanced from the *Nihon shoki*. Books for popular audiences as well as scholarly treatises have generally been based on the *Kojiki*. This is because we are reading the *Kojiki* as an emotional novel, in accordance with Motoori's theory of *mono no aware*. As we read the inner feelings of the characters into the *Kojiki* and *Nihon shoki*, we share Motoori's understanding as epitomized in his commentary on the tale of Yamatotakeru. This affective approach to the ancient texts laid the basis for the emotional debates on the nature of the heroic age that were repeatedly played out during the postwar era. The debate between the Marxist historians Ishimoda Shō and Tōma Seita, for instance, revolved around whether or not the Yamatotakeru of the *Kojiki*, seen as a national hero, committed himself to a tragic death in the face of state authority.[5]

In contrast, when we read the tale of Yamatotakeru in the *Nihon shoki*, we, like Motoori, feel a sense of aloofness. However, it would be an abuse of our authority to then conclude that the *Nihon shoki* lacks literary character as a myth. On the whole, interpreters unconsciously affirm and impose their own values and norms in the process of signifying a distinct sense of relevance to the past. Karatani Kōjin (1941–), a literary critic influenced by post-modernism, explains this notion concisely:

> When we read what is called premodern literature...we feel as if it lacks "depth."...What does it mean to say that their literature has no "depth"? We cannot return to their "reality" or "inner feelings," nor should we forcibly read a "depth" into their literature. On the contrary, we should inquire what "depth" is and by what [means] is it achieved.[6]

Within research on intellectual history, in particular, there is the startling tendency "to familiarize the unfamiliar" in the name of tradition.[7] Clearly, this tendency has given birth to the dogmatization of the worldview of the textual interpreter. What is needed now is to avoid imposing our own gaze once again. We must instead recognize that the viewpoints that have become so widespread were actually the personal ideas of the interpreters themselves.

The *Nihon shoki* was upheld as a canon from the time it was compiled as an official national history in the Nara period up to the first part of the Edo period. If we feel uncomfortable with this text, it is not due to a lack of literary merit or any other deficiency in the text itself. Instead, our discomfort arises from the peculiarities of our own understanding, which differs from the way the myths were understood in ancient times. The gaze of the comprehending subject should not suppress the differences between it and the object of its understanding. Once we have recognized that the interpretation of texts is a means for the interpreter to proclaim his own values, we can better comprehend the switch that was initiated in the middle of the Edo period, namely, when the *Nihon shoki* was replaced by the *Kojiki* as the most widely interpreted text. Freed from theoretical disputes over historical precedence, we can understand the shift from the *Nihon shoki* to the *Kojiki* as a turning point from the ancient image to a modern image of the myths.

In this chapter, I would like first to clarify the understanding of the myths in the early-modern and modern periods through a consideration of Motoori's theory of the Ancient Way (*kodōron*). Then, by comparing the early-modern and modern perspectives on ancient mythology, I will consider the transfigurations of the myths within the *Kojiki* and the *Nihon shoki* through the ages, as well as account for the process underlying this transformation.

Motoori Norinaga's Exposition of the Ancient Way

When analyzing the intellectual stance of an individual, one must be cautious and not divide that person's words into fragments, but instead question the logic of the discourse through which his argument is constructed and worldview is assembled. Motoori's works on the Ancient Way can be classified into three genres: commentaries on the Japanese classics, epitomized by the *Kojikiden*; Shintō writings, such as *Tamakushige* or *Naobi no mitama*; and his compiled text, *Kamiyo no masagoto*. Studies of Motoori have tended to emphasize the objectivity of the commentaries and the subjectivity of the Shintō works, or else, based on a different method of assessment, have addressed the former within the field of Japanese literature and the latter as intellectual history.

However, as clarified by Motoori's own statements, the *Kojikiden*—his grand commentary on the *Kojiki*—did not exist in isolation, but in the end embodied the development of his approach to Shintō thought and the compilation of texts. Of course, today, even in the areas of philology and positivist historiography, there is no room for a naive objectivity that abstains from engaging with subjectivities.[8] In this section, while placing *Tamakushige* (Commentary on *The Tales of Genji*) at the center of my argument, I address Motoori's Shintō works as the culmination of his annotative activities. In *Tamakushige*, written in 1787, Motoori aimed at a theory of government, which he explained from the viewpoint of the existential constructs of the world and the patterns of human life that act in concert with such formations. At the time he wrote *Tamakushige*, Motoori was finishing his commentary on the volume on the "Age of the Gods" in the *Kojikiden*. It is apparent that, based upon the results of that research, he held his ground in various disputes with Confucianists and Nativist scholars. Thus, *Tamakushige* was representative of the period in which Motoori firmly established his approach to the Ancient Way.

The Way of Sincerity

What Motoori Norinaga called the Ancient Way, or "the way of sincerity," was a selfless attitude in which "in general, one does not depend upon one's personal judgment for any action."[9] Based on this attitude, "when both vassals and the common people...identify with the emperor's will and, earnestly respecting the imperial court, obey the rule of the emperor,...then those above and those below will be in harmony, the realm will be auspiciously governed,"[10] and order would be introduced into the world.

The foundation of this order was the emperor. "Because this age, this realm and its people exist above all due to the benevolence of [the imperial ancestor] Amaterasu Ōmikami," wrote Motoori, "there can be no individual ownership."[11] Mythically ordained as the land's sole sovereign, the emperor fulfilled the function of denying the egotistical desires of all humans, from the warrior ruling classes to the commoners. Above all else, the emperor himself was made into a selfless executor who "takes the will of the heavenly deities as his own." As he stated, "The emperor does not deal with matters according to his own will, but acts and governs according to the precedents of the Age of the Gods."[12] Following this line of logic, then, in Motoori's idealized Japan, a person who could assert his personal desires did not conceptually exist.

Motoori discovered a mythological basis for the emperor's status, as the sole sovereign of the realm in the foundation myths and in the myth of the descent of the imperial grandson of Amaterasu, the sun goddess, writing:

> Heaven and earth, all the gods and all phenomena, were brought into existence by the creative spirits of two deities—Takami-musuhi-no-kami and Kami-musuhi-no-kami. The birth of all humankind in all ages and the existence of all things and all matter have been the result of that creative spirit... It was the original creativity of these two august deities which caused the deities Izanagi and Izanami to create the land, all kinds of phenomena, and numerous gods and goddesses at the beginning of the Age of the Gods.[13]

First, Motoori asserted that Izanagi and Izanami themselves give actual birth to the realm and all things by receiving Takami-musuhi-no-kami and Kami-musuhi-no-kami's power of creation. Subsequently, Izanagi's child, Amaterasu Ōmikami, appears as the sun goddess who rules the heavens (Takama-ga-hara) and illuminates the world.

> Amaterasu Ōmikami directed her imperial grandson to govern the Abundant Reed Plain (Ashihara-nakatsu-kuni, i.e., the earth), so he descended from the heavens to the land. In the oath that Amaterasu Ōmikami made at this time, she pronounced that the reign of the imperial throne was eternal, together with heaven and earth. This oath is itself the great fundamental essence of the Way.[14]

In other words, Amaterasu entrusted control of the land to her imperial grandson Ninigi, and he, accepting the commission, descended to earth. According to Motoori, actual history substantiated the unbroken continuity of the imperial line as foretold by Amaterasu. "Although the great imperial country—as stated in the sacred oath of its eternal existence—has persisted through ten thousand generations," he wrote, "lords are still lords and vassals are still vassals. There has been no change in their positions."[15]

Motoori's reactions to the myths, beginning with the scene portraying the creation deities with which he begins the narrative on the age of the gods in the *Kojikiden*, were modeled primarily on the *Kojiki*, with variant texts from the *Nihon shoki* deployed at important junctures.[16] The epitome of this mixing of the *Kojiki* and the *Nihon shoki* is his treatment of Amaterasu Ōmikami's sacred oath. This oath, which for Motoori guaranteed an eternal imperial line, is not related in the *Kojiki* or the main text of the *Nihon shoki*, but rather is told in a variant of the *Nihon shoki*. Likewise, by introducing a variant into the myth that relates the ceding of the land by the reigning deity Ōkuninushi-no-mikoto to Amaterasu's grandson Ninigi, Motoori transformed the myth into a covenant assigning the "visible world" (*utsushigoto*) to Ninigi and the "invisible world" (*kamigoto*) to Ōkuninushi-no-mikoto.[17] In this manner, although Motoori focused on the text of the *Kojiki*, by interweaving the alternative version of variants from the *Nihon shoki*, he was able to reflect his own interpretation onto the written text, namely, that the imperial house, signifying the highest existence in the human world, would persist eternally.[18]

Thus, Motoori's interest lay in using myth–history to legitimate an attitude of selflessness, which was the Ancient Way of supporting the order of things. For this purpose, he wrote about the creation of the land and its inhabitants, as well as the establishment of the right of sovereignty, asserting the appropriateness of the imperial house as the ruler of Japan, given its genealogical link to the creator deities. Yet, this is not to say that Motoori treated the emperor as a historical subject. Until the very end, he espoused the imperial system as an apparatus of selflessness, while expounding on the unselfish nature of the Japanese people.

Mono no aware

Since the development of medieval Shintō thought, it has been commonplace to understand the myths of the *Kojiki* and the *Nihon shoki* as being normative with regard to an individual's way of life. Within this interpretive tradition, Suika Shintō, the prominent school of Confucian Shintō, and Motoori's thought are closely related in attaching great importance to the way of the ruler and the ruled, with respect to the emperor. Motoori's innovation lay not in his emphasis on the way of the sovereign and the subject itself, but rather in the foundations that he proposed to substantiate the Ancient Way.[19]

In Motoori's work, "the way of sincerity" was supported from within by the aesthetic of *mono no aware*. "The understanding of *mono no aware* extends in its broadest sense to the way of governing oneself, one's household, and the country as well," he wrote. "When [the ruler] sympathizes with the toil and suffering of the people, then there will be no malevolent ruler."[20] Motoori believed that, given a *mono no aware*-like sensitivity, people will naturally feel sympathy and concern for others and harmony will be brought to society. *Mono no aware* was something that acknowledged the movements of the heart and mind without suppressing them. This did not mean that *mono no aware* made any particular emotion permanent. Rather, as Motoori himself stated, "*aware* is to be moved by things,"[21] whereby the issue is not the content but "the degree, the depth of feeling" itself.[22]

Motoori's theory of *mono no aware* is developed in his works on poetics and *The Tale of Genji*. This concept occupies an important place in his works on the Ancient Way as well, although the phrase itself does not appear in the text. For instance, in one passage of *Tamakushige* (Commentary on *The Tale of Genji*), Motoori expounded how, long ago, every movement of the heart, whether enjoyable or sad, was recognized, and that this sensitivity to feelings was a fundamental characteristic of human beings in their original form. He wrote,

> In ancient times when the hearts of people were naive and not yet adulterated with doctrines from other lands, there was no useless, devious thought of indiscriminately creating theories about where people go after death. When they died, people simply went to the Land of Yomi, the world of the dead, and there was nothing to do but prepare themselves for it and grieve.[23]

He went on to criticize harshly the Confucian-like demeanor that suppresses individual feelings:

> To esteem and consider it good not to rejoice at anything joyful, not to grieve over anything sorrowful, to be unmoved by anything surprising: these are all foreign fallacies. They are superfluous; they do not exist in the true nature of people.[24]

In Motoori's theory, the most profound aspect of *mono no aware* was the deep emotion prompted by "anything that does not follow one's desires," as in sadness or love, for instance.[25] As the prototype of sadness-like *mono no aware*, he cited the mortal parting of the divine couple, Izanagi and Izanami in the *Kojiki*, stating, "since they will without fail go to the defiled land of Yomi, there is nothing as sad as death in this world."[26] The grief of Yamatotakeru also signified a similar response.

A world ordered on the feelings of individuals was precisely what formed the basis of Motoori's studies on the Ancient Way. To borrow the words of Maruyama Masao (1914–96):

> [Motoori Noringa] elevated the sense of *mono no aware*, which was "the essence of Japanese poetry," to the level of the essence of Shintō itself... If this can for the time being be called a "politicization of literature," with Noringa this politicization... [means] that the principle of literature (that is, the sense of *mono no aware*) is to be validated as a political principle.[27]

As a result of what Maruyama calls its literary character, we are today still captivated by Motoori's explication of the myths. The interiority and emotions that he read into the protagonists of the *Kojiki* and the *Nihon shoki* could appear in a modern novel. In that respect, Motoori was the progenitor of the modern interpretation.

Yet, although he generalized the *mono no aware*-like emotionality of "ancient times when the hearts of people were naive," the relevant passages that Motoori actually cited in the myths, even with respect to the *Kojiki*, included only the death scene of Izanagi and Izanami, and a few other passages. Based on a few scattered references, one must conclude that Motoori overexaggerated the presence of *mono no aware*-like understanding in his interpretation of the myths. By extending *mono no aware*-like sensitivity to the age of the gods in its entirety, Motoori introduced into the myths of the *Kojiki* and the *Nihon shoki* an interiorized understanding of the different characters.

The worldview of the non-ruling strata

The basis of *mono no aware* can be seen in *jōruri* (a type of sung narrative employed in traditional Japanese puppet theatre) and other cultural representations among the non-ruling classes in a broad sense. As Hino Tatsuo suggests, after having examined the cultural background of Motoori's thesis:

> The desire to rescue human emotions from the restraints of public norms...exists strongly through popular culture in any era... The reception of the classics of *jōruri*, *haikai* and vernacular works, as reaffirmations that even adultery is love, has its roots, after all, in this characteristic of popular culture...I have no doubt that the precursor of [Motoori] Noringa's argument about "knowing *mono no aware*" can be found in this aspect of the popular culture that was contemporary and to which Noringa was closely attached.[28]

In other words, the worldview of Motoori Norinaga was based on popular culture rather than the ethics of the ruling classes affiliated with Confucianism. Yet, Motoori's theory was distinct due to its stance on self-criticism.

In fact, Motoori espoused *mono no aware* not merely to glorify sentimentality, but rather to avoid an over-reliance on human logic. He used the concept to criticize Confucianism as blind faith in reason—that which is rigorously subjugated by reason and which ignores the fundamental sensitivity of human beings. In contrast, he understood the spontaneous *mono no aware*-like sensitivity as a natural force that sweeps rigidity away. Since all existence was influenced by this natural creative force, Motoori placed a single creative deity (Musuhi-no-kami) at the very beginning of his interpretation of the myths.

> In accordance with their status in this world, all living things... know and carry out what they should do in order to live, and this is thanks to the power of Musuhi-no-kami. Of all living beings, humans are especially superior, and in accordance with our superior ability, we know and do what we should know and do. Why pursue the matter any further? [29]

By positing an original deity, Musuhi-no-kami, as the source of all beings, encompassing the creation of heaven and earth, Motoori reasoned that humans are endowed at birth with "the way of sincerity." Thus, the practice of the Ancient Way became a simple activity that did not require rigid application, since, "on the whole, the kami...rejoice in the people of the world freely enjoying themselves."[30] It is clear that although Motoori couched his description of the social order in Confucian terms such as "the way of lord and subject, father and son, and the rest,"[31] the process that he proposed for attaining this ideal arrangement differs fundamentally from Confucianism.

Creator deities (*musuhi-no-kami*) appear in the opening passage of the *Kojiki*. However, one cannot say that the one creator deity (Musuhi-no-kami), as Motoori understood it, conforms to the passage in the *Kojiki*. In the opening of the *Kojiki*, three deities—Amenominakanushi-no-kami, Takami-musuhi-no-kami, and Kami-musuhi-no-kami—appear together. Yet, Motoori re-read them as a single original deity, Musuhi-no-kami. Thus, Amenominakanushi-no-kami lacks any concrete meaning, and even the two other deities, Takami-musuhi-no-kami and Kami-musuhi-no-kami, are actually seen as one.[32] Likewise, in the text of the *Kojiki*, the narrative begins at a point where heaven and earth are already separate. Yet, Motoori, by introducing the main text of the *Nihon shoki*, gave his creator deity, Musuhi-no-kami, an existence that preceded the separation of heaven and earth.[33]

In the opening of the *Kojiki*, the Musuhi-no-kami and other deities remain fundamentally no more than an enumeration of the names of gods; they lack a concrete connection to the history of the Age of the Gods. Since the *Kojiki* describes them as "having hidden their bodies," these *kami* or gods may be construed as supreme deities, namely, *kami* who retreat from history.[34] Motoori, however, added his own unique interpretation by re-reading the Musuhi-no-kami as the source of all beings, existing since before the creation of heaven and earth, a single fundamental deity from which all things were "born into the world." Accordingly, the values and norms that Motoori read into the myths became legitimated as being natural, each bestowed by the creator deity, Musuhi-no-kami. Even today, theories about the creation myths generally follow Motoori's identification of "*Kojiki*'s Musuhi-no-kami" as the fundamental source of all beings. Yet, Motoori developed his theory of Musuhi-no-kami as a criticism of the rigid Confucian ethics of a warrior society. One should be aware that his theory is indeed distinct from the ancient myths themselves.

As we have seen above, the significance of the *Kojiki* that Motoori summoned and valued was not derived from the *Kojiki* alone. While Motoori continually cited parts of the *Kojiki* in the crux of his arguments, he eventually wrote an authoritative text with its own original title, *Kamiyo no masagoto* (The True Language of the Divine Age), wherein he incorporated variants, such as the alternative passages from the *Nihon shoki*. *Kamiyo no masagoto*, for him, represented true events and the mentality of ancient Japan better than the *Kojiki* itself, and was the purified product of his commentaries. As we have already seen, Motoori created this composite text in order to read into the myths of the *Kojiki* and the *Nihon shoki* a world ordered around the basis of *mono no aware*.

Surely, as mentioned earlier, the *mono no aware*-like sensitivity that Motoori read into his text had its roots in the non-ruling strata of society. While Confucian Shintō and medieval Shintō studies before Motoori had analyzed the *Kojiki* and *Nihon shoki* myths as a way of understanding individual norms, they had attributed historical significance only to the elite political circles of the court and shogunate. Motoori, however, did not limit the mythical implications of the texts in terms of the ruling classes. He always envisioned the "imperial land" as including both "the revered and the humble"—namely, all the people who lived in Japan, from the nobles and warriors to the common people. This proposal, to link the myths in both the *Kojiki* and *Nihon shoki* closely to the non-ruling strata, was groundbreaking for its time and does not surface again until the advent of Nativism.

Phases of interpretation

Interpreters since Motoori have traditionally devoted themselves to the establishment and compilation of a single authoritative text, aiming primarily to reconcile the discrepancies between the *Kojiki* and the *Nihon shoki*, as well as between the main text and variants within the *Nihon shoki*. Yet today, as scholars have increasingly reconsidered the interpretative history of the *Kojiki* and the *Nihon shoki*, it has become clear that what each commentator believed to be a recapturing of the original form of the classic texts remained in the end no more than his own personal exegesis. Indeed, as far as can be ascertained from historical documents, there was never a time when the myths in the *Kojiki* and the *Nihon shoki* constituted a single unified text. Rather, a multitude of variants and correlating interpretations have always coexisted side by side.

This awareness of the distinct nature of each mythic text is related to a wider movement in interpretive studies which propounds a move away from the background of the text to the text itself. In other words, whether it is an ancient classic or a commentary upon it, each text is seen as an expression of a discrete worldview.[35] Thus, in Motoori's exposition of the Ancient Way, "the demand to restore or recreate a past so remote as to have little relevance to the present may," as E. J. Hobsbawm has said of invocations of antiquity elsewhere, "equate total innovation."[36]

In Motoori's interpretation, as we have already seen, as the content read into the Kiki texts changed, so too did its social relevance. In other words, the very relationship between the myths and human beings also transformed, including an understanding of the myths from the interpreter's point of view, or the social function of the myths from the vantage of the myths themselves.[37] The distinctiveness of Motoori's understanding of the relationship between the myths and human beings becomes apparent when his interpretation is compared to the way myths were regarded in ancient times.

In the following sections, I will elucidate the key points which support this conclusion stemming out of the analysis of ancient myths, based both on earlier studies and my own understanding.

Motoori Norinaga and Antiquity

For the ancient Japanese, as for Motoori, the purpose of mythic history was to explain the creation of the Japanese land and the birth of its rulers. The common themes that appear in different versions in the *Kojiki* and the *Nihon shoki*—as in Izanagi and Izanami giving birth to the land, the descent of the imperial grandson, and the abdication of Ohnamuchi—were regarded as tales explaining the process by which the rulers of the realm were selected. In this regard, the ancient understanding of the texts was no different from Motoori's perspective.

Yet, in ancient times, the subjects who were legitimated by the myths—in other words, the constituency signifying and signified through the myths—was comprised of the imperial family as well as the entire Yamato court surrounding the emperor.[38] The kingship myths at the time were drawn from two types of text: the imperial household histories (*teiki* and *kuji*) and the clan histories (*ujibumi*). The imperial household histories were orthodox texts that confirmed the power of the court. In a similar manner to the *Kojiki* and the *Nihon shoki*, these texts comprised a history of kingship centered on the imperial household. In contrast, clan histories were handed down within each clan and respectively elucidated their own distinct relations to the court.

For the clans, histories about their relationship to royal authority related the origins of their service to the kings. As the dispute in the early Heian period between the Takahashi and Azumi clans clearly demonstrates—in which each clan cited myths to support its claim as belonging to the line of imperial chefs—such histories were summoned as proof to substantiate political roles and offices. By linking clan histories to the imperial household histories, the kingship myths became not merely ideal tales but writings that fulfilled a political function, placing the clans that created the myths within the sphere of authority.[39]

Through the mediation of the clan writings, the constituency signifying the myths in ancient times was limited to clan members who were integrated according to their political functions in the Yamato court, centered on the imperial house. The people who appeared in the myths were the ancestors of the clans that constituted the court. According to the clans, as a result, the kingship myths were literally their own history. This intimate relationship between the myths and the people who comprised the court was also evident in their sense of history. Mediated by the continued process of compiling official state histories (*Rikkokushi*) until 887—when the *Nihon shoki* was the first to be included—the original time of the myths was flowing linearly up to the age in which each interpreter was active.

Thus, the people who lived in the land of Japan did not look to the myths of the *Kojiki* and the *Nihon shoki* for a portrayal of the origins of "the people" (*aohitogusa*). Rather, in contrast to Motoori's interpretation, in antiquity, the common people appeared only as objects in the rule of the Yamato court. In ancient times, there existed a solemn distinction between the subject that narrated and signified the myths and the object that was contained in the myths. The kingship myths of antiquity were not the product of the folk but were creations of the ruling body, which was the court.[40] As a result of their political functions, the myths were possessed exclusively by the court.

Given this situation in antiquity, it becomes even more obvious that the relationship of humans and myths in Motoori's thought is an apolitical ideal that lacks the understanding of restrictions which made up the social collectivity. This apolitical idealism, and the attendant emancipation of the constituency signifying the myths in early-modern interpretations, first materialized due to the loss of real political power by the royal court centered on the imperial household.

With the rise of the political power of the military families in the medieval period, the ancient political system in which the emperor was the direct symbol of authority weakened. By the early-modern period, the court had lost political power entirely. The imperial family became a traditional authority that did not hold real power,[41] while, at the same time, the kingship myths lost their political function. The clan writings lost their former *raison d'être* for situating their histories as a part of the political order. Indeed, the clan writings and the clans themselves virtually disappeared entirely at the beginning of the early-modern period.

By this time, the dual structure of the clan writings and the Kiki no longer existed. Even those clan writings that continued to thrive had lost their original political function. They had come to be seen as mere alternative versions of the *Kojiki* and the *Nihon shoki*, such as the *Kogoshūi* of the Imbe clan, or even forgeries, such as the *Sendai kuji hongi* of the Mononobe clan. Since there was no longer any function for the clan writings to fulfill, in politically linking the myths and their constituencies, the myths became apolitical and unrestrained. Thus, the *Kojiki* and *Nihon shoki* myths as we understand them became monotonous, devoid of the clan writings. Our mode of understanding was created in terms of a different structure of relations between humans and myths as compared to ancient times, one that came into existence in the early-modern period.

Through this process, the myths of the Kiki were freed from their political constraints in the early-modern period to become relevant to a wide range of social classes. The constituency signifying the myths expanded to include all people who lived in the Japanese archipelago. Here, the dynamic with regard to the subject who relates the myths and the object that is related was constituted. Yet, the actual ancestors for the new constituency as the nation's people were not defined and there is nothing akin to the clan writings that links the population of Japan as a whole concretely to the myths. Rather, the only entity directly connected to the myths was the imperial house. Motoori's interpretation, which found the right to govern Japan only in the emperor as elucidated in the *Kojiki* and the *Nihon shoki*, arose under the premises of the early-modern view of the Japanese emperor.

Compared to the ancient period, a gap opened up in the early-modern period between the myths and their signifying constituency. As a result of this fissure, it became possible to conceive of the liberation of the dominated class. The Kiki myths did not directly explain the history of the people of the non-ruling classes. However, in the *Kojiki* and the *Nihon shoki*, there exists the story about the creation of the Japanese archipelago where "such people" actually lived their daily lives. In this manner, even if only as the object of governance, it became possible for the people of the non-ruling classes to be linked to the Kiki myths. Since by now the myths did not contain any direct referent, anyone could take part in them by simply having lived in Japan.

The publishing technology created in the Kan'ei era (1624–44) did effectively manage to connect the myths and the people of the non-ruling classes. Prior to this development, the dissemination of written texts had been largely constrained by the technological limitations of hand-copying and block printing. With the establishment of woodblock printing, large-scale production of written texts became possible.[42] The *Kojiki*, beginning in 1667, and the *Nihon shoki*, beginning in 1682, were printed repeatedly, and innumerable commentaries on them circulated in the cities. Concerning the changes brought about by this large-scale production of written texts, Konta Yōzō concludes:

> The printing establishments that sprang up during the Edo period published all of the notable products of the spiritual movements of the Japanese people that had been amassed as hand copies since the ancient period... The classics of aristocratic society began to transform into the classics of the Japanese folk. One could call this the liberation of the classics... Anyone who wanted to could become familiar with the classics, and the social and geographic expansion of cultural reception proceeded on an unprecedented scale.[43]

Together with the establishment of book-lenders, the large-scale publication of written texts made it possible for anyone to pick up the Kiki in his own hands and read it. In other words, with the development of printing technology alongside the loss of the prescriptive (political) power of the Kiki, even an individual who did not belong to a particular group, such as the court or a Shintō religious association, could freely read the myths and their commentaries.

Motoori lamented the limited nature of the hand-copied texts and the closely guarded thought of his time. "Secret transmissions and the like," he wrote, "truly [embody] the dirty, selfish feeling of holding something for oneself without revealing it to other people, yet bragging of it to the world at large."[44] The national characteristics of the *Kojiki* and the *Nihon shoki* that came to be seen as self-evident in the modern period were first established only with the spread of printed texts and the loss of the prescriptive power of the classics. We must fully recognize that our understanding of the myths, as being essentially apolitical and limited to the people of Japan, was a product of Motoori and the period that followed. Based on this logic of Norinaga, the people of the non-ruling classes, who had newly become the reading audience of the myths, read the Kiki as tales about feelings and emotions, using the *mono no aware*-like sentimentality which represented a distinct cultural understanding.

Entering the modern period

By not taking membership in a closed group as its premise, but instead establishing a more open relationship between humans and myth, Motoori's interpretation opened up the horizon for the modern interpretation of the Kiki. During the last years of the Tokugawa shogunate, at about the same time that people began to understand the imperial system in political terms, Nativism permeated more deeply among the non-ruling classes. No longer concerned with the domain of regional intellectuals alone, Nativism put down roots in the daily lives of local communities. Led by the thought of Hirata Atsutane (1776–1843), Motoori's self-proclaimed disciple, Nativism had become a grass-roots phenomenon by the end of the Edo period.

However, as the Kiki myths were taken up amidst "the management of actual life and society in the countryside,"[45] and their interpretation became systematized and habitual, the inclination to interpret the myths as an epistemological issue, along Motoori's lines, dissipated. Although Motoori belonged to the non-ruling class, he was an intellectual and therefore distinct from people rooted in local communities. In denying the stability of feelings and criticizing actions undertaken on the basis of such supposedly unwavering sentiments, Motoori's theory of *mono no aware* problematized the depths of emotion. Markedly, his theory came into being from a tension-ridden relationship with Confucian studies, which at that time dominated social ethics.

In Motoori's words: "There is a limit to all human knowledge. Since the principle of sincerity cannot be understood intellectually, one should not recklessly assess and comment upon matters related to the gods."[46] Thus, reality could be measured by human reason, while value judgments of reality were criticized as resulting from actions that made humans exceed the authority of the gods. Furthermore, while attacking the Tokugawa Confucian audaciousness concerning human reason, Motoori asserted that "'overcoming emotions' is no great thing. It is also not proper to overindulge in your own emotions."[47] Here, Motoori warned against the danger of being swept away by the content of one's own emotions. Whether in Confucian studies or with regard to *mono no aware*-like feelings, Motoori refused to attribute a substantive quality or even a unilateral legitimacy to material objects.

This mental attitude, akin to being an ascetic monk, was not something that a person could easily achieve in actuality. One could even say that it was unconnected to the daily lives of ordinary people. However, as the interpretation of the Kiki became incorporated in the daily life of the people, people's opinions gained social legitimacy, which in turn brought with it a dogmatization of interpretation. Matsumoto Sannosuke, the Japanese scholar of politics, has summarized the peculiarities of this domesticated Nativist thought as

> diligence in one's household occupation, prohibition of abortion, respect for social distinctions, warning against luxury, the ethical ways of a husband and wife, the education of children, prenatal care, the rules for a neighborhood group to help each other, respect for village elders, prohibition of meat-eating, and the like.[48]

This understanding was derived from Morinaga's perspective because of the focus on individual life, but it overstepped Morinaga's sentiments in substantializing a rigid lifestyle: this was beyond Motoori's conceptions. No longer was there the tension with opposing philosophies like Confucianism. Rather, Motoori's interpretation was unilaterally actualized as a principle that supported the ethics of everyday life. In the place of Confucianism that had once enveloped society, the discourse of Nativism was systematized and circulated as the governing principle dictating public culture.

In this respect, the Nativist interpretation of the Kiki, following Hirata Atsutane's efforts, became embedded in everyday life while becoming dissociated significantly from Motoori's criticism regarding one's consciousness. Likewise, ever since Hirata's Nativism, the way in which people unilaterally read emotions into the myths—understanding mythology like a novel which concerned private lives (the "I-novelized myths")—has prevailed in substantive interpretations of the Kiki. Our "novelized" interpretations of the mythic tales have thus been dissociated from Motoori's critical stance.[49]

Yet, at the same time, one can see that Motoori's intention to liberate the Kiki myths from limited readership within the ruling class to include the general public is what made it possible to link people rooted in local communities to the imperial system. Once this openness to signifying a wider relevance to the myths was achieved, it instigated a process whereby the myths could be used assertively to attract people of the non-ruling classes—reconstituted in the modern period as national subjects—to be a part of the imperial state. From the late Edo into the Meiji period, anthologies of Motoori's commentaries were repeatedly edited and published. Yet, while this shows that many people at the time were fascinated with the Kiki, it also demonstrates that their understanding was superficial, merely reading in Motoori's statements what resounded as pertinent to their everyday lives.[50]

The Authority of the Original Past

In the end, Motoori's greatest achievement in the history of Kiki interpretation can be found in his adaptation of ruling class-based traditions in accordance with the norms of the non-ruling classes. As Tsuda Sōkichi, the historian who significantly influenced contemporary Kiki studies, states:

> Human nature...although it always existed in actuality, had been constrained by Chinese thought through the form of literary knowledge, and had therefore not appeared in the theoretical dimension. But little by little, human nature emerged because of the distinctive accomplishment of the Nativists in the intellectual world.[51]

Prior to Motoori, *mono no aware*, as grounded within the culture of the non-ruling classes, had always remained in the obscure realm of everyday impressions. The notion had not been granted social legitimacy, which would have enabled it to oppose the rationalism of Confucian thought. In these circumstances, Motoori evoked the Kiki myths which had provided the basis for the historical legitimacy of the ruling classes, and inscribed into them his own worldview, which included the non-ruling class.

The historian of China J. B. Henderson has written that "commentary dominated much of the intellectual life of postclassical, pre-modern man not only by virtue of its importance as a genre or form, but also through the habits of mind and modes of thought it fostered."[52] Indeed, much in the way that Motoori used the Kiki, people in pre-modern societies in both the East and West have frequently chosen the traditional classics of their respective societies as the site for the development of their own distinct philosophies. By engaging with a site that had been granted social authority, it became possible for the non-ruling classes, through their worldview, to defend their social foundation against the ruling classes.

This appears in a straightforward form in Motoori's stylistic assessments. For instance, he asserted that the *Kojiki* was more authentic for indigenous Japan than the *Nihon shoki* because it was written in Japanese and Chinese, in contrast to the *Nihon shoki*, which was written only in Chinese. Today, scholars dispute the validity of Motoori's position, on grounds such as the chronological precedence of classical Chinese over phonetic representations, and the relationship of oral culture and writing.[53] However, to reduce this question to such objective dimensions alone misses the point. The Chinese style in the *Nihon shoki* was the symbol of the Chinese educational prerogative of the ruling classes, as represented by Confucian studies. Moreover, classical Chinese was not conducive to the emotional expression that Motoori desired. By designating the *Kojiki* as the indigenous tradition of Japan, Motoori decried the cultural traditions relating to China and the ruling classes, who comprised the constituency identifying the *Nihon shoki* as being historically Chinese. In doing so, he succeeded in asserting the legitimacy of his own worldview with respect to that which he considered to be indigenous.

However, the attempt to appropriate the logic of the ruling class in order to prove the legitimacy of the non-ruling classes necessarily served to co-opt the hearts of the non-ruling classes into the historical authority made by the imperial tradition, as symbolized through the Kiki. In other words, through a commentary, the interpreter projects the worldview of a new constituency onto the texts so that people are not conscious that what they read into the texts is a part of their worldview. Eventually, they understand their own reading as the restoration of the ancient tradition held by the imperial household. As a result, the worldview of the interpreter becomes united with the narrative of the classic myths, so that the imperial system appears inconspicuously as the fundamental source of authority for the interpreter's cultural perspective.

Throughout the Edo period, since the emperor lacked political power, references to the Kiki myths by Motoori and others remained only at the level of culture. The political significance of Motoori's praise for the classic myths was not apparent as of yet. Later, in the modern period, when the imperial system was once again politicized and systematized by the new government, Nativist commentaries began once again to represent the source of culture, resembling the interpreters' projected worldview, which then merged with the political authority of the imperial system. Consequently, one can say that the cultural character of the imperial system began to conceal its own political nature by utilizing Nativist interpretations of the Kiki.

Strikingly, this perspective can be witnessed in the modern period with the viewpoint that the imperial system was a "cultural community," a view that was prevalent among liberal intellectuals like Watsuji Tetsurō and Tsuda Sōkichi.[54] After Japan's defeat in World War II, when the imperial system was redefined as the central symbol of state authority, it could no longer continue as the apparatus of selflessness that it had been for Motoori. Voluntary submission to the emperor as a symbol of cultural tradition, as espoused by modern intellectuals, was institutionalized and transformed into a mode of compliance under the authority of the modern state. Thus, Motoori's re-reading of the myths based on the non-ruling classes was in the end inevitably tied to the concept of the new constituency made up of Japanese subjects accepting the imperial state.

Towards an intellectual history of perspectives

The practice of seeking a relationship to an original past in order to legitimize one's own worldview can be found throughout history, from pre-modern to modern times. An original past, one which provides "an ideological foundation capable of guaranteeing the existence of man and of the universe, its stability and its permanence,"[55] confers the authenticity of historical origins upon the content of a given exposition. However, the myths fail to be relevant in new circumstances without a process of re-reading, which defines their renewed pertinence from an individual and socio-political standpoint. This process involves reinterpreting both the compilation of the mythic texts and the relationship between humans and myths. Indeed, one would hope that it has already become impossible to believe that one's own interpretation is a means to reclaim the original intention of the myths.

When one looks back upon the history of the interpretation of Kiki from this standpoint, one notices that interpreters most often fall into the trap of searching for an original past. Such unconscious orientation toward an original past conceals a lingering gap in our contemporaneous interpretation of the original text; this in fact works to conceal the dogmatism inherent in defining an object with our own gaze. As long as we seek to identify culturally with the Kiki, we cannot deny the possibility that, depending on the circumstances, we may once again be politically captured by the imperial system.

Today, a distinct new movement is propelling us to consider reducing the history of Kiki interpretation to solely concern the worldviews which have been projected onto the texts. This is an effective form of criticism with regard to an interpreter's literal belief in old legends. Yet, if this perspective simply concerns worldviews, it loses sight of the unique significance of research on the history of Kiki interpretations that elucidates, for example, how worldviews have been co-opted into supporting the prevailing discourse of a given age. Therein emerges the gap that I allude to in contemporary interpretations of ancient worldviews. In other words, there is the danger of interpreting the Kiki only in the dimension of the worldview of each period, which will dissolve within the general field of intellectual history and revive a form of historical relativism that simply points to different orientations spanning the ages.

The significance of studying the interpretative history of Kiki *per se* lies in the ability to examine the fundamental intentionality of the epistemological subject. That is, despite different worldviews, it compels one to ask: why have people consistently turned to the Kiki in order to legitimize themselves? Furthermore, in current times, how are we to re-examine the basic intentionality toward an original past? A naive intellectual history that simply concerns the object of study, no matter how well it is grounded in fashionable theories of the time, will always bring forth new myths that are characteristic of a given age and its rationale. Rather, what is required is a study situating the interpreters' disposition to familiarize the myths—what amounts to a meta-intellectual history unraveling the perspectives of the interpreters themselves.

6 The Space of Historical Discourse: Ishimoda Shō's Theory of the Heroic Age

Postwar Thought and Ishimoda Shō

Subjectivity and the theory of the Heroic Age

The collapse of the 1950s debate on the Heroic Age cast a dark shadow over subsequent research on the *Kojiki* and the *Nihon shoki* as well as, I daresay, the study of Japanese history. The departure point of this debate was an article by the Marxist historian Ishimoda Shō (1912–86), entitled "Kodai kizoku no eiyū jidai: Kojiki no ichi kōsatsu" (The Heroic Age of the Ancient Nobility: A Study of the *Kojiki*). According to this article, democratic communities ruled throughout Japan at the end of the primitive era (*genshi jidai*), but were defeated around the sixth century by the imperial state which had newly gained power. The Heroic Age refers to the final stages of the primitive era, which were marked by rivalry among these democratic communities. This era was not, however, a harmonious one. What confronted the formation of the ancient state was rather a period of disorder and upheaval, from within which emerged a national (*minzoku*) spirit.

Although epic poetry is generally the form in which such heroic ages are later recounted, this genre never crystallized in Japan. Instead, memories of the past can only sparingly be glimpsed within the *Kojiki* and the *Nihon shoki*, texts that were produced by the imperial state. The subsequent Heroic Age debate was what developed around Ishimoda's views, questioning his gaze at the past.

Beginning in the postwar era, Ishimoda consistently engaged in historical research focusing upon "the *tennō* [emperor] system," which for him was "the greatest task" of criticism. This research did not simply point out the hegemonic nature of the Japanese imperial system. Rather, it attempted to explore the "issue of confronting the Japanese people, most of whom were under the spell of the Japanese imperial system."[1] While Ishimoda saw the people as constituting a force which shapes history, this view was by no means an optimistic one:

> The knowledge that the people are the driving force behind historical progress and revolution remains unchanged. When this correct principle is seen from

a negative perspective, however, it must be said that the stagnation or regress of the people's strength and consciousness has brought about the stagnation and regress of historical development... As can typically be seen in the case of state power, domination always rules over the people by means of a powerful framework. Yet no political [form of] power could survive if this domination were merely naked force. The particular conditions of a people have to correspond with the domination, permitting its survival.[2]

Ishimoda's statement urging one to pay attention to historical stagnation emerged from his experience of an era ruled by the prewar Japanese imperial system. Emancipation from this system was brought about externally by means of the Occupation Army. Painful memories lingered of the Japanese who were unable to oppose imperial fascism in and of themselves, as could be seen in such phenomena as grassroots fascism and the imperially instigated conversion of intellectuals. It was in order to overcome this failure that Ishimoda set out to explain the "various conditions and contradictions of the people, who made possible the maintenance and survival of this *tennō* (Japanese emperor) rule itself."[3]

Ishimoda's project can be understood as part of simultaneous movements which went beyond the genre of scholarship. These included the political scientist Maruyama Masao (1914–96), who published "Chō kokkashugi no ronri to shinri" (The Logic and Psychology of Ultra-nationalism), the economic historian Ōtsuka Hisao (1907–96), the theory of the "nation" as set forth by the Chinese literature scholar Takeuchi Yoshimi (1910–77), the subjectivity debate involving the philosopher Umemoto Katsumi (1912–74), and the *tenkō*-conversion theories of the Shisō no Kagaku Kenkyūkai (Research Association for the Science of Thought). Convinced of the need to go beyond a simplistic theory of infrastructure (namely, the economic determinism of Russian Marxism), these thinkers appealed to the actual consciousness of the ordinary people (which included intellectuals) so as to found a humanity commensurate with the revolutionary subject of history. While the word "subjectivity" was at this time used in many different ways, a shared underlying trait was apparent. As the philosopher Ichikawa Hiroshi writes:

> The practices of democratization and socialization in postwar society did not take place as "commands given by an authorized theory" but rather with respect to the "spontaneity found within individuals' lives"... This notion [of individual spontaneity] was grounded upon the wartime collapse of the socialist movement as well as upon urgent reflection on the individual's experience of intellectual defeat.[4]

The common trait of this subject of thought and action was that it did not rely upon external authority but rather willed and decided on the basis of its own judgment. Besides, the imperial system had not yet become an issue of the past. Instead it began to set forth its own traditions as the cultural symbol of the Japanese nation. Immediately after the war, in January 1946, Tsuda Sōkichi—who was considered the leader of the Reform camp—published an article entitled "Kenkoku no jijō to bansei ikkei no shisō" (The Founding of the State and the Notion of the Unbroken Imperial Line). Meanwhile, in the autumn of the same year, the Ministry of Education distributed a national textbook, *Kuni no ayumi* (The Historical Course of the Nation). It was also reported that some 90 percent of the populace were in favor of the continuation of the *tennō* (emperor) system on a cultural basis.[5]

Although depicted as being new and symbolic, the postwar *tennō* system still represented the head of state power and claimed to literally represent the historical origin of Japan. Hence it had to be opposed by scholarship which dealt with history. This is one of the reasons why the "History Division" came to play the leading role in the Minshushugi Kagakusha Kyōkai (Association of Democratic Scientists), which was formed in January 1946, including survivors of prewar leftwing groups. It was within this atmosphere that Ishimoda finished writing "The Heroic Age of the Ancient Nobility" (hereafter abbreviated as the essay on the "Heroic Age") in September 1947. In his words:

> To oppose historical-materialist methods to the hermeneutic-idealist methods which have hitherto dominated literary history is truly a simple matter as far as method is concerned. Yet it is extremely difficult to concretely put these methods into practice…[Traditionally] materialist literary history has merely discovered social and economic reflections within literature; namely, it grasps this process crudely and uni-dimensionally without seeing it as dynamic, as one mediated in various ways. This facile understanding first became possible by rejecting the multifaceted complexity of historical structure. A correct materialist literary history must fight against such vulgar methods.[6]

These lines appear at the beginning of the essay on the Heroic Age. Here, Ishimoda resists a "nationalist view of ancient history," which directly incorporates the figures from the *Kojiki* and the *Nihon shoki* as national heroes. Yet, he also reveals a desire to go beyond a "vulgar materialism" that attempts to reduce historical complexity to a principle dictated by the economic structure. The nationalist view of ancient history regarded the *tennō* state as existing from time immemorial. For Ishimoda, on the one hand, this was nothing more than an attempt to conceptually hide the class character of the state. On the other hand, materialist history at the time only repeated the determination of the superstructure by the infrastructure in a dogmatic manner. In other words, it did not set forth any effective criticism of the nationalist view of history.

Certainly, Ishimoda also adopted this materialist position and thus he recognized shifts in the infrastructure as a matter of "historical necessity."[7] He refused, however, to adopt an inflexible determinism and sought an alternative position made possible through the notion of "human subjectivity within history."[8] He writes:

> What is important for historiography is..."actual possibilities," in other words, possibilities which have their ground in given historical conditions themselves. Such possibilities are formed within real history... Real history advances only through the opposition and struggle brought about when people seek to transform these possibilities into reality... Because history contains several actual possibilities as elements, it was able to become a process filled with abundance and life.[9]

Ishimoda's notion of subjectivity opened a way for the possibility of man's intentional decisions vis-à-vis historical necessity. It represented an understanding of subjectivity, which at this time swept over an entire generation, and in which Ishimoda tried to discover a "history created by man."[10] Those people who were suited to act as revolutionary subjects of history were called "heroes" and they constituted the subject-matter for his essay on the Heroic Age. In this manner, his exposition was written on the basis of critical concerns which were widely shared among intellectuals in the immediate postwar period. From a wider perspective, this was a time when historiography attained an authoritative position at the forefront of research within intellectual circles.

The debate on the nation and the Heroic Age

Ishimoda's essay appeared in a volume entitled *Ronshū: Shigaku* (Collected Essays: Historical Studies), in December 1948, one year after it was written. In 1949, Saigō Nobutsuna and Kawasaki Tsuneyuki discussed "the Heroic Age" in a special issue of the journal *Bungaku* [Literature], entitled "Henkaku ki no rekishi to bungaku" [History and Literature of the Revolutionary Period]. Subsequently, in 1950, a "Heroic Age Symposium" was held under the auspices of the sectional meeting on history by the Minshushugi Kagakusha Kyōkai (Association of Democratic Scientists). Debate over the Heroic Age gradually increased, reaching its peak in the years 1951–52 at the general meetings of the Rekishigaku Kenkyūkai (Historical Science Society), entitled "The Question of the Nation within History" and "On National Culture."

Yet there were certain aspects of the Heroic Age debate of the 1950s which are not to be found in Ishimoda's essay, written in 1947. This discrepancy is explained by Tōma Seita (1913–), who was both Ishimoda's friend and a participant in the debate:

> Ishimoda's theory of the Heroic Age...sought to criticize the *tennō* system and the ideology that based itself upon it. It was grounded in the question as to why Japan's ancient literature was only able to describe the petty ancient nobility as heroic. I, however, regarded the *Kojiki* tale of "Yamatotakeru" as

representative of a "national" hero and national culture. I also related it to such modern poets as Park Yongcheol from Korea. Although we both took up the Heroic Age theory, great differences existed between Ishimoda and myself as far as the interpretation of "Yamatotakeru."[11]

With the increasing tension between the USA and the Soviet Union, brought about by the founding of the People's Republic of China, the outbreak of the Korean War and the rise of Communist influence in East Asia, the Occupation Army changed its ruling policy in Japan from one of eradicating domestic nationalism to that of building an anti-Communist outpost. The Japanese government responded to this change by enacting policies which hindered democratization, such as the Red Purge and the protection of monopoly capital. It was within these political conditions that Tōma took up the Heroic Age theory as a form of intellectual praxis for the Japan Communist Party's (JCP) movement for national independence.[12] Although the JCP first viewed the Occupation Army as a leader of democratic reform, it set out on a path of anti-American imperialism after 1948, eventually calling for a "Democratic National Front." Within this setting, the Heroic Age was pushed to the forefront, as denoting the historical origin of national independence. Hence, discussion was focused along the lines of whether the Heroic Age had actually existed and, if so, at what time.[13]

As I have already mentioned, the aim of Ishimoda's essay was not simply to oppose power. Even if it were, however, he tried to explain how legitimizing power was a problem involving the people (the governed) on the basis of its premise that the people's authoritarian nature could not be overcome. This was not a binary division between the ruling power and those ruled. Rather, the essay focused on the secret that underlay power by firmly grasping the nature of the relations between the two opposing sides. In this manner, Ishimoda attempted to find a means by which the people could establish their national subjectivity. For Tōma, however, the Heroic Age debate of the 1950s downplayed the significance of the people's wrestling with power. In fact, this debate became a historic symbol of the anti-authoritarian camp in its resistance to American imperialism and call for national independence. This signified a return to the binary mode of thinking which, as pointed out by both Ishimoda and Maruyama Masao, was due to the weakness of the prewar resistance movement.

This trend did not stop with the Heroic Age debate. Issues regarding national culture were widely addressed in historiography and Japanese literature. Beginning with the aforementioned general meetings of the Historical Science Society in 1951–52, this topic of concern then spread to the Nihon Bungaku Kyōkai (Japanese Literature Society) and the Nihonshi Kenkyūkai (Japanese Society for Historical Studies). Special issues were successively put together in the journals *Bungaku* [Literature] and *Kikan riron* [Theory

Quarterly]. Furthermore, this movement evolved along the lines of increasing the political and cultural solidarity between intellectuals and the people, as witnessed by the emergence of a national history movement within the field of historiography and a national literature movement within the field of Japanese literature.

Ishimoda had himself become one of the leaders of this movement, although his writings at this time were not directly related to the Heroic Age. In a volume entitled *Rekishi to minzoku no hakken* [The Discovery of History and the Nation], published in 1952, Ishimoda sought to establish his own standpoint on "national emancipation and the struggle against imperialism." In order to organize a national front, he wrote, it was the task of historiography to awaken the "proper national consciousness latent within the masses."[14]

In this manner, the postwar Heroic Age debate, which began as an analysis of the people's thought, had changed within the climate marked by the intensified political struggle of the 1950s. It had become the basis for the political standpoint which regarded anti-Americanism as being equivalent to the founding of a national unified front. Since the debate recognized partisanship as being a self-evident truth, it changed its course in such a way as to provide legitimacy to this perspective. This change moreover produced a split within the Reformist camp, resulting in the National Front's opposition to the International People's United Front, as well as to the anti-nationalist forces whose goal was the overthrow of the *tennō* system. This can be seen quite clearly in Kitayama Shigeo's (1909–84) criticism of Tōma and Ishimoda:

> It is very problematic to "eulogize" a conqueror with links to the imperial line, whose basic essence is excluded from *Kojiki* legends, on the basis of a pile of unreliable suppositions. For, by so doing, ancient autocratic rule is not taken seriously, and the *tennō* or imperial prince—who embodies this rule—is unjustifiably and ahistorically romanticized... Rather than criticizing antiquity, the Heroic Age debate actually obscures it. This debate profits the Reactionary camp (which is planning its rejoinder) through its encouragement of nationalism.[15]

What underlies this criticism is a difference in opinion as to how the nation was to be understood. At this time, the notion of "*minzoku*/nation [this latter term is given in English]" was interpreted as something that denied the existence of class[16] while being a "socio-historic category." The former interpretation was entrenched in prewar nationalism and took the *tennō* system as its symbol. As is apparent, this interpretation was affirmed by conservatives. In this sense, such members of the Reform camp as Kitayama Shigeo and Inoue Kiyoshi (1913–2001) criticized the nation as feudalistic, one that was hostile to the working class. The latter interpretation was typically that of 1950s Marxists who argued in favor of the nation, such as Tōma and Ishimoda. This group called for political independence as part of its opposition to imperialist rule. Although, as Uehara Senroku (1899–1975) has pointed out, debate must begin from the analysis of actual conditions in Japan, it is also apparent that both camps sought their legitimacy in different essays by Stalin. Although differences existed in their interpretation of the concept of the nation, the former criticized the latter as reactionary, while the latter criticized the former for its lack of awareness of the situation.

Even though this difference, with regard to the interpretation of the nation, was not all-pervasive, it overlapped with the political situation whereby a division existed within the JCP. This division was not something that could be entirely resolved through scholarship. In any case, the debate evolved while containing such internal fissures. However, this movement was gradually forced to retreat before the actual political denouement represented by the September 1951 pronouncement of Independent Peace with regard to the U.S.–Japan Security Treaty of 1955. The Heroic Age debate, which had grown considerably, quieted down in 1954.

In 1953 Ishimoda acknowledged the strategic error of the theory of the nation as set forth by the Marxists (among whom he included himself) in the following manner: "We were unable to take as our common starting point the understanding as to how the postwar concept of the 'nation' should distinguish itself from the prewar concept."[17] As if chastised for this, the JCP underwent a period of self-criticism in 1955, while Stalin was criticized in the Soviet Union after his death in 1956. While the stage for historiography retreated into positivism, Marxist historiography entered a period of stagnation.

The disintegration of the debate on the Heroic Age

The Heroic Age debate represents the period in the postwar era when the *Kojiki* and the *Nihon shoki* attained their prominence and were most sharply disputed. This was so much the case that its collapse had a substantial effect on the study of the Kiki texts, which consequently lost their marked significance in the forefront of historical research. In turn, all that remained in the field of Japanese literature and mythology was research dwelling on the ancient form of myth and legend as evident in the texts. Subsequently, niches were formed whereby historical research dealt solely with political and economic history, and Japanese literature began to be concerned only with literary history. The *Kojiki* and the *Nihon shoki*, which were placed in the domain of Japanese literature, were transformed into objects for positivist research. As a result, the significance of conducting such research went unquestioned.

Positivist research does not have neutrality, through which one supposedly ousts all interpretive bias. It is rather an engagement in which a tense exchange ensues between the scholar's interpretive horizon and the reading demanded by the text. In this case, however, it was reduced to a mere handling of documents in which the established interpretive framework was thought to be self-evident. Far from being a form of social criticism, this unconscious appeal to established interpretations had an exclusionary quality which gave greater weight to dominant viewpoints. This qualitative decline in research on the *Kojiki* and *Nihon shoki* originated in the Heroic Age debate of the 1950s. Although it is rather crude at this juncture to expound on its significance for "scholarship," one must note that the existence of the Heroic Age was at the time perceived as an "established fact."[18] It was believed that it was indeed possible to return to the ancient age, as explicated in the texts that were upheld as national legends, if adequate historical research was devoted to it.

What Ishimoda had originally attempted in his Heroic Age essay was an explanation of human nature as being dependent upon authority. In explaining this problem, he shed light on that period of history which pre-existed the formation of the *tennō*-state. Insofar as this explanation took the form of historical research, however, it was in fact a cognitive act through which past events were revealed. Yet, this act was formulated so as to clarify the circumstances informing our knowledge of history.[19] The question as to why people still supported the *tennō* system in the postwar era was grounded upon our inexplicable tendency to separate everyday sensation from thought. Herewith, there was no blind self-confidence to believe that one's own epistemological horizon could attain clarity, nor a naiveté in gazing at the past from the safety zone marking the interpreter's scope of reason.

As such, if contemporary research on the *Kojiki* and the *Nihon shoki* is to regain its critical force, it will do so not by continuing such exhausted inquiries into the ancient forms of these texts, but rather by re-visiting Ishimoda's essay, "The Heroic Age of the Ancient Nobility." In other words, research today must begin by explaining the achievements as well as the limits of Ishimoda's exposition. It is important for researchers to proceed in accordance with the internal logic of this praxis-based article, as opposed to dwelling on their individual intentions alone. After all, historical research advances arguments by taking as its starting point those actions and events that have actually taken place, and in turn it problematizes the writer's original intentions and inconsistencies from such a perspective. Therefore, within this work, the logic and values which inform Ishimoda's essay must be brought to light. As a result, we will be able to discover clues to understanding the fundamental question as to why the *Kojiki* and the *Nihon shoki* have survived over the ages and how is it that they have prevailed on the basis of authority.

The Heroic Age of the Ancient Nobility

The origin of subjectivity

Ishimoda's essay, "Kodai kizoku no eiyū jidai: Kojiki no ichi kōsatsu," consists of six parts, with a "Preface" and "Conclusion" added onto four main sections. While its diffuse style combined with its lengthy exposition has frequently left readers at a loss, the essay's logical construction is in itself extremely clear.

To begin with, the essay's aims and methodological premises are presented in the Preface. In "Section 1: Epic Poetry and the Heroic Age," a theoretical intervention is introduced whereby Hegel's notion of the "Heroic Age"—which forms the basis of this section—is transformed, in light of its aesthetic relevance, into a historical notion. Sections 2 and 3 are paired. In "Section 2: On the Existence of the Heroic Age in Japanese Antiquity," Ishimoda argues that the Heroic Age also existed in Japan as a universal law in light of the development of world history. Subsequently, in "Section 3: On the Features of the Heroic Age," Japan's distinct form of universal law is considered. In contrast to these two sections in which the Heroic Age itself is discussed, "Section 4: On the Heroic Narrative (*monogatari*) within Ancient Literature" deals with the problem of historical knowledge, inquiring into the manner that the ancient nobility understood the Heroic Age. In the Conclusion, Ishimoda offers his perspective on the significance of his own essay within the field of Japanese intellectual history as well as on the process through which the Heroic Age developed within Japanese history as a diachronic notion.

Seen from this perspective, it can be understood that the essay is logically constructed around two basic axes. The first is that of the Heroic Age understood as historical fact and its relation to epic literature, namely, its epistemological product. The second is that of the basic law of world history (advocating a materialist worldview of history) and its relation to Japan, which represents a particular construct of the law. By allowing these two axes to intersect with each other, Ishimoda sets up both universal and particular categorical types within both the Heroic Age and epic literature. He then goes on to search for Japan's (the Japanese imperial system's) distinctness in the course of its transition from the Heroic Age to the period of the formation of epic literature. However, difficulties emerge within this logic.

Firstly, there arises the question whether the very existence of the Heroic Age can ever be proven. In order to discuss this issue, I would like to clarify Ishimoda's perspective on the Heroic Age as elaborated in the first section of the essay.

The Heroic Age refers to the period when there existed "a relationship between heroes who acted as independent individuals and [the same heroes] who appeared as *models of social groups* to which they belonged"[20] (italics added). Ishimoda writes that this was a transitional period in which existing institutions had collapsed and a new order had not yet been established. During this period, such phenomena (i.e., these heroes) were often seen diachronically and from a global perspective. Above all, Ishimoda places great value on the transitional period from primitive society to the formation of the ancient state, during which, as he writes, heroes fully embodied "the worldview of the national spirit and the totality of the period and its people."[21] Although such an argument was originally set forth by Western scholars, Ishimoda claims that the Heroic Age existed in Japan as well. In this manner, he argues that Japan also experienced an era in which individuals acted by means of their subjectivity rather than relying upon state authority.

Ishimoda sought out the characteristics of the hero, namely, the truth of their subjectivity, via notions of "individuality" and "national spirit." Both of these concepts derive from Hegel's work, *Aesthetics: Lectures on Fine Art*. For Ishimoda, "individuality" signifies "immediate human authority unmediated by system or law." In other words, "individuality in which man takes the lead in the real world by means of his extraordinary purpose, eminent greatness, and the force of his personality."[22] As he adds, "Above all, the distinguishing characteristics of the Heroic Age are to be found in tumultuous instability, inchoate contradictions and the chaos that emerged in the midst."[23] Hence, only the individual's strength and courage could protect the life and property of the hero as well as those who followed him. On the other hand, state structure and law are rejected as "external autonomous institutions that oppose individuality."[24] Since the state and the law regard abstraction and generality as essential, they allow man to stop thinking for himself and therefore create an attitude that promotes blind obedience to authority.

Therefore, individuality that has been realized does not imply an indulgence of desires. Rather, it is backed by a foundation which bestows propriety. However, this foundation differs between Ishimoda and Hegel. Just as Hegel writes that "true independence consists solely in the unity and interpenetration of individuality and universality,"[25] individuality does not merely oppose the state but must above all first be supported by universal values. Yet, it is impossible to find a word in Ishimoda's essay which corresponds to Hegel's "universality." Just as "it is necessary for the individual to truly oppose state life so as to be independent,"[26] Ishimoda's notion of individuality derives its meaning through its persistent opposition to the state.

Hegel's notion of universality refers to the ultimate form of "Reason," known as the "Absolute Spirit." Here the finiteness of man's knowledge is "sublated," enabling him to attain a godlike infinity. While it is unclear as to what degree Ishimoda was aware of his differences with Hegel, his standpoint was that of Marxism, and thus it was natural for him to focus less upon such conceptual questions than on the political aspect of independence with respect to the state. Once this independence was attained, it would transform into communality rather than universality, which bequeathed propriety upon individuality.

In the Heroic Age, the patriarch *qua* hero is believed to possess "a holistic individuality which contains, utterly within itself, the most diverse personalities of the people." Yet Ishimoda explains that this individuality is not grounded upon the community's undifferentiated unity. Rather it was produced by "a single social group which contained, within itself, complex oppositions."[27] In other words, independent and self-supporting peasants had not yet diminished in this pre-slave society. Meanwhile, the patriarch, whose identity was determined by members of this society, took democratic action. This communality was not characteristic of only one community. Instead it was believed to hold true for the "national spirit" as a whole, which permeated the struggles associated with the formation of the state.

This type of communality is also cited by Hegel as a necessary condition for the Heroic Age. Yet, ultimately for Hegel, it is the state itself which constitutes the ideal community that realizes freedom as its final goal. He views the state as the existence of "Reason," whose purpose is to bring diverse individuals into harmony.[28] In contrast, Ishimoda understands the state as the ruler's power-structure. For him the Heroic Age is essentially incompatible with the state. Ishimoda himself spoke of the need to reinterpret Hegel's aesthetics from the standpoint of "class opposition", as set forth in the materialist view of history.[29] Yet, this would entail a fundamental shift in conceiving the relationship between state and individuality. While research on the Heroic Age had been conducted in Japan since the prewar period, Ishimoda's essay may be considered epoch-making in its introduction of class opposition within this research.[30]

In this manner, Ishimoda's theory of the Heroic Age represents the sum-total of his views on the individual and the state. He set forth this argument in order to claim that subjectivity had also existed at the dawn of Japanese history. In the conclusion of his essay, he writes:

> Heroes could not exist apart from the Heroic Age. Neglecting this age was a basic demand of the nationalist view of ancient history. The formation of the ancient state is seen as the work of the imperial household and the Japanese emperor as opposed to a class-based project of the ancient nobility. Hence they refuse to recognize the existence of the Heroic Age. In marked contrast, the perspective which recognizes the Heroic Age sees the state as the result of class contradictions within the ancient nobility. It recognizes the existence of a driving force which generates man's greatness precisely within these

contradictions, one which reveals his hidden characteristics while forming new men and history. It understands that this is the basis upon which men can be made into heroes.[31]

According to the explanation given in the *Kojiki* and the *Nihon shoki*, it was fated that, together with the emergence of heaven and earth, the imperial family would be the rulers of the earthly world. This authority of rule was guaranteed eternally by the gods. Against this view, Ishimoda argued that the historical origins of the Japanese imperial system lack proof. He criticized the national psychology of dependence on the imperial as merely derivative of later generations. Ishimoda believed that man acted on the basis of his own will prior to the formation of the imperial system, and that the nation was formed on the basis of these actions. What Ishimoda conceives of here as the nation signifies a national community unmediated by state power. As goes without saying, this nation represents the communality of the Heroic Age.

As I have mentioned, Ishimoda argued that the Heroic Age did not take place only at the dawn of ancient history but was instead something that appeared frequently during changes in eras. In a book written at the end of the Asian–Pacific War (1931–45), entitled *Chūseiteki sekai no keisei* [The Formation of the Medieval World], Ishimoda discusses the state of affairs of the warrior class which thrived during the "medieval Heroic Age." He finds this to be a "popular" movement based on solidarity among the classes.[32] However, what unexpectedly appears in this essay is an account of the Heroic Age of the proletarian class: "Only the proletariat hero allows for the individual–group relation to be ideally guaranteed, such that the hero appears as the model of the social group to which he belongs while acting as an independent individual."[33]

According to Ishimoda, on the one hand, class conflict would be overcome under a dictatorship of the proletariat and a state would come into being which possessed the right of national self-governance with its origins in the working class.[34] On the other hand, the Heroic Age at the end of primitive times always contained class conflict: "Ancient heroes, who appeared as rulers and oppressors, directly opposed the social group; this relation was of a different nature."[35] This age can be conceived as a transitional state of equilibrium that was on the verge of collapsing.

Further, Ishimoda announces at the end of this essay that the time was imminent for the dictatorship of the proletariat to come into being: "We are now certainly experiencing a class-based Heroic Age on a global scale."[36] Yet this dictatorship could not be realized solely by political action. Rather, it was necessary to support such action internally by means of a heroic subjective will. His aim in writing the Heroic Age essay was to unearth and rehabilitate the historical tradition of human subjectivity.

That is to say, Ishimoda placed the Heroic Age of the proletariat at the end of a trajectory leading to a class-based society and the Heroic Age of the ancient patriarch as marking its beginning. In this manner, he tried to show that the *tennō*-state, which existed between these two ages, was temporally obsolete, and its fate was now at an end. He claimed we must understand that the historical origins of the modern state do not lie in the *tennō* system but can in fact be traced back to the ancient Heroic Age. In fact, in this essay, Ishimoda constantly employs words like "nation" and "people/citizens" (*kokumin*) in relation to the Heroic Age community. This usage reveals his desire that political independence needs to be attained in such a way that the modern national community conforms to the original cultural community.

At this time, Stalin's essay entitled "On Marxism within Linguistics" (1950), in which he sets forth the historical nature of the nation, had not yet been published. Therefore, Ishimoda's understanding of the nation should have been similar to that of other Marxists, namely, that it was basically a "product of the capitalist era" and did not exist prior to modernity.[37] Nevertheless, it is clear that during the actual writing of the essay on the Heroic Age, Ishimoda conceived a proto-nation as having existed during ancient times. As was also the case with Hegel, the theory of the Heroic Age itself was originally set up with the aim of seeking the origins of the modern nation in the past:

> The history of pre-capitalist society is not to be reduced or distorted into something that existed for the sake of the formation of the bourgeois nation. Rather this society stands on a much more expansive ground of the socialist nation. It provides new possibilities for a qualitatively different nation.[38]

While these lines emerged from within the 1950s debate on the nation, the logic is identical to that of the Heroic Age essay of 1947 (except for the fact that Japan's situation at the time was understood to be that of a bourgeois nation, rather than a feudal nation). In both these cases, though, Ishimoda's criticism of the *tennō* system endorses a logic of historical origins that is precarious to the extent that it relies on the system itself. Yet, Ishimoda claims that it is his own standpoint that accords with this logic, namely, it is not derivative of the Japanese emperor system. In this sense, it can be said that a form of essentialism that is both a romanticized ideal and a strategic rendering, by which an attempt is made to historically legitimate the existence of the universal and individual elements, deeply permeates Ishimoda's research at the time.

The missing communality

In engaging with the theory of the Heroic Age through historiography, both archival proof and logical conformity need to be demanded of statements. So it propels one to ask: how does Ishimoda prove the existence of the

Heroic Age in this essay? In the following discussion, let us focus upon his attempt to provide such proof via historiography, through an examination of "Section 2: On the Existence of the Heroic Age in Japanese Antiquity."

Here, Ishimoda argues that "we," the people of succeeding generations, are able to discuss the Heroic Age due to the fact that texts of epic literature which recorded this age were left behind. Epic literature refers to the narrative form which develops through the social experiences of a hero, whose individuality can be seen in both thought and action. In particular, the epic literature of ancient times describes the formative process of each nation as the "childlike consciousness of a people [that] is expressed for the first time in poetic form."[39] In the case of Japan, this literature is represented by the *Kojiki* and *Nihon shoki* texts.

However, both these texts solely write about the *tennō* and, as a result, give the impression that the history of the imperial family is the history of Japan itself. According to Ishimoda, their exemplary figure is Emperor Jinmu, the "despotic sovereign." Emperor Jinmu appears in the *Kojiki* and the *Nihon shoki* as ontologically denoting the "abstract existence of the political idea."[40] In other words, having been made subordinate to the idea of the state, he loses his individuality, which allows him to act through his own free will. As I have already pointed out, Ishimoda conceives of the state as requiring people to act uniformly. He finds it to be incapable of adapting to circumstances in the manner of the hero. As is widely known, the political idea expressed here refers to the notion that "Japan must be ruled by the Imperial Household."[41]

In contrast to these texts, Ishimoda suggests that "actual history was a grander and more severe experience, one which differed from that which is narrated in the *Kojiki* and *Nihon shoki*."[42] He asserts that these texts "utterly robbed 'epic independence.'"[43] History at its origin, he states, was repressed and rewritten during the formation of the imperial system. As goes without saying, Ishimoda here refers to the history of the people; he points out that the Kiki texts contain a double structure:

> As seen in the *Kojiki* and the *Nihon shoki*, the ancient nobility of the seventh century, which nearly completed Japan's state structure and legal system, forgot most of the historical facts essential to the process of state formation. They remembered only that the Heroic Age had once existed, and that without the heroic actions of that age it would have been impossible to create the state.[44]

While the *Kojiki* and the *Nihon shoki* are themselves products of the imperial state, they contain within them memories of the concealed Heroic Age. Now it is in fact songs (*kayō*) that reveal these traces. Two literary forms exist within the *Kojiki* and *Nihon shoki*: the prose that constitutes the body of the text and the songs inserted therein. According to Ishimoda, these forms originally distinguished two periods, namely, the prose was written during the formation of the imperial state, but the songs were composed earlier during the Heroic Age.

As mentioned above, epic literature is believed to have crystallized in the later recollections of the Heroic Age. Focusing on the gap between the texts and the Heroic Age, Ishimoda finds a perversion of the image of the Heroic Age as a moment in the formation of class society. As a result, these texts are seen as being distorted, serving the purpose of legitimating state power. According to Ishimoda, memories of the past are accurately inscribed only in the few songs which appear therein. It is on the basis of this division between prose and song that he analyzes the account of Emperor Jinmu:

> Contained within the narrative of Jinmu's eastern expedition are the two opposed worlds of prose and song: the abstract and bloodless man, who is merely the ontological premise of a political idea; and the independent hero, who, as the group ruler, appeals to the group with all his strength, and who knows the vivid reality of group life. As opposed to the considerable generality of description and the emptiness of content, there can be seen poetic intimacy and attachment to the details of everyday life. Prosaic monotony opposes epic tension. In sum, the prosaic, vulgar world and the epic, heroic world are opposed to one another.[45]

Basing his ideas on the Japanese literature scholar Takagi Ichinosuke's (1888–1974) pioneering essay, "Nihon bungaku ni okeru jojishi jidai" (The Epic Period in Japanese Literature), published in 1933, Ishimoda believed that the features of the Heroic Age could actually be confirmed in the so-called "Kumeuta" song, as presented in the account of Jinmu.[46] However, this analysis holds true only if one presupposes the specific interpretation that the Heroic Age also existed in Japan as a universal stage in world history. As proof, Ishimoda cites the appearance of a "heroic individual" (the song's subject) in the "Kumeuta," as well as the focus upon the everyday life of hunting and cultivating that is seen alongside the battle narrative. Yet, one must note that such themes as battle and everyday life are not limited to the Heroic Age but are rather frequently employed in the song. Furthermore, the existence of a heroic spirit is limited to the reader's own impressions; it would be difficult to even recognize this existence as a literary feature. One could go so far as to say that there was no way that the existence of the Heroic Age in ancient Japan—which was his focus in the second section of the essay—could have been proven by the use of historic materials.

First, the notion that the song reflects the true shape of the Heroic Age can only be propounded by universalizing Hegel's theory of art. Hegel highly esteemed poetry as "the original presentation of the truth" and regarded prose as artistically inferior, something that was produced by later generations.[47] Behind this evaluation could be seen a characteristic set of values which inquired into the degree to which the individual embodied universality, which for Ishimoda implied unity with the community. While poetry was still based upon a state of fusion with universality, this unity was damaged by the time of prose. Needless to say, such an analysis did not merely concern Hegel. Poetry was also classically understood as having put an end to the stage of oral tradition which existed prior to the introduction of writing. Grounded upon these values, Ishimoda considered the *Kojiki* and the *Nihon shoki* as texts which contained both temporal and qualitative gaps, constituted as a result of the duality emerging through the prose and the poetry.

Certainly, contemporary Western scholarship on epic poetry reveals that Hegel's division in literary form is rather vague. This division is put to question as a determinant factor, something that can be principally relied upon. Questions emerge as to "whether it is possible, desirable or necessary to separate oral epic from written epic." The perspective that poetry is a model of the Heroic Age, as Ishimoda contends, is critically put to question in this regard, as with the resonant critique that "the Marxist variant sees …folk poetry as founded on a pre-feudal, classless society."[48]

In contrast to what Ishimoda believed, no arguments proving the existence of the Heroic Age could ultimately be supported through historical data. Ishimoda's actual reasoning was such that, in order to compensate for this lack of data, he posited that the notion of the Heroic Age was a universal fact and in turn used this perspective to fill in the deficiencies. Just as the "basic laws of world history" could typically be seen within materialist historical perspectives at the time, individual events and theories were, if appropriate, believed to be substantial facts. While historical research is certainly an act by which potentiality is presented, it is essential that the argument be grounded in historical data, so as to ascertain its relevance in terms of historical phenomena. The reasoning that interpretative presuppositions conceal a lack of historical data is not fully persuasive. In this regard, Ishimoda's reasoning confuses means and ends, by presupposing the existence of the Heroic Age as fact instead of aiming to prove its historical validity.

Yet Ishimoda's investigation does not simply end with this point. His essay develops into a discussion of the community in the latter half of Section 2. He concludes that this community was insufficiently differentiated and within it patriarchal authority was in a state of transition, namely, that it was represented by the ruler but at the same time was not extended beyond the level of the community member. This conclusion was based on the following developments: the domestic conquests and the advance into Korea by powerful clans; the mixture of ruling and mass elements, as seen in the giant tumuli; and the constant battles among powerful clans to form the state in the fourth and fifth centuries. Yet, in Ishimoda's exposition, no matter how antagonisms of this period are described, everything ultimately returns to a basis of harmony. It is not surprising that Ishimoda was criticized on this point.

Among critics, the historian Kitayama Shigeo faulted Ishimoda's understanding of the fifth century, stating as follows:

> The essential problem lies rather in the fundamental opposition between the *tennō*, or various powerful clans, and the masses. The latter existed within the complex social relations of the old community placed under subjection to the former.[49]

In contrast to Ishimoda's understanding of the patriarch at the time as a public leader who served the good of the community, Kitayama saw him as an authoritarian figure who oppressed the community. Questions regarding Ishimoda's notion of harmony extended beyond intracommunity relations to the dynamics between communities. He apparently conceived of the nation as a cultural community which emerged through the disputes between existing communities in the process of state formation. Kitayama and Inoue Kiyoshi, however, criticized this reading, arguing that it merely projected upon past societies the homogeneity that was characteristic of the modern nation.

Among the complexities of his argument, Kitayama criticized the state of the debate, stating that "demonstration which is not grounded in documentary evidence does not constitute a body of scientific historical research."[50] Yet, this criticism can be applied to all standpoints, including that of Kitayama. From the point of view of lived history, oppositional elements are generally mixed together with non-oppositional elements in any given period. When judging which of these elements are dominant, the researcher's own disposition comes strongly into play. While all historical research takes the researcher's epistemological horizon as its starting point, the irrefutable existence of historical data generally resists and changes the reading. In cases such as the Heroic Age, where contemporary documents are scarce, however, it is exceedingly difficult to grasp the nature of society as a whole on the basis of fragmentary data.

In particular, because the documents do not reveal the nature of conditions within the community, there is virtually no record of the relations between patriarch and group, nor records from the viewpoint of community members. These records, including those made by later generations, are unilateral accounts as seen from the center of political and cultural power. Hence it is extremely difficult to shed light on their substance. Because of this, the desire on the part of all researchers to be projected into the ancient community assumed a concrete form. In the case of Ishimoda, the notion of communality that was projected therein was filled with harmonious relations both within and surrounding the communities, and nowhere could there be witnessed any decisive heterogeneity or antagonisms. On the basis of this understanding, power was derivative, something introduced later by class-based society. Power was thus excluded from any essential consideration of community.

In the materialist view of history, although power comes into being together with the formation of class society, it signifies the constant domination required to maintain labor and its inequalities. The state becomes the organ which systematically guarantees this act of exploitation. This period is charged with being historically unjust in terms of the fixed relations of exploitation in class-based society. In contrast, pre-class society is conceived of as a time in which power relations did not exist, due to a lack of surplus products. While it is certainly true that this form of domination has been prevalent, nevertheless power relations can and do exist outside of class society. Even if the gap between rich and poor were small and relations between the two were fluid, disparities would continue to exist and relations of exploitation would always be present. In this sense, power is something that exists in all social formations, not only within the state.

The primary weakness of Ishimoda's theory on the Heroic Age lay in the notion of a pure community as having historically existed. In later years, Ishimoda reflected on the Heroic Age debate and stated that "the presentation of the problem of the 'nation' itself was not 'national.'"[51] Yet, insofar as he regarded the nation in an undefiled state, problems in his line of argument were vague. Even if one were to adopt the viewpoint of Inoue Kiyoshi's Popular United Front, in which the "people" are hailed and "nation" is despised, the same perspective would hold. Regardless of whether the term summoned is the "nation" or the "people," power would have to be identified as an act of violence which imposed itself from without in order for a powerless communality to have actually existed. In turn, only a sense of reformism would prevail in the conception of community and it would be impossible to understand power as an essential problem within communality.

One can therefore argue that Ishimoda unconsciously projected his own values upon the past in his discussion of the Heroic Age. On the one hand, his theory of the Heroic Age took as one of its goals the radical criticism of the ultra-nationalist theory of the national hero. Yet, as a countermeasure to this ultra-nationalism, on the other hand, it excavated a different history of the national community, one which was excessively glorified and endowed with an ideal subjectivity. Certainly, as a result of his elucidation of the process through which this subjectivity collapsed, Ishimoda distanced himself from later scholars like Tōma Seita, who spoke only about the subjective origins of the people. Nevertheless, in terms of their distinct attempts to understand the self as being absolute, by way of the epistemological subject, both Ishimoda and Tōma can be thought of as naive adherents of positivism.

However, what was required was that one not construct yet another history. As we have already confirmed, the Heroic Age could not be proven theoretically or through the use of historical data. In view of such limitations, the Heroic Age can only be understood as Ishimoda's rendition of the "past" that is missing—namely, his projection of a communality which stems from the fissure within Kiki accounts. His perspective avoids privileging a "metaphysics of speech/presence" in terms of what Derrida calls "logocentrism."[52] Rather, for Ishimoda, it is the gap between epic literature and the Heroic Age and the binary division between prose and song that enables this "imaginary past" to attain an actual visual presence. Yet, Ishimoda's logic is inverted, since his means replace the projected ends. By conferring an original value upon oral accounts which he presupposed were marginally decipherable in the texts, he argued that the existing texts derived from the ruined figure of the Heroic Age.[53]

Ever since the emergence of the *Kojiki* and *Nihon shoki*, the proclivity to search for historical grounds becomes apparent through the long history of interpretation. This orientation has been consistently adopted by those who have worked on these texts, such as Motoori Norinaga and Tsuda Sōkichi. Furthermore, such propensity also reflects the logic which grounds these texts. The most powerful argument in favor of the *tennō* system is that it constitutes the basis of the nation's historical origins. It is difficult to overthrow this system so long as one adopts this supposition. In contrast to the so-called ascertained proof the Kiki possess, being the oldest written texts, the history set forth by the advocates of the Heroic Age was curtailed, unable to go beyond speculation. Particularly since modern historical research demands clear documentary evidence, it became difficult for claims that lack "historical clarity" to be persuasive, making them incapable of making an argument that overturns its pre-eminence. Rather, what would have represented true criticism had to begin with the examination of one's historical aims and the proclivity, whether for strategic reasons or not, to objectify identity as being grounded in historical tradition.

If we wish to be free from the spell of the *tennō* system, we must realize that the notion of grounding the national community as having historical origins replicates the logic of this system. We must realize that even forms of resistance are governed and subsumed by this logic. Therefore, we must understand that the inclination to discover origins is the essential problem that haunts us. Insofar as we are unable to face this standpoint, we are doomed to continue drifting, perpetually caught within the very same domain that upholds the imperial system.

Degeneration of the Theory of Subjectivity

The goal of Ishimoda's Heroic Age essay was not simply to set forth the historical origins of national subjectivity in Japan. Rather, as stated at the beginning of this chapter, it was one that explained why the people wished to submit to the historical authority of the *tennō* system, examining the reasons behind their loss of subjectivity. Clearly, this is what is attempted in "Section 3: On the Features of the Heroic Age."

Concretely, Ishimoda tried to explain the subservience of the people by focusing on the specificity of the period in which "autocratic aspects" emerged. He believed that, beginning in the fourth and fifth centuries, the imperial house at the time of the Heroic Age not only possessed patriarchal features (as prevalent in other powerful clans) but also autocratic characteristics. He concludes that the existence of such autocratic qualities, which could not be seen in other regions, allowed local sovereign power centered in the Five Home Provinces around Kyoto to develop into the ancient state, which in turn extended across a broad area. Here, autocracy refers to the "political system of caste and patriarchalism" which divided the functions of sovereign power among the clans. This system was the basis for the imperial house, which established the hereditary system.[54] On the basis of this organizing principle of the patriarchal caste, Yamato sovereign power appropriated the large expanse of undifferentiated regional communities. Ishimoda concludes this line of reasoning in the following manner:

> An oriental hereditary monarchy was not prevented, a republican system of the nobility could not be set up, and it proved impossible to develop a heroic and epic antiquity. It seems that these failures were due to the rapid degeneration of people's political authority in Japan at this time, which was the only force capable of sustaining [the contrary].[55]

The reason for this loss of subjectivity is explained merely as the result of the autocracy politically defeating "the communal organization of the people."[56] This form of logic aptly expresses the essence of Ishimoda's theory of the Heroic Age. Just as the image of Emperor Yūryaku is regarded here as "a typical personality of an emperor of the late fifth century,"[57] this argument is essentially a political and historical theory of class struggle that adopts its material from the *Kojiki* and the *Nihon shoki*.

As Ishimoda explains at the beginning of the section, literature is something that has its own laws so as to overcome a dogmatic notion of infrastructural determinism. Here, the structure of literature is never thematized along the lines of Max Weber. Rather, it is considered to possess a relative autonomy within the field of thought. For Ishimoda, autonomy *vis-à-vis* economic movement does not have significance *per se* in thought or literature, but rather involves politics. Literature's distinctness concerns its capacity for reflecting shifts in the political sphere.

Upon acknowledging the infrastructure's regulatory force, Ishimoda tries to discover within man's political actions the power of choosing among historical possibilities. He writes that if man accurately recognizes historical necessity and takes proper action, he will be able to bring historical trends closer to himself. In this sense, what Ishimoda refers to as "hero" represents an image of the "'practical and political man,' someone who, unlike the contemplative philosopher, changes reality and so produces a new era."[58] Here we see the practical features of Ishimoda's historical research which, while grounded on a theory of social formation, opens the way for actual social revolution. According to Ishimoda, the people were defeated when class society came into being. If, however, popular resistance movements could be brought together in the present (when class society has disappeared), then the dictatorship of the proletariat would be realized. In his words, historical research plays the role of awakening the original traditions in people's movements of the past:

> It is the work of organizing and systematizing the experiences of the masses, expanding these to the point of those national experiences which the masses have not directly undergone, learning lessons from these experiences, and acquiring devotion, confidence and pride for and in the nation and fatherland.[59]

However, as Ishimoda's political theory has elsewhere been criticized, it is unclear as to how far historical necessity extended and human possibility could be projected. Once the situational analysis is confused with a revolutionary vision, human subjectivity loses its tension with reality and becomes merely conceptual. The unity of the people's movement is then presupposed as being self-evident, with no power relations abounding therein. In fact, words like "subjectivity" and "nation" conceal actual contradictions that must be unraveled. On this point, Suzuki Ryōichi's remark concerning the people's lack of independence is apt, even though it addresses a different context, as part of a discussion on the Middle Ages:

> Revolution is generally on the side of the people. And yet, this is not always the case: unable to unite independently, the people became the lower classes under the samurai during the so-called revolution from antiquity to the Middle Ages. At the time of the Tsuchi riots, they could fight with the samurai-village leaders on the condition that they drew a common battleline. This consequently allowed the samurai to compromise with the ancient nobility and form the Kamakura shogunate. Or yet again, it gave way to a pure form of feudalism constituting the daimyo of the Sengoku period from among the village leaders and samurai. In other words, the so-called "revolution from below" was always defeated by the "revolution from above."[60]

Ishimoda sketches out a design in which the subjectivity of the Heroic Age has unavoidably collapsed under autocracy. However, in addition to not being able to prove the existence of the Heroic Age of Japan, he fails to answer the question concerning the masses and their dependence upon authority, given his presumption that a unity supposedly prevailed among the people at the time. One could say that he merely agitates the capacity for political resistance, while the vital notion of resistance itself is undermined.

The fact that Ishimoda's logic misses the mark is due to the intensity of his political praxis. The scholar poisons himself in his own desires when such political praxis goes unanalyzed and positivism vainly upholds its ideals. Herewith, positivism, which is eloquent in confirming sound facts and guarding against unclear interpretations, falls short of substantiating Ishimoda's historical projection.

Hegemony and Discourse

Language as power

In Ishimoda's essay, "Section 4: On Heroic Narrative within Ancient Literature" begins with a theory about Yamatotakeru. Ishimoda here ironically discusses the traces of heroic epic poetry in the Nara period:

> Japanese literature of the ancient nobility was able to produce prosaic heroes and romantic heroes... There is no fact that better symbolizes the fate of the ancient nobility than the scarcity of epic heroes within this literature. This class of nobility, which played a heroic role in the creation of the state and the unification of the [Japanese] archipelago, finally came under the control of the imperial household through the intense oppositions and hostilities that took place within their ranks during the fifth and sixth centuries. The imperial household spoke of this result, namely, the ancient nobility's achievement, as a fact that had been absorbed into imperial history. The ancient nobility lost its independence and subjectivity: they confessed their decadence, leading to the self-deceptive notion that they were related through lineage and blood to the ancestors of the imperial household, and that they constituted one branch of the family tree of gods within the *tennō* system. This decadence was one in which they sought to discover their own value and sense of unsurpassed pride.[61]

The inevitable collapse of subjectivity within the imperial state is described, as is the blockage that took place politically as well as at the level of human interiority. What Ishimoda refers to as "prosaic heroes" are beings who, like Emperor Jinmu, embody the idea of autocracy. "Romantic heroes" are the symbols of the ruined clans that were once powerful, whose freedom from the autocratic rule of the *tennō* system was attained at the price of isolation from the community. They are represented in the *Kojiki* by the figure of Yamatotakeru-no-mikoto. Both these heroes had their place in the epic literature which crystallized at the time of the juridical state. The current of the times was already such that the nobility, which had given up all hope of political independence, was turning to composing "lyrical poetry" in order to express its deepest concerns.

However, it is now impossible to discuss Yamatotakeru on the basis of this schema when the existence of the Heroic Age is in doubt. As described in the *Kojiki* and *Nihon shoki*, Yamatotakeru is clearly a conqueror. He subjugated the borderlands from the southern to the northern area of Japan. Yet the battles he fought were not those between equals who mutually acknowledged their respective character, in the way Ishimoda idealized the Heroic Age struggle. What is actually narrated in the *Kojiki* and the *Nihon shoki* concerns the manner in which the "logic of coercion (*kotomuke*)" is culturally valued. Supported by a belief in the virtuous rule of the emperor, this form of coercion idealizes the scenario whereby the conquered voluntarily join the *tennō* system of order.[62] Yamatotakeru's Emishi expedition is a clear example of this:

> When Yamatotakeru-no-mikoto arrived at the Emishi frontier, the chiefs of the Emishi...feared his majesty and power, and knew in their hearts that they could not gain victory over him. They all flung away their bows and arrows, bowed down towards him, and said, "When we look upon your face, we see that it is more than human. Are you perchance a deity? We desire to know your name." The prince answered and said, "I am the son of the current divine emperor." Hereupon the Emishi were all filled with awe...and they submitted themselves for punishment. He therefore pardoned their offense.[63]

This is a prototypical instance of the logic of coercion. Upon seeing Yamatotakeru, the Emishi realize their wrongdoing and even go so far as to fetter their own bodies. The context is such that the refusal to submit to sovereign power is itself an "offense." This mode of fighting, which presupposes an absolute world order as marked by the emperor, can never be a battle between equals. The opponent is forgiven only when he kneels before this world of order. Otherwise, he is ruthlessly killed, as in the instance of Yamatotakeru murdering Kumasotakeru.

This act of conquest goes beyond physical violence. It is in fact grounded in conceptual self-legitimacy as virtuously represented via the conqueror, and the guilt that is naturally embraced by those subjugated. Upon defeat, the conquered are given what is called a clan name with a standing that is designated by the emperor, such as "Katsuragi-no-omi" or "Karakanuchi-no-obito." This was an identity index that revealed one's position and duties within the sovereign order. One's attachment to a clan and family was legitimated via such names. From today's perspective, one could say that social identity was stamped upon the surname itself. Names in Japan reflected extremely powerful relationships, which were exemplified through one's idyllic relation to the emperor. This system proliferated alongside the growing sphere of influence of the Yamato sovereignty, given that before this period there were only individual names (like "Sotsuhiko").[64]

In other words, people who lacked clan names were not recognized as human by the Yamato rulers. Such non-humans included both the emperor and the outcasts and the nameless. As slaves who were deprived of human rights, outcasts were placed in the lowest strata in the Yamato order, while the nameless pointed to those who had not yet been appropriated within the order. Yet, it was unnecessary for the emperor, as the source of this order, to have a designated name within the Yamato system, given his exclusive authority to bestow all names. In other words, although he was named, he could not be named. As is apparent in the following passage, in the *Kojiki* and the *Nihon shoki*, even nature or the natural land was designated with a name determined by the emperor: "Now, Yamatotakeru-no-mikoto was always regretful when thinking about Oto-tachibana-hime. Therefore, when he ascended to the summit of Usuhi and looked down towards the southeast, he sighed three times, and said, 'Alas! My wife!' Therefore the provinces east of the mountains were given the name of Azuma."[65]

In the *Kojiki* and the *Nihon shoki*, as well as the *fudoki* (provincial gazetteers ordered to be compiled by the Yamato court in 713), narratives about the origins of names of places are too numerous to mention. These are attempts "to refashion a given environment as one's own life-space, by burying it with newly created proper nouns."[66] Everything within Japan's national territory, whether in the realm of nature or human life, is named by the emperor and placed within his order. Indeed, this history of naming is recounted in the *Kojiki* and the *Nihon shoki*, which begin with the creation of the land of Japan. Naming represents the will to grasp and own the world. The essence of the object thus seized is determined by the name bestowed by the emperor. Epistemological objects constitute one part of the world-order as configured by the emperor. This process of naming is explained by Ichimura Hiromasa in the following manner:

> In being named, the "world" became the world for man. Through names, man opens up a rift in the world understood as the continuum, thus punctuating the object...[and] allows things to come into being through mutual separation. Man comprehends phenomena by setting up names for them...The power of names is revealed via the determination of the form of space and things which they must possess in the world of experience. For naming is "ownership."[67]

In other words, via this process of naming places and people, the emperor, as the designator, and the place or clan name, as the designated, enter a relationship that can be characterized as one between "the observing subject and the gazed object." It is an epistemological act which results in intellectual hegemony, whereby the named object is essentially determined by the naming subject. Now, *tennō* as a designation in fact traces back to the ancient seer. Although he determines the existence of others, his own existence is indeterminate. Indeed, it would be appropriate to identify him as the "manifesting divine emperor" or even a "demigod." Consequently, Yamatotakeru, who extended the world-order of the Yamato kingdom from the southern to the northern regions of Japan, is his greatest servant. Such an epistemological system is propounded not only in the *Kojiki* and the *Nihon shoki* but also in the oral myths that are regionally distinct. Conquest, after all, is the extension and enforcement of an epistemological system entrenched in one's own culture.

Ishimoda attempted to distinguish and rescue the original character of Yamatotakeru from the distortion in the conqueror's nature that ensued in the autocratic state. Yet, if one were to argue that the state does nothing but consistently engage in acts of conquest and that such accounts of conquest are witnessed in diverse cultures, within myths prior to the formation of the state, it makes little difference if Yamatotakeru is seen as a symbol of the juridical state or as a patriarch of the Heroic Age.

Conquest involves contact between two epistemological systems and results in political conflict as well as a discord in worldviews. In other words, when the mode of situating things is negated by a different epistemological system, a reversal takes place whereby one's own status as seer is transformed into the loss of status in being seen. As a result, the conqueror expands his own epistemological system by appropriating the other, whereas the conquered undergo a repositioning at the level of perception. In this sense, the conceptual elements defining myths or historical narratives are complicit within the act of violence.

The epoch-making quality of the *Kojiki* and the *Nihon shoki* results from having secured this means of appropriation as pertaining to the greater part of the Japanese archipelago. State structure and written records enabled this grand schema to unfold. Politically, this appropriation was grounded in the juridical state and the stability of rule. The appearance of biographical records as transcriptions facilitated both the perfect textualization and the semipermanent preservation of this epistemological system.

While the juridical state prototypically seeks to possess vast territory, oral tradition is such that regional expansion brings about a diversification of content, thus provoking a loss in authority. Yet, since written records preserve the original text as it existed at the time of transcription, they play the canonical role by suppressing the diversity in textual reception. At the same time, due to the fact that written records are replicable, the growing complexity of myths, including various local folktales, could be accurately preserved.[68]

Certainly, local oral traditions were also being transcribed in the course of their appropriation within the *Kojiki* and the *Nihon shoki*. This is related in the local folklore as left behind in the *fudoki* and in clan writings, such as the *Takahashi ujibumi* (Record of the Takahashi Clan) and *Kogoshūi* (Gleanings from Ancient Stories). These oral traditions were fixed within the order of the Yamato kingdom on the basis of their relation to the history of the imperial household and as deemed by the emperor. While originally including a vast range of information, this knowledge was streamlined to constitute peripheral accounts which followed the format of written records. Both written records and the state structure first appeared in the transformation from "barbarism to civilization." The *Kojiki* and the *Nihon shoki*, as well as the imperial system, assumed canonical positions by being the first to introduce the Yamato rule that prevailed in the Japanese archipelago.

In ancient times, these written records formed part of an oligopoly and overwhelming differences existed within communities. One can say that narrative accounts represented an act through which the possessor of writing and knowledge objectified those without such knowledge on the basis of a domineering worldview, such that a one-sided regulative force operated between the narrator and the narrated. While the regulated entity was also endowed with writing and language, it lacked proof with regard to the dissemination of its knowledge as passed on to later generations and society at large. This goes to show how the dynamic relation in language produces a fissure between the witnessing subject and the witnessed object. As Hani Gorō (1901–83), a modern Japanese historian influenced by Marxism, states: "Speech and writing bear class characteristics."[69]

The "seer" par excellence is the Japanese emperor, who possesses the most ancient written records in Japan, whereas the masses are the "seen," always determined via linguistic representations that originate in the seer. As is widely known, a debate took place in the early 1950s concerning the question of national culture, which asked: Should such cultural legacies of the ruling classes, like the Yamatotakeru legend, be re-read as part of "Japanese culture"? While a conclusion was never reached, what did become clear was that popular culture lacked an independent voice. As the scholar of Japanese literature Masuda Katsumi (1923–) has pointed out, "even if the imperial family glorifies the Heroic Age, it cannot glorify the masses themselves. Our problem lies in the fact that 'national culture' cannot be 'Marxist-Leninist national culture.'"[70]

By providing a history of this undocumented world of the Heroic Age, Ishimoda's essay sought to fashion a body of tradition from the perspective of a seer who would not be co-opted into the imperial system. Yet, this attempt had to fail, since the imperial system possessed the *Kojiki* and the *Nihon shoki*, the oldest records of Japan. In spite of this fact, however, these texts, according to Ishimoda, were merely one interpretation of the formation of the Japanese archipelago that was proclaimed at a given time in history. The masses lacked their own records to refute this interpretation, and so inevitably were made to depend upon these texts to claim their origins. The very act of participating in a debate on historical origins, which continues alongside the interpretative history of the *Kojiki* and the *Nihon shoki*, in fact puts to question the emperor as necessarily being the primary source of legitimacy. In the midst, what often gets reinstated through such debates is the narrative substantiating the emperor's supremacy as documented within the written records.

One can suggest that Ishimoda should have adopted a strategy that focused on the cultural hegemony of written records rather than reclaiming, through the very same written records, a marginally documented and forgotten world. From this vantage, Ishimoda should have objectified the relations between the patriarch and community members, as well as culturally developed and culturally underdeveloped regions. Topics of intellectual history which could not be treated comprehensively by infrastructural theory should have been analyzed on the basis of cultural hegemony. This would have stimulated reflection among historians who were determined to discover another trajectory of thought by way of its relation to written culture.

Towards discursive historical research

Ishimoda's theory of the Heroic Age projected an ideal community onto history. This ideal community was moreover modeled upon the national solidarity movement and the political situation in 1950, when opposition was directed toward the *tennō* system and the U.S. government. As a matter of fact, this movement grew to unprecedented heights, instigating a stream of "national historical research."[71] At the time, Ishimoda had elaborated on the "proper task of historical research" in the following manner:

> It is the work of organizing and systematizing the experiences of the masses, expanding them to the extent of those national experiences which the masses have not directly undergone, learning lessons from these experiences, and acquiring devotion, confidence, and pride for and in the nation and fatherland. Without this work, the masses cannot reach the level of national consciousness.[72]

The task was to aim at building political solidarity, and was to be achieved by stirring up the people via the nation's true history as unearthed by historians. Here, Ishimoda compared historians to the patriarchs of the Heroic Age, and the people to community members, who together tried to pave the way for an actual revolutionary movement. However, just as the community in the Heroic Age could not be proven to have existed, this solidarity inevitably failed in the face of the political denouement as represented by the signing of the U.S.–Japan Security Treaty. This implied more than political defeat, for it confronted Ishimoda with the fact that the relation between intellectuals and the masses was not monolithic.

In revisiting the idea of the task of history, what should have been problematized first was the form of solidarity itself. There was markedly the issue of difference between the intellectuals and the masses as it came to be formulated in terms of the political and the cultural realms, which had to be reconciled. Within the cultural realm, there was the undeniable disparity between those with the power of linguistic representation and those without. There was also the mechanism of discourse that circumscribed an era's rationale sustained via the production and dissemination of written records. In Japan, the Western discourse of modernity, the Buddhist discourse of the Middle Ages and the Chinese discourse of ancient times may be cited as representative examples of this. Yet, therein, in a self-proclaimed fashion, the legend of Yamatotakeru as found within the *Kojiki*, the *Nihon shoki*, and the *fudoki* stands out as precisely the dominant discourse of ancient times.

Discourse that attains a position of dominance does not simply represent reality; rather, it exacts upon reality a specific epistemological mode. While this amounts to conceptually constricting the production of knowledge, which is an act of violence, the formation of the idea of cultural identity and distinction works to conceal the violence and instead implant an emotive sense of pride. In that sense, those who are made to listen to language welcome it as true knowledge, while those who speak flatter themselves in thinking that their language represents an ideal form of illumination. We must remind ourselves of Michel Foucault's insight that physical violence is only the crudest form of power.[73]

Intellectuals can no longer simply believe in the objectivity of language. Hence Ishimoda's essay "'Koe naki koe' o daiben suru kakushin" [Conviction to Speak for 'Voiceless Voices'][74] seems now to be merely an instance of a good intention that is already co-opted from its premise. Certainly, discourses appeal to contexts in which people are situated (namely, the period, class, etc.). Furthermore, we must not spare our efforts in exposing those discourses which help us understand the motives behind the "order of things." We ought to note also that the fissure between the gaze and the object gazed at is principally inherent to discursive practice. It therefore becomes impossible and futile to enter a pre-discursive interior world in which writing and language are absent. While modernity has come to re-evaluate "oral culture" and "folk culture," these forms of culture have also been signified by writing culture and the dominant discourses of intellectuals. Oral and folk cultures have lacked the authority to determine their own value. So, with this understanding, while the question of unearthing the so-called "voiceless voices" is important in light of reconstituting historiography, such a project has to be undertaken in a more systematic and strategic manner. Likewise, the intentions of historians, like Ishimoda, have to be contextualized in light of the distinct discursive spheres which influence their conceptions.

Putting it another way, if one were to conceive of reality, as constituted discursively, to be a site where diverse languages converge, it becomes important to examine the dynamics of such language systems as both influencing and being influenced via modes of communication. In order to confine the violence of language, we must specify its discursive intentions, and appropriately locate and situate its determining forces. Upon clarifying the differences between intellectuals and the masses as produced by linguistic representation, we must excavate a sense of humanity founded upon differing interests. Herein, historians must have the courage to reflect upon criticism that exposes their inherent capacity in being producers of historical discourse. In this sense, it becomes important to note how the death of Yamatotakeru attains its symbolic significance for Ishimoda, who conceived the prince as his own heroic ancestor.

Yamatotakeru dies on his return from the Eastern Expedition, when he makes a careless remark at Ibukiyama. In this regard, there is no striking difference between the exposition in the *Kojiki* and the *Nihon shoki*. The former describes the scene as follows:

> He went up the mountain. Then on the mountain he met a white boar... Thereupon he spoke out and said: "This is the deity's messenger, who, here, has transformed into a white boar. I will not kill it now, but will kill it when I return." He went up. At this time, [the deity of the mountain] caused a violent hailstorm and dazed Yamatotakeru-no-mikoto.

The text continues: "It was not the deity's messenger which had been transformed into a white boar, but the deity himself. He was dazed because he had spoken out (*kotoage*) [to it]."[75]

Yamatotakeru is attacked because he verbalizes his underestimation of the god of Ibukiyama. In ancient times, a "verbal declaration"[76] was an important act. When a word was uttered which did not correspond to reality, it was believed that misfortune would befall the speaker. While the speaker here is Yamatotakeru, who, as you recall, suppressed both man and nature by giving them names, he ironically falters by relying upon his own language. I am proposing a distinct way of reinterpreting the ending here. In a resonant manner, one can argue that Yamatotakeru's death overlaps with the figure of the modern intellectual who unquestioningly trusts his own language.

In his essay, however, Ishimoda did not take up this aforementioned scene of *kotoage*, perhaps because he did not realize that language causes man to stumble and was generated from multiply layered narratives espousing a plethora of configurations for witnessing the seer and the seen. In the late 1950s, Ishimoda published his theory on the Izumo myth, which was akin to his theory on the Heroic Age.[77] In this elucidation as well, he did not pay attention to the notion of difference as related to language. All the while hoping to further elaborate on "the question of the 'Heroic Age,'"[78] Ishimoda died in 1986.

In the postwar period, amidst the repercussions of defeat that permeated the social milieu, Ishimoda's theory of the Heroic Age was indeed a splendid critical force. If we were to follow in his footsteps and once again bestow his radiance on historical research, we would have to begin by dissolving the very values which he regarded as self-evident, such as subjectivity, community, and historicity. Furthermore, the object of analysis would have to be understood as being heterogeneous. In turn, we would have to ask: how is language being used and what kind of force has it exercised? Certainly, it is the ontology of language within society that would come into question here. If and when this were to occur, historical research on the *Kojiki* and *Nihon shoki* would become a site for self-reflection as it amounts to becoming structured in distinct historical periods, rather than a self-appraisal which reconstitutes the search for the past in a manner that ironically resonates and is complicit within the dominating discursive paradigm.

Notes

The following abbreviations are used in the notes:
ISC   *Ishimoda Shō chōsakushū* (Tokyo: Iwanami Shoten, 1988–90)
MNZ   *Motoori Norinaga zenshū* (Tokyo: Chikuma Shobo, 1968–93)
NKT   *Nihon koten bungaku taikei* (Tokyo: Iwanami Shoten, 1964)
NST   *Nihon Shisō taikei* (Tokyo: Iwanami Shoten, 1970–82)
SKT   *Shintei-zōhō kokushi taikei* (Tokyo: Yoshikawa Kōbunkan, 1964–86)
ST   *Shintō taikei* (Tokyo: Shintō Taikei Hensankai, 1977–94)
TSZ   *Tsuda Sōkichi zenshū* (Tokyo: Iwanami Shoten, 1963–89)

Introduction

1. Martin Heidegger, *Ontology: The Hermeneutics of Facticity* (1923), trans. John V. Buren (Bloomington: Indiana University Press, 1999); Hans-Georg Gadamer, *Truth and Method*, trans. Joel Weinsheimer and Donald G. Marshall, 2nd rev. edn (New York: Continuum, 1994).
2. On the dissemination of ideology, see Michel Foucault, *Archaeology of Knowledge*, trans. A. M. Sheridan Smith (New York: Routledge, 1982); Martin Jay, "Should Intellectual History Take a Linguistic Turn? Reflection on Habermas–Gadamaer Dabate," in Dominick LaCapra et al. (eds), *Modern European Intellectual History: Reappraisals and New Perspectives* (Ithaca: Cornell University Press, 1982). From the point of view of the logic of reception, see Iser Wolfgang, *The Act of Reading: A Theory of Aesthetic Response* (Baltimore: Johns Hopkins University Press, 1978); Hans Robert Jauss, *Toward an Aesthetic of Reception*, trans. Timothy Bahti (Minneapolis: University of Minnesota Press, 1982).
3. William A. Graham, in *Beyond the Written World: Oral Aspects of Scripture in the History of Religion* (Cambridge: Cambridge University Press, 1987); Miriam Levering (ed.), *Rethinking Scripture: Essays from a Comparative Perspective* (Albany: State University of New York Press, 1989).
4. For the significance of oral tradition, see Walter J. Ong, *Orality and Literacy: The Technologizing of the Word* (London: Methuen, 1982). With regard to the relation between the canon and cultural practice, see David Johnson (ed.), *Ritual and Scripture in Chinese Popular Religion: Five Studies* (Berkeley: The Chinese Popular Culture Project, 1995).
5. See Harry Y. Gamble, *Books and Readers in the Early Church: A History of Early Christian Texts* (New Haven and London: Yale University Press, 1995).
6. Roger Chartier, *The Cultural Origins of the French Revolution* (1990), trans. Lydia G. Cochrane (Durham, NC: Duke University Press, 1991).

7. Wilfred Cantwell Smith, *What Is Scripture?: A Comparative Approach* (London: SCM Press, 1993); James Bar, *Holy Scripture: Canon, Authority, Criticism* (Oxford: Oxford University Press, 1983).
8. In terms of analyses to date of the canonization process, see Werner Jeanround, "The Development of Theological Hermeneutics: From the Beginnings to the Enlightenment," in *Theological Hermeneutics: Development and Significance* (New York: The Crossroad Publishing Company, 1991); John B. Henderson, "Integration, Development, and Closure of Canons," in *Scripture, Canon, and Commentary: A Comparison of Confucian and Western Exegesis* (Princeton: Princeton University Press, 1991).
9. Henderson, *Scripture, Canon, and Commentary*.
10. Shlomo Biderman's work, entitled *Scripture and Knowledge: An Essay on Religious Epistemology* (Leiden: E. J. Brill, 1995), while recapitulating research elucidating the authority of the canon, reveals the limits of such a perspective.
11. Graham, *Beyond the Written World*, p. 3; Smith, *What Is Scripture?*, pp. 9–10.
12. With regard to questions on comparative methodology within religious studies, see Jonathan Z. Smith, "No Need to Travel to the Indies: Judaism and the Study of Religion," in Jacob Neusner (ed.), *Take Judaism, for Example: Studies towards the Comparison of Religions* (Atlanta: Scholar Press, 1992); Kimberley C. Patton and Benjamin C. Ray (eds), *A Magic Still Dwells: Comparative Religion in the Postmodern Age* (Berkeley: University of California Press, 2000); *Numen: International Review for the History of Religions*, 58–3 (2001).
13. Jonathan Z. Smith, "Sacred Persistence: Towards a Redescription of a Canon," in *Imagining Religion: From Babylon to Jonestown* (Chicago: The University of Chicago Press, 1982).
14. In terms of the relationship between canonization and hermeneutics in the vein of H. G. Gadamer or P. Ricoeur, see Biderman's elucidation in *Scripture and Knowledge* (pp. 28–35).
15. Jon Davis and Isabel Wollaston (eds), *The Sociology of Sacred Texts* (Sheffield: Sheffield Academic Press, 1993).
16. Bernard M. Levinson, *The Hermeneutics of Innovation: The Impact of Centralization upon the Structure, Sequence, and Reformulation of Legal Material in Deuteronomy* (Ann Arbor: University Microfilms, 1991).
17. Watsuji Tetsurō, *Nihon kodai bunka* (Tokyo: Iwanami Shoten, 1920).
18. Kōnoshi Takamitsu, *Kojiki no sekaikan* (Tokyo: Yoshikawa Kōbunkan, 1986).
19. Isomae Jun'ichi, "Kokushi to iu gensetsu kūkan: Gendaishisō," *Gendaishisō*, 27:12 (1999).
20. Yamada Yoshio, *Kojiki jyobun kōgi* (Tokyo: Isobekōyōdō, 1935); Miyake Kazurō, *Kiki shinwa no seiritsu* (Tokyo: Yoshikawa Kōbunkan, 1984).
21. Tsuda Sōkichi, *Nihon koten no kenkyū* (Tokyo: Iwanami Shoten, 1948), vol. 1.
22. See Chapter 1.
23. Ishimoda Shō, *Nihon kodai kokkaron dai ni bu: Shinwa to bungaku* (Tokyo: Iwanami Shoten, 1973); Mizubayashi Takeshi, *Kiki shinwa to ōken no matsuri*, (Tokyo: Iwanami Shoten, 1991); Kōnoshi Takamitsu, *Kojiki to Nihon shoki: Tennô shinwa no rekishi* (Tokyo: Kōdansha, 1999).
24. In terms of the belief that a text can actually be re-experienced, in a literal manner, see Iida Isamu, *Chinkon, Tennōrei o kangaeru* (Shisō, 820), p. 40.

25. Kōnoshi, *Kojiki to Nihon shoki*.
26. Maruyama Masao, *Nihon seiji shisōshi kenkyū* (Tokyo: Tōkyō Daigaku Shuppankai, 1952); in a parallel sense, with regard to research in the Western context, see Peter Addinall, *Philosophy and Biblical Interpretation: A Study in Nineteenth-Century Conflict* (Cambridge: Cambridge University Press, 1991).
27. See Chapter 1.
28. In a parallel sense, with regard to the study of historical narration in Ancient Greece and Rome, see John Marincola, *Authority and Tradition in Ancient Historiography* (Cambridge: Cambridge University Press, 1997). For an analysis of the power of the text in the medieval period, see Jesse M. Gellrich, *The Idea of the Book in the Middle Ages: Language Theory, Mythology, and Fiction* (Ithaca: Cornell University Press, 1985).
29. Mircea Eliade, *The Quest: The Meaning and History in Religion* (Chicago: The University of Chicago Press, 1969).
30. Isomae Jun'ichi, *Kindai Nihon ni okeru shūkyō-gensetsu to sono keifu: Shūkyō, Kokka, Shintō* (Tokyo: Iwanami Shoten, 2003), pp. 147–8. Also see Chapter 1.
31. The phantasmal discursive space that I allude to here is evoked and understood by Jacques Derrida in light of the idea of "Khōra" and by Homi Bhabha in terms of the idea of "metaphor." See Jacques Derrida, *On the Name*, trans. Thomas Dutoit (Stanford: Stanford University Press, 1995); and Homi Bhabha, *The Location of Culture* (London: Routledge, 1994), chap. 8. In terms of research on the Kiki, with regard to characterizing the notion of "Japan," see Kōnoshi Takamitsu, *Nihon to wa nanika* (Tokyo: Kōdansha, 2005).
32. Gadamer, *Truth and Method*, pp. 305–11.
33. Narita Ryūichi, *Rekishigaku no style, shigakushi to sono shūhen* (Tokyo: Azekura Shobo, 2001); Naoki Sakai, *Translation and Subjectivity: On "Japan" and Cultural Nationalism* (Minneapolis: University of Minnesota Press, 1997).
34. For an extensive discussion on historical essentialism and the inclination to reinterpret the nature of time, see Bhabha, *The Location of Culture*, chap. 8.

Chapter 1

1. See Ishimoda Shō, "Kodai kizoku no eiyū jidai," originally published in 1948, and Tōma Seita, "Nihon ni okeru eiyū jidai," originally published in 1950, in Hara Hidesaburō (ed.), *Rekishi kagaku taikei*, vol. 1 (Tokyo: Azekura Shobo, 1972).
2. See Kōnoshi Takamitsu, *Kojiki no sekaikan* (Tokyo:Yoshikawa Kōbunkan, 1987), and Mizubayashi Takeshi, *Kiki shinwa to ōken no matsuri* (Tokyo: Iwanami Shoten, 1991).
3. See Saul Friedlander (ed.), *Probing the Limits of Representation: Nazism and the "Final Solution"* (Cambridge, MA: Harvard University Press, 1992).
4. Ise Shintō (Mie prefecture) rose in power within Shintōism during the medieval period, when the imperial line was enshrined in Ise Jingu that was structurally comprised of two independent shrines, Naikū (inner sacred structure) and Gekū (outer sacred structure). Repeatedly, from the middle ages to the modern

era, there were struggles between the two shrines over the issue of their predominance, which was enacted through theological arguments. The Gekū claimed to enshrine the main deity, Kunitokotachi-no-mikoto. This is the deity who first appears in the Kiki and is said to have blessed the country's land eternally. In terms of medieval texts, see Takahashi Miyuki, *Ise Shintō no seiritsu to tenkai* (Tokyo: Taimeidō, 1994).

5. Yoshimi Yoshikazu, "Sōbyōsha shoku tōmon," in *Daijigūsōsho Watarai Shintō-taisei kōhen* (Mie Prefecture: Jingūshichō, 1955), p. 554.
6. It is believed that the divine pair who appear in the beginning of the *Kojiki*, Takamimusuhi and Kamimusuhi, preside over creation. Their names literally denote the power to materialize objects.
7. Motoori Norinaga, *Naobi no mitami*, in *MNZ*, 9:59 (1968).
8. See Kōnoshi Takamitsu, *Kojiki to Nihon shoki: Tennō shinwa no rekishi* (Tokyo: Kōdansha, 1999).
9. See John B. Henderson, *Scripture, Canon, and Commentary: A Comparison of Confucian and Western Exegesis* (Princeton: Princeton University Press, 1991), and Miriam Levering (ed.), *Rethinking Scripture: Essays from a Comparative Perspective* (Albany: State University of New York Press, 1989).
10. See Tsuda Sōkichi, *Jindaishi no atarashi kenkyū* (1913), chap. 4, and *Kojiki oyobi Nihon shoki no shinkenkyū* (1919), chap. 5, first section; also in *MNZ*, supplementary vol. 1, new edition (1966).
11. Tsuda Sōkichi, *Nihon koten no kenkyū* (1948), vol. 1; also in *MNZ*, 1:308–9 (1963).
12. Ōta Shōjirō, "Jindai ni okeru Nihon shoki kōkyū" (1939), in *Ōta Shōjirō chosakushū* (Tokyo: Yoshikawa Kōbunkan, 1992), vol. 3; Seki Akira, "Jindai ni okeru *Nihon shoki* kōdoku no kenkyū" (1942), in *Seki Akira chosakushū* (Tokyo: Yoshikawa Kōbunkan, 1997), vol. 5.
13. Nishimiya Kazutami (ed.), *Shinchō Nihon koten shūsei Kojiki* (Tokyo: Shinchōsha, 1979), p. 21.
14. *Shoku Nihongi*, article 790, July 11.
15. *Shoku Nihon shoki*, article 714, Feb. 10; *Ruijū kokushi,* article of "Kokushi."
16. This refers to the clan ancestor related to Ame-no-Futodama-no-Mito as the priest for the imperial household. In the imperial court in the Nara period, when the Nakatomi clan attained power, there emerged a dispute over the authority of the clan priest.
17. This refers to the clan responsible for the food offered to the imperial family. In approximately 789 CE, there was a dispute with the Azumi clan over its official authority in the regard.
18. A book on the family lineage of ancient clan families as selected by governing authorities.
19. *NKT*, 67:153 (1967).
20. Nishimiya Kazutami (ed.), *Kogoshūi* (Tokyo: Iwanami Bunko, 1985), pp. 127–8.
21. One of the powerful maritime clans in ancient times, whose ancestral deity is Watatsumi-no-kami.
22. By "canon," akin to its etymology in the Judeo-Christian tradition, we mean that which has been established as the "normative" text, which functions as the

"law and rule, fundamental axiom, principle or standard." See Kendall W. Folkert, "The 'Canons' of 'Scripture'," in Miriam Levering (ed.), *Rethinking Scripture: Essays from a Comparative Perspective* (Albany: State University of New York Press, 1989), p.173. The "canon" also includes the sense of being a "fixed" text. See Bernard M. Levinson, "The Human Voice in Divine Revelation: The Problem in Religious Tradition in Biblical Law," in Michael A. Williams, Collett Cox and Martin S. Jaffee (eds), *Innovation in Religious Traditions: Essays in the Interpretation of Religious Change* (Berlin: Mouton de Gruyter, 1997), p. 36. Having stated this, for our purposes here, I will refrain from questioning and elaborating further as to whether the canon is inherent to the Judeo-Christian tradition or yet whether it necessarily has to have a religious connotation.

23. Abe Yasurō, "Nihongi to setsuwa," in *Setsuwa no kōta* (Tokyo: Benseisha, 1993), vol. 3, p. 199.
24. While, according to the description in the Kiki, the emperor's reign is said to run from 71 to 130 CE, in reality, it is questionable whether the emperor actually existed.
25. The Kusanagi sword enshrined in Nagoya city in Aichi prefecture is said to be one of the regalia of the royal prerogative.
26. *Yamatohime no mikoto seiki*, in *SKT*, 7: 53–4 (1966).
27. *NKT*, 67: 304; *Kogoshūi*, p. 136.
28. *NKT*, 67: 305; *Kogoshūi*, p. 136.
29. *The Tale of Heike* was compiled prior to 1240, and the *Taiheiki* is said to have been compiled around 1370.
30. Ichiko Teiji (ed. and trans.), *Shinpen Nihon koten bungaku zenshū: Heike monogatari* (Tokyo: Shōgakukan, 1994), vol. 2, p. 398.
31. According to the description in the Kiki, Emperor Sūjin reigned in 100 BCE, although it is questionable whether he actually existed.
32. Takagi Makoto, "Seitosei no shinwa ga hōtei suru shunkan: Heike monogatari 'tsurugi ni maki' no katari," in *Heike monogatari: Sōzo suru katari* (Tokyo: Shinwasha, 2001), pp. 227–8.
33. *Ibid.*, p. 238.
34. Literal interpretation examines the text as being self-evident, primarily involving modes of linguistic and grammatical interpretation. Contrarily, allegorical interpretation aims to unravel the underlying meaning of the text. Herein, the actual adaptation of the Kiki, in light of such interpretations, is evident in the pioneering work by Herman Ooms, "Yamazaki Ansai, Jindai no maki ni okeru kaishaku-gaku," in *Shūkyo kenkyū to ideorogī bunseki* (Tokyo: Perikansha, 1996).
35. *SKT*, 8:198 (1965).
36. Yoshida Kanetomo, "Kanetomo-bon Nihon shoki Jindaikan-shō," in *Kanetomo Senken bon Nihon shoki Jindaikan-shō* (Tokyo: Zokugunsho Ruijūkankōkai, 1984), p. 1208.
37. According to medieval perceptions, there were no independent Shintō doctrines and related organizations. See Kuroda Toshio, "Chūsei Shintōshi ni okeru shūkyō no ichi," in *Nihon chūsei shūkyō to shakai* (Tokyo: Iwanami Shoten, 1990).
38. Scriptures that were based on the Protestant tradition were for the most part passed down as sacred religious texts. Here, for our purposes as well, I am stating this in accordance with that which is commonly accepted as knowledge.

However, today this notion is expanding to include the Qur'an, Vedas and other non-Christian oral religious traditions. See William A. Graham, "Scripture," in Mircea Eliade (ed.), *The Encyclopaedia of Religion* (New York: Macmillan, 1987), vol. 7.
39. Yoshida Kanetomo, "Kanetomo-bon Nihon shoki Jindaikan-shō," pp. 97–8.
40. This stream of Shintō explains the world of deities in accordance with the Shingon-shū doctrine of Buddhism.
41. In the *Nihon shoki* and the *Kojiki*, within the tale about the emperor's ancestor descending from heaven, Ho-no-Ninigi refers to the deity who first appears to bestow fertility upon an ear of rice.
42. A tool that is representative of the Esoteric Buddhist tradition, which symbolizes the annihilation of human desire.
43. *Reikiki*, in *Shintō taikei Shingon Shintō* (Tokyo: Shintō Taikei Hensankai, 1993), vol. 1, pp. 31–4, 130–2, 146; Ogawa Toyoo, "Chūsei shinwa no métier," in *Chūsei no chi to gaku* (Tokyo: Shinwasha, 1997), pp. 165–6.
44. Kuroda Toshio, "Chūsei kokka to shinkoku shisō," in *Nihon chūsei no kokka to shūkyō* (Iwanami Shoten, 1975); Imahori Taitsu, *Jingi shinkō no tenkai to Bukkyō* (Tokyo: Yoshikawa Kōbunkan, 1990).
45. Nitta Ichirō, "Kyōgen wo ōseraruru kami," in *Rettō no bunka-shi*, vol. 6 (1989).
46. *Yōmei tennō shokunin kagami*.
47. Kaigo Tokiomi, *Reikishi kyōiku no rekishi* (Tokyo: Tōkyō Daigaku Shuppankai, 1969); Murakami Shigeyoshi, *Kokka Shintō* (Tokyo: Iwanami Shoten, 1970).
48. Nihonshi Kenkyūkai and Kyoto Minka Rekishi Bukai, *Ryōbo kara mita Nihon-shi* (Tokyo: Aoki Shoten, 1995).
49. In modern times, in terms of the emergence of the superiority of the epistemological subject, see Martin Heidegger, *Off the Beaten Track* (1950), trans. Julian Young and Kenneth Haynes (Cambridge: Cambridge University Press, 2002); and Michel Foucault, "What Is an Author?" (1969), trans. Donald F. Bouchard and Sherry Simon, in Donald F. Bouchard (ed.), *Language, Counter-Memory, Practice: Selected Essays and Interviews* (Ithaca: Cornell University Press, 1977), pp. 113–38.
50. Kazamaki Keijirō, "*Kojiki* kenkyū no sai-shuppatsu," in *Kojiki taisei kenkyō shihen* (Tokyo: Heibonsha, 1956), pp. 177–81.
51. Urabe Kanekata, *Shaku Nihongi*, in *SKT*, 8: 84 (1965).
52. Motoori Norinaga, *Tamakushige*, in *MNZ*, 8:314 (1972).
53. See Katō Genchi's (edited) *Shintō shōseki mokuroku*, and *Meiji Taishō Shōwa Shintō shōseki mokuroku* (Tokyo: Meiji Seitoku Kinen Gakkai, 1938 and 1953).
54. Tanaka Satoshi, "Jyōko no kakutei kinenronsō o megutte," in *Edo no shisō*, 8 (1998).
55. Ōbayahi Taryō, "Nihon shinwa no kenkyūshi," in *Nihon shinwa no kisen* (Tokyo: Kadokawa Shoten, 1973); Isomae Jun'ichi and Fukusawa Hidetaka, *Kindai Nihon ni okeru chishikijin to shūkyō – Anesaki Masaharu no kiseki* (Tokyo: Tōkyōdō Shuppan, 2002).
56. Tsuda Sōkichi, *Kojiki oyobi Nihon shoki no shinkenkyū*.
57. In accordance with religious studies in the West, the concept of the "religious," as elaborated by Mircea Eliade and others, has been criticized for being Western-centric, overly simplistic and furthering "orientalist" forms of thought. See Russell

T. McCutcheon, *Manufacturing Religion: The Discourse on Sui Generis Religion and the Politics of Nostalgia* (Oxford: Oxford University Press, 1997); Timothy Fitzgerald, *The Ideology of Religious Studies* (New York: Oxford University Press, 2000); and Talal Asad, *Genealogy of Religion: Discipline and Reason of Power in Christianity and Islam* (Baltimore: The Johns Hopkins University Press, 1993).

Chapter 2

1. Tsuda Sōkichi, *Nihon koten no kenkyū* (1947), vol. 1, in *TSZ*, 1:671 (1963).
2. *Ibid.*, p. 560.
3. *Ibid.*, p. 561.
4. Mishina Shōei, "Kokushi to shinwa densetsu," in *Mishina Shōei ronbunshū ichi* (Tokyo: Heibonsha, 1970), p. 66.
5. Motoori Norinaga, *Kenkyōjin Ueda Akinari no ron ni atauruben*, in *MNZ*, 8:406 (1972).
6. Motoori Norinaga, *Kojiki den*, in *MNZ*, 9:8 (1968).
7. Motoori Norinaga, *Jindaiki Uzunoyamanokage*, in *MNZ*, 6:518 (1970).
8. *Kojiki* (Nishimiya Kazutami, *Shinchō Nihon koten shūsei Kojiki*, pp. 21–2).
9. Sakamoto Tarō, "Kiki kenkyū no gendankai" (1963), in *Sakamoto chosakushū* (Tokyo: Yoshikawa Kōbunkan, 1988), vol. 2, p. 13.
10. Tsuda Sōkichi, *Nihon koten no kenkyū*, vol. 1, p. 46.
11. *Ibid.*, p. 73.
12. *Nihon shoki*. See the chronicle of Emperor Tenmu, the article of the Third Month, Year 10, in *NKT*, 68–2:446 (1965).
13. Miyake Kazuo, *Kiki-shinwa no seiritsu* (Tokyo: Yoshikawa Kōbunkan, 1984), chap. 2.
14. Tsuda Sōkichi, *Nihon koten no kenkyū*, vol. 1, part 1.
15. Mizoguchi Mutsuko, *Nihon kodai shizoku keifu no seiritsu* (Tokyo: Gakushūin University, 1982), chap. 4.
16. In terms of "Alleged books' records," as in the example of record 6.1, the first number (6) displays the paragraph number of the *Nihon shoki* followed by the variant number 1 located within the same paragraph 6. In principle, each paragraph of the *Nihon shoki* has several alleged records as variants to the commentaries in the main text, so the variant number implies the order of the record in each paragraph.
17. Tsuchihashi Yutaka, "Pledged Augury Kō" (1980), in *Nihon kodai no juju to setsuwa* (Tokyo: Haniwa Shobō, 1989), p. 55.
18. Tsuchihashi Yutaka, "Pledged Augury no bunkajinruigaku 'Jujutsu no kami to kami no chikara'," in *Nihon kodai no juju to setsuwa* (Tokyo: Haniwa Shobō, 1989).
19. Claude Lévi-Strauss, *Anthropologie structurelle* (Paris: Plon Press, 1958), chap. 11.
20. *Kojiki* (p. 48).
21. *Nihon shoki*, in *NKT*, 68-1:106.

Notes to Chapter 2

22. Mizubayashi Takeshi, *Kiki shinwa to Ōken no matsuri* (Tokyo: Iwanami Shoten, 1991), chap. 1.
23. *Nihon shoki*, in *NKT*, 68-1:104.
24. *Kojiki*, p. 49.
25. *Kojiki*, p. 88.
26. *Nihon shoki*, in *NKT*, 68-1:134.
27. *Nihon shoki*, in *NKT*, 68-1:107-8.
28. *Nihon shoki*, in *NKT*, 68-1:110.
29. *Nihon shoki*, in *NKT*, 68-1:119-20.
30. *Nihon shoki*, in *NKT*, 68-1:120.
31. *Nihon shoki*, in *NKT*, 68-1:110-11.
32. *Nihon shoki*, in *NKT*, 68-1:116.
33. *Nihon shoki*, in *NKT*, 68-1:119.
34. Motoori Norinaga. *Kojiki den*, in *MNZ*, 9:384 (1968).
35. *Nihon shoki*, in *NKT*, 68-1:127.
36. *Nihon shoki*, in *NKT*, 68-1:102.
37. *Nihon shoki*, in *NKT*, 68-1:100.
38. *Nihon shoki*, the chronicle of Emperor Kinmei, Third Month, Year 2 clause (*NKT* 68-2: 68).
39. William A. Graham, "Scripture", in Mircea Eliade (ed.), *The Encyclopedia of Religion* (New York: Macmillan, 1987), vol. 7; Kendall W. Folkert, "The 'Canons' of 'Scripture'," in Miriam Levering (ed.), *Rethinking Scripture: Essays from a Comparative Perspective* (Albany: State University of New York Press, 1989).
40. *Nihon shoki*, in *NKT*, 68-1:90.
41. *Nihon shoki*, in *NKT*, 68-1:96.
42. Ishimoda Shō, *Nihon no kodai kokka*, in *ISC*, 3, chap. 1 (1989).
43. Ibid.
44. With regard to the debate in the West concerning the formation process of canons, see Werner G. Jeanround, "The Development of Theological Hermeneutics: From the Beginnings to the Enlightenment," in *Theological Hermeneutics: Development and Significance* (New York: Crossroad Publishing Company, 1991); John B. Henderson, "Integration, Development, and Closure of Canons," in *Scripture, Canon, and Commentary: A Comparison of Confucian and Western Exegesis* (Princeton: Princeton University Press, 1991).
45. The book of Sui dynasty, *Gishiwajiden, Gokanshowaden, Sōshowakokuden*, ed. and trans. by Wada Kiyoshi and Ishihara Michihiro (Tokyo: Iwanami Shoten, 1951), p. 69.
46. *Nihon shoki*, the chronicle of Emperor Ingyō, Ninth Month, Twenty-eighth Day, Year 4 clause, in *NKT*, 67-1:437-8.
47. Ibid., p. 438.
48. *Nihon shoki*, the chronicle of Empress Suiko, Year 28 clause (*NKT* 68-2:203).
49. Uematsu Shigeru, "Takahashi ujibumi," in *Kōza Nihon no shinwa 2* (Tokyo: Yūseidō, 1976); Kamada Jun'ichi, *Sendai kuji hongi no kenkyū: Kenkyū no bu* (Tokyo: Yoshikawa Kōbunkan, 1962).
50. Urabe Kanekata, *Shaku Nihongi*, in *SKT*, 8:4 (1965).

51. For further discussion in a comparative frame, see John B. Henderson, "Origins, Dimensions, and Apotheosis of Commentaries," in *Scripture, Canon, and Commentary*.
52. *Nihon shoki shiki (Kōhon)*, in *SKT*, 8:9–10 (1965).
53. *Nihon kōki*, Enryaku 18, Twelfth Month, Sixth Day clause, in *SKT*, 3:27 (1966).
54. *Sandaikyaku*, Dajōkanpu of Enryaku 17, Second Month, Eighth Day, in *SKT*, 25:514 (1965).
55. *Shinsen shōjiroku*; *Shinsen shōjiroku no kenkyū: Kōshōhen* (Tokyo: Yoshikawa Kōbunkan, 1981), vol. 1, p. 167.
56. *Kojiki* (p. 23).
57. *Nihon shoki shiki (kōhon)*, in *SKT*, 8:8–9.
58. *Shinsen shōjiroku no kenkyū: Kōshōhen*, vol. 1, p. 153.
59. *Nihon shoki*, the chronicle of Emperor Ingyō, Ninth Month, Ninth Day, Year 4 clause, in *NKT*, 67-1:437.
60. *Nihon shoki shiki (kōhon)*, in *SKT*, 8:10.
61. *Nihon shoki*, the chronicle of Emperor Kinmei, Third Month, Year 2 clause, in *NKT*, 68, last vol., p. 68.
62. *Shinsen shōjiroku no kenkyū: Kōshōhen*, vol. 1, p. 152.
63. Several works expound on the use of the past for contemporary interests, including Ernest Gellner, *Nations and Nationalism* (Oxford: Blackwell, 1983), and Prys Morgan, "From a Death to a View: The Hunt for the Welsh Past in the Romantic Period," in E. J. Hobsbawm and Terence Ranger (eds), *The Invention of Tradition* (Cambridge: Cambridge University Press, 1983).
64. *Nihon kōki*, Daidō 4, Second Month clause, in *SKT*, 3:81.
65. *Nihon shoki shiki (kōhon)*, in *SKT*, 8:7.
66. Forthright arguments against the reconstruction of written works in the West include Michel Foucault, *The Archaeology of Knowledge*, trans. A. M. Sheridan Smith (London: Tavistock, 1972), originally published in 1969. Works from an opposite perspective include E. D. Hirsh, Jr., *Validity in Interpretation* (London: Yale University Press, 1967). For a general survey with regards to such matters see Richard Crossman, "Do Readers Make Meaning?" in Susan Suleiman and Inge Crossman (eds), *The Reader in the Text* (Princeton: Princeton University Press, 1980).

Chapter 3

1. In terms of Kumaso, see Nakamura Akizō, "Kumaso no jittai to Kumaso kannen no seiritsu ni tsuite," in Inoue Kaoru (ed.), *Nihon kodai no kokka to shūkyō* (Tokyo: Yoshikawa Kōbunkan, 1980), vol. 2.
2. For the worldview established through the three sacred items enshrined, see Kōnoshi Takamitsu, "Kogoshūi no hyōka," *Kokubungaku* 39, 6 (1994): 72–8; and Tsurumaki Yumi, "Sanshu no shiki no sōtei to Heike monogatari," *Gunki to katarimono*, 30 (1994): 41–53.
3. Saigo Nobutsuna, "Yamatotakeru no monogatari," in *Kojiki kenkyū* (Tokyo: Miraisha, 1973), p. 232.

4. For the relationship between father and son in the Yamatotakeru legend, see Ishimoda Sho, "Kodai kizoku no eiyū jidai: Kojiki no ichi kōsatsu" (1948), in *ISC*, 10 (1989).
5. See Araki Toshio, "Hitsugi no miko to kōtaishi," in *Ritsuryō seika no kōtaishi, Kodai Nihon no kōtaishi* (Tokyo: Yoshikawa Kōbunkan, 1985).
6. *NKT*, 2:441 (1958).
7. *Shoku Nihongi*, 713, Fifth Month, *kinoene* clause, in *NKT*, 1:197–8 (1989); in terms of the purpose behind editing *fudoki*, see Sakamoto Tarō, "Fudoki ni tsuite," in *Nihon kodaishi no hisoteki kenkyū*, vol. 1, reprinted in *Sakamoto Tarō chosakushū* (Tokyo: Yoshikawa Kōbunkan, 1988), vol. 4.
8. Sakamoto Tarō, "Fudoki to Nihon shoki," in *Nihon kodaishi no hisoteki kenkyū*, vol. 1, reprinted in *Sakamoto Tarō chosakushū*, vol. 4, pp.17–20.
9. Sakamoto Tarō, "Nihon shoki to Kyūshu chihō no fudoki," in *Sakamoto Tarō chosakushū*, vol. 4, pp. 102–6; Tanaka Takashi, "Kyūshu fudoki no seiritsu" (1950), in *Tanaka Takashi chosakushū* (Tokyo: Kokusho Kankōkai, 1994), vol. 10.
10. Mizuno Yū, "Yamatotakeru-no-mikoto to Yamatotakeru Tennō," *Shikan* 43/44 (1955): 266–70.
11. *Shoku Nihongi* (chronicle complied in 797, covering the period 697–791), vol. 1.
12. Kamata Jun'ichi, *Sendai kuji hongi no kenkyū: Kenkyū no bu* (Tokyo: Yoshikawa Kōbunkan, 1962).
13. *Kuji hongi*, in *SKT*, 7:106 (1966); *Shoki*, in *NKT*, 67-1, p. 298 (1967).
14. *Kuji hongi*, p. 106.
15. *Kuji hongi*, p. 105; *Shoki*, p. 283.
16. Yatomi Hamao, "Nihongi kyōenka no kenkyū," *Kokugakuin zasshi*, 36 (1930): 2–4, 6–8, 10, 11.
17. "Nihongi kyōenka," in *Zokugun shoruijū*, 15, vol. 1, p. 58.
18. On the life of Fujiwara Arizane, see *Mizunoetora-jyo*, compiled in 906, in *Kugyōbunin*, *SKT*, 1:140–60 (1966).
19. Nishimiya Kazutami, *Kogoshūi* (Tokyo: Iwanami Shoten, 1985), p. 224.
20. *Nihon shoki*, vol. 8 (*honbun chuissho*), the chronicle of Emperor Keikō, 40-year clause, in *NKT*, 67-1:122, and 1:304; *Kojiki*, in *Shincho Nihon koten shūsei Kojiki*, ed. Nishimiya Kazutami (Tokyo: Shinchōsha, 1979), pp. 162–3.
21. *Kogoshūi*, p. 40.
22. *Ibid.*, pp. 46–7.
23. *Ibid.*, p. 47.
24. Tsuda Sōkichi, "Kogoshūi no kenkyū," in *Nihon koten no kenkyū*, in *TSZ*, 2 (1963).
25. With regard to the Old Testament and Deuteronomy, see research by Malcolm revealing how the power of rule establishes the canon. Namely, how the capacity among the masses to accept the rules bestowed via texts denotes the power of the canon. Levinson B. Malcolm, "The Hermeneutics of Innovation: The Impact of Centralization upon the Structure, Sequence, and Reformulation of Legal Material in Deuteronomy" (Ann Arbor: UMI Dissertation Services, 1991); and Levinson B. Malcolm, "The Human Voice in Divine Relation: The Problem of Authority in Biblical Law," in Michael A. Williams, Collett Cox and Martin S.

Jaffee (eds), *Innovation in Religious Traditions: Essays in the Interpretation of Religious Change* (Berlin: Mouton de Gruyter, 1992).
26. *Genji monogatari* [*The Tale of Genji*], in *NKT*, 2:432 (1958).
27. Yoshie Akio, *Shinbutsu shūgo* (Tokyo: Iwanami Shoten, 1996); Kawane Yoshiyasu, "Ōdo shisō to shinbutsu shūgo," in *Chūsei hōken shakai no shuto to nōson* (Tokyo: Tōkyō Daigaku Shuppankai, 1984).
28. *Yamatohime no mikoto seiki*, in *NST*, 19:17–28 (1977); *Nihon shoki*, the chronicle of Emperor Keikō, Tenth Month, 40-year clause, in *NKT*, 1:303–4; *Kogoshūi*, p. 40.
29. *Yamatohime no mikoto seiki*, p. 31.
30. Watarai Yukitada, "Jyūko shinmeihisho," in *Zokugun shoruijū*, vol. 3-2, pp. 843–4; *Kojiki*, pp. 162–3.
31. *Shoku Nihongi*, *SKT*, 8:107–44 (1965).
32. Urabe Kanefumi, in Ono Mitsuo (ed.), *Kojiki uragaki* (Tokyo: Bensei Bunko, 1982), p. 25.
33. Ozaki Tomomitsu, *Atsuta Jingū bunka sōsho: Owarikoku Atsuta Daijingū engi* (1967).
34. *Ibid.*, p. 23.
35. *Ibid.*, p. 27.
36. *Ibid.*, p. 23.
37. *Ibid.*, pp. 26–7.
38. Kitabatake Chikafusa, *Jinno seitōki*, *NKT*, 87:75 (1965).
39. *Ibid.*
40. Okada Shoji (ed.), *Kanetomo-bon, Nobukata-bon Nihon shoki jindai no maki sho* (Tokyo: Zoku Gunsho Ruijū Kankokai, 1984), p. 170.
41. *Ibid.*
42. *Ibid.*
43. Niida Noboru, "Gunbōrei clause 11," in *Tourei shūi* (Tokyo: Tōkyō Daigaku Shuppankai, 1933).
44. Kawai Masaharu, "Ise Jingū to buke shakai," in Hagiwara Tatsuo (ed.), *Ise shinkō* (Tokyo: Yuzankaku, 1985), vol. 1.

Chapter 4

1. Arai Hakuseki, "*Sakuma Gendō Ataurusho*," in *Hakuseki Sensei shukan*, in *Shin Arai Hakuseki zenshū* (Tokyo: Kokusho Kankōkai, 1977), vol. 5, p. 562.
2. Arai Hakuseki, *Koshitsū*, in *Shin Arai Hakuseki zenshū*, vol. 3, p. 219.
3. *Ibid.*, p. 210; excerpt by Isomae Jun'ichi.
4. Ise Sadatake, *Shintō Dokugo*, in *Kinko bungei onchi sōsho* (Tokyo: Hakubunkan, 1881), vol. 6, p. 11.
5. Arai, *Koshitsū*, p. 318.
6. Yamagata Bantō, *Yume no shiro*, in *NST*, 43:278 (1973).
7. See Motoori Norinaga and Ueda Akinari, *Kagaika*, and Ueda Akinari, *An'an'gen*, in *Ueda Akinari* (Tokyo: Chūō Kōronsha, 1990), vol. 1.
8. Yamagata, *Yume no shiro*, p. 293.

9. Ever since the publication of the *Kojiki oyobi Nihon shoki no shinkenkyū* by Tsuda Sōkichi in 1919, there has been doubt concerning the actual existence of a number of emperors mentioned in the Kiki, particularly from the first Emperor Jinmu to about the fourteenth Emperor Chūai, who were said to exist before the fifth century. However, the Kiki texts envisage a world on the assumption that they did exist, by describing the centuries which correspond to each distinct emperor's lifespan.
10. Yamagata, *Yume no shiro*, p. 272.
11. *Ibid.*, p. 275.
12. Urabe Kanekata, *Shaku Nihongi*, in *SKT*, 8:84 (1965).
13. Arai, *Koshitsū*, p. 212.
14. Arai, "*Sakuma Gendō ataurusho,*" p. 558.
15. Arai, *Koshitsū*, p. 212.
16. Arai, "*Sakuma Gendō ataurusho,*" p. 518.
17. *Ibid.*, p. 562.
18. Yamagata, *Yume no shiro*, p. 293.
19. To Teikan, *Shōkōhatsu*, Sanchōura, p. 6.
20. *Honchō tsūkan* (Tokyo: Kokusho Kankōkai, 1918); *Dainihonshi* (Tokyo: Dainihon Yūbenkai, 1928).
21. Asaka Tanpaku, "Shin'anshukan furoku," in *Hakuseki Sensei shukan*, p. 359.
23. Aizawa Seishisai, *Tokukuzubana, Tokumaganohire*, in *Nihon jurin sōsho* (Tokyo: Tōyō Tosho Kankōkai, 1929), vol. 4.
23. Motoori Norinaga, *Kuzubana*, in *MNZ*, 8:127 (1972).
24. Ichikawa Tazumaro, *Maganohire*, in *MNZ*, 8:194.
25. *Ibid.*, p. 183.
26. *Ibid.*
27. *Ibid.*, p. 184.
28. The ideological/psychological interpretation also generated the allegorical interpretation, as with Fujitani Mitsue. Stating that the Divine Age in the *Kojiki* did not exist, Mitsue maintained that this represented the teachings of the Emperor Jinmu. Stating that, although the content therein was not to be taken literally, if one let Kotodama (the spirit of language) exercise its power, he held that one would understand the teaching that human beings are not able to curb their avarice via reasoning. While regarding Motoori's literal interpretation as irrational, this school of thought divorced the Kiki from such explanations by bringing forth the concept of Kotodama and situating it in light of the dogmatic. See Fujitani Mitsue, *Kojiki no tomoshibi*, in *Fujitani Mitsue shū* (Tokyo: Kokumin Seishin Bunka Kenkyūkai, 1936), vol. 1.
29. Yamagata, *Yume no shiro*, p. 298.
30. Ichikawa, *Maganohire*, pp. 192, 194.
31. Shimada Kenji, *Shushigaku to Yōmeigaku* (Tokyo: Iwanami Shinsho, 1967).
32. Motoori Norinaga, *Naobi no mitama*, in *MNZ*, 9 (1968).
33. Motoori, *Kuzubana*, p. 167.
34. Ichikawa, *Maganohire*, p. 193.
35. Fujii, *Shōkōhatsu*, and Murata Harumi, *Nishigorinoyazuihitsu*, in *Nihon zuihitsu taisei* (Tokyo: Yoshikawa Kōbunkan, 1927), vol. 3.
36. Ise, *Shintō dokugo*; Motoori and Ueda, *Kagaika*; Ueda, *An'an'gen*.

37. Tani Seigo, "Hirata Atsutane no koshi kenkyū," in *Suzuki Shigetane no kenkyū* (Kyoto: Shintō Shingakkai, 1968).
38. For matters concerning modern-period textbooks, see Kaigo Tokiomi, *Rekishi kyōiku no rekishi* (Tokyo: Tōkyō Daigaku Shuppankai, 1969).
39. Miyake Yūjiro, "Bukkyō tōraimae no shūkyō," in *Nihon Bukkyōshi*, vol. 1.
40. Kume Kunitake, "*Shintō wa saiten no kozoku*" (1891), in *Ronshū Nihon bunka no kigen* (Tokyo: Heibonsha, 1971).
41. Mori Ōgai, *Kanoyōni* (1912), in *Mori Ōgai zenshū* (Tokyo: Iwanami Shoten, 1972), vol. 10, p. 53.
42. Tsuda Sōkichi, *Shindaishi no atarashii kenkyū* (1913), in *TSZ*, supplementary vol. 1.
43. Tsuda Sōkichi, *Bungaku ni arawaretaru waga kokuminshisō no kenkyū: Kizoku bungaku no jidai* (1916), in *TSZ*, supplementary vol. 2, p. 42.
44. Tsuda Sōkichi, *Kojiki oyobi Nihon shoki no kenkyū* (Tokyo: Iwanami Shoten, 1924), pp. 502–3.
45. Wajima Seiichi, "Nihon Kōgogaku no hattatsu to kagakuteki seishin," in *Nihon Kōgogaku no hattatsu to kagakuteki seishin* (Okayama: Wajima Seiichi Chosakushū Kankōkai, 1973).
46. Tsuda Sōkichi, *Kojiki oyobi Nihon shoki no shinkenkyū* (1919), in *TSZ*, supplementary vol. 1, p. 201.
47. Tsuda Sōkichi, *Jindaishi no kenkyū* (Tokyo: Iwanami Shoten, 1924), p. 52.
48. Tsuda, *Kojiki oyobi Nihon shoki no shinkenkyū*, pp. 491, 495–9.
49. Tsuda, *Jindaishi no atarashii kenkyū*, p. 122.
50. Ibid., p. 144.
51. Tsuda, *Bungaku ni arawaretaru waga kokuminshisō no kenkyū: Kizoku bungaku no jidai*, p. 43.
52. Tsuda, *Jindaishi no kenkyū*, p. 564.
53. Tsuda, *Jindaishi no atarashii kenkyū*, p. 123.
54. Tsuda, *Bungaku ni arawaretaru waga kokuminshisō no kenkyū: Kizoku bungaku no jidai*, p. 34.
55. Ienaga Saburō, *Tsuda Sōkichi no shisōshiteki kenkyū* (Tokyo: Iwanami Shoten), p. 446.
56. Watsuji Tetsurō, *Nihon kodai bunka* (Tokyo: Iwanami Shoten, 1920), p. 274 onward.
57. Non-Japanese researchers who have engaged in modern Kiki interpretations, and have been overlooked, include Basil Hall Chamberlain and William George Aston. Such works should be given proper recognition in association with the history of (Japan's intrinsic) research on the Kiki.
58. Watanabe Yoshimichi, *Kojiki kōwa: Jindai hen* (Tokyo: Hakuyōsha, 1936), pp.186, 446–7.
59. Watanabe Yoshimichi, "Shinwa densetsu to kofun bunka," in *Nihon rekishi kyōtei* (Tokyo: Hakuyōsha, 1937), vol. 2, p. 15.
60. Watsuji, *Nihon kodai bunka*, p. 59.
61. Watsuji Tetsurō, *Shinkō Nihon kodai bunka* (Tokyo: Iwanami Shoten, 1951), p. 62.
62. Kurano Kenji, *Kojiki no shinkenkyū* (Tokyo: Shibundō, 1927).
63. Yoshii Iwao, *Tennō no keifu to shinwa* (Tokyo: Hanawa Shobō, 1976), vols. 1–2.

64. Ishimoda Shō, "*Yowasa o ikani kokufukusuruka*" (1953), in *ISC*, 14 (1989); Naoki Sakai and Harry Harootunian, "Japanese Studies and Cultural Studies," *East Asia Cultures Critique* 7:2 (Fall 1999): 593–647.

Chapter 5

1. See Motoori Norinaga's *Kojikiden*, in *MNZ*, 11:219.
2. See Chapter 3.
3. Hans R. Jauss, *Toward an Aesthetic of Reception*, trans. Timothy Bahti (Minneapolis: University of Minnesota Press, 1982).
4. Following Martin Heidegger, I understand the act of interpretation as completing the formation of understanding of the conscious subject. See Martin Heidegger, *Gesamtausgabe Band 63 Ontologie: Hermeneutik der Faktizit* (Frankfurt am Main: Vittorio Klostermann, 1988).
5. Refer to Chapter 6.
6. Karatani Kōjin, *Origins of Modern Japanese Literature*, trans. Brett de Bary (Durham, NC: Duke University Press, 1993), p. 137.
7. See Harry D. Harootunian, "The Consciousness of Archaic Form in the New Realism of Kokugaku," in Tetsuo Najita and Irwin Scheiner (eds), *Japanese Thought in the Tokugawa Period 1600–1868: Methods and Metaphors* (Chicago: The University of Chicago Press, 1978), p. 67.
8. See Hayden White, *Tropics of Discourse: Essays in Cultural Criticism* (Baltimore: Johns Hopkins University Press, 1978).
9. *Tamakushige*, in *MNZ*, 8:321.
10. *Ibid.*
11. *Ibid.*, p. 319.
12. *Naobi no mitama*, in *MNZ*, 9:49; Sey Nishimura, "The Way of the Gods," in *Monumenta Nipponica*, 46:28 (1991).
13. *Tamakushige*, in *MNZ*, 8:309.
14. *Ibid.*, p. 310.
15. *Kuzubana*, in *MNZ*, 8:146.
16. As already mentioned in Chapter 2, the *Nihon shoki* has the structure to include several variant versions as commentaries to the main text, while the *Kojiki* is comprised of only one main text.
17. *Kamiyo no masagoto*, *MNZ*, 7:528 (1971); *Tamakushige*, *MNZ*, 8:310; *NKT*, 67–68, second alternate variant of section 9 (1967).
18. *Kamiyo no masagoto*, p. 526; *Tamakushige*, pp. 320–1; *NKT*, 67, second alternate variant of section 9, chapter 2, p. 151 (1967).
19. Muraoka Tsunetsugu, "Suika Shintō no shisō," in *Zoku Nihon shisōshi kenkyū* (Tokyo: Iwanami Shoten), vol. 2, pp. 185–9.
20. *Genji monogatari tama no ogushi*, in *MNZ*, 4:225 (1969).
21. *Ibid.*, p. 202.
22. Kanno Kakumyō, *Motoori Norinaga* (Tokyo: Perikansha, 1991).
23. *Tamakushige*, p. 316.
24. *Ibid.*

25. *Genji monogatari tama no ogushi*, p. 202.
26. *Tamakushige*, p. 316.
27. Maruyama Masao, *Studies in the Intellectual History of Tokugawa Japan*, trans. Mikiso Hane (Tokyo: University of Tokyo Press, 1974), pp. 170–4.
28. Hino Tatsuo, *Norinaga to Akinari* (Tokyo: Chikuma Shobō, 1984), p. 205.
29. *Naobi no mitama*, p. 59.
30. *Tamakushige*, p. 323.
31. *Kuzubana*, p. 136.
32. *Kojikiden*, MNZ, 9:131 (1968).
33. Kōnoshi Takamitsu, *Kojiki no sekaikan* (Tokyo: Yoshikawa Kōbunkan, 1986), p. 43.
34. See Mircea Eliade et al. (eds), *The Encyclopedia of Religion* (New York: Macmillan, 1987).
35. Kōnoshi, *Kojiki no sekaikan*.
36. Eric J. Hobsbawm, "The Social Function of the Past: Some Questions," *Past & Present*, no. 55 (1972), p. 8.
37. Increasingly, works attempting to clarify historical phases in the social contextualization of sacred texts have emerged from within European and American religious studies. In such works, the treatment of sacred texts, as purely doctrinal expressions of an individual's inner state, is repeatedly criticized for being an approach that de-historicizes modern individual viewpoints. Instead, such works make an attempt to demonstrate the relationship between sacred texts and society as situated in the past. See, for example, Helmut Koester, "Writings and the Spirit: Authority and Politics in Ancient Christianity," in *Harvard Theological Review* 84-4 (New York: Macmillan, 1991); Thomas K. Srull, "The Quaker Book of Discipline: A Sacred Text by Committee?" in Jon Davis and Isabel Wollaston (eds), *The Sociology of Sacred Texts* (Sheffield: Sheffield Academic Press, 1993).
38. Tsuda Sōkichi, *Nihon koten no kenkyū* (1948), vol. 1, in *TSZ*, 1 (1963).
39. Mizoguchi Mutsuko, *Nihon kodai shizoku keifu no seiritsu* (Tokyo: Gakushūin, 1982).
40. Tsuda Sōkichi, "Kamishiro no monogatari," in *Nihon koten no kenkyū*, vol. 1 (1963).
41. Fukaya Katsumi, *Kinsei no kokka, shakai to tennō* (Tokyo: Asekura Shobō, 1991).
42. Kawase Kazuma, *Kokatsuji-ban no kenkyū [Study of the Early Typographic Edition of Japan]* (Tokyo: Antiquarian Booksellers Association of Japan, 1967).
43. Konta Yōzō, *Edo no honyasan* (Tokyo: Nihon Hōsō Shuppankai, 1977), p. 1.
44. *Tamakatsuma*, MNZ, 1:284 (1968).
45. Matsumoto Sannosuke, "Bakumatsu Kokugaku no shisōshiteki igi: Shutoshite seiji shisō no sokumen ni tsuite," in *Nihon shisō taikei*, vol. 51, in Matsumoto Sannosuke et al. (eds), *Kokugaku undō no shisō* (Tokyo: Iwanami Shoten, 1971), p. 634.
46. *Kojiki den*, MNZ, 9:126.
47. *Genji monogatari tama no ogushi*, MNZ, 4:207.
48. Matsumoto Sannosuke, "Bakumatsu Kokugaku no shisōshiteki igi: Shutoshite seiji shisō no sokumen ni tsuite," p. 642.

49. In recent years, Umehara Takeshi's *Yamatotakeru* (Tokyo: Kōdansha, 1986) has received much attention.
50. See, for example, Kurita Hijimaro's *Jindaiki ashikabi* (1810); Murakami Tadamasa's *Murakami Tadamasa Kojiki hyōchū* (1874).
51. Tsuda Sōkichi, *Bungaku ni arawaretaru waga kokumin shisō no kenkyū: Heimin bungaku no jidai* (1921), vol. 2, in *TSZ*, supplementary vol. 5, p. 467.
52. John B. Henderson, *Scripture, Canon, and Commentary: A Comparison of Confucian and Western Exegesis* (Princeton: Princeton University Press, 1991), p. 81.
53. Kotani Hiroyasu, *Mokkan to senmyō no kokugo gakuteki kenkyū* (Tokyo: Izumi Shoin, 1986).
54. See Watsuji Tetsurō, *Nihon rinri shisōshi* (1952), in *Watsuji Tetsurō zenshū* (Tokyo: Iwanami Shoten, 1962), vols 12 and 13; and Tsuda Sōkichi, *Bungaku ni arawaretaru waga kokumin shisō no kenkyū*.
55. See Raffaele Pettazzoni, "Myth of Beginnings and Creation-Myth" (1947–48), in *Essays on the History Religions*, trans. H. J. Rose (Leiden: Brill, 1954), p. 29; and David Gross, *The Past in Ruins: Tradition and the Critique of Modernity* (Amherst: University of Massachusetts Press, 1992), chapter 1.

Chapter 6

1. Ishimoda Shō, "'Kokumin no tame no rekishigaku' oboegaki: Keimō shugi to sono kokufuku no mondai" (1960), in *ISC*, 14: 350–1 (1989).
2. Ibid., p. 357.
3. Ibid., pp. 357–8.
4. Ichikawa Hiroshi, "Shutaisei ronsō," in *Kindai Nihon shisō ronsō* (Tokyo: Aoki Shoten, 1963), p. 319; Victor Koschmann, *Revolution and Subjectivity in Postwar Japan* (Chicago: University of Chicago Press, 1996).
5. Takeda Kiyoko, *Tennō kan no sō kaku: 1945 nen zengo* (Tokyo: Iwanami Shoten, 1978), pp. 267–9, 305.
6. Ishimoda Shō, "Kodai kizoku no eiyū jidai: Kojiki no ichi kōsatsu," in *ISC*, 10:214 (1989).
7. Ishimoda Shō, "Rekishi jojutsu to rekishi kagaku" (1954), in *ISC*, 13:24–5 (1989).
8. Ibid., p. 92.
9. Ishimoda Shō, "Rekishikan ni tsuite" (1963), in *ISC*, 15:304 (1990).
10. Ishimoda, "Kodai kizoku no eiyū jidai," p. 92.
11. Tōma Seita, "Sekaishi no hōhōron toshite no minzoku riron" (1974–75), in *Kindai higashi Ajia sekai no keisei* (Tokyo: Shunjūsha, 1977), p. 509.
12. Tōma Seita, "Oboegaki," in *Higashi Ajia sekai e no mosaku* (Tokyo: Azekura Shobō, 1982), p. 206.
13. The following texts provide detailed accounts of the circumstances compelling the Heroic Age debate: Tōyama Shigeki, *Sengo no rekishigaku to rekishi ishiki* (1968), in *Tōyama Shigeki chosakushū* (Tokyo: Iwanami Shoten, 1992), vol. 8, pp. 77–90; Tōma Seita, "1950 nendai ni okeru minzoku mondai no ronsō," in *Kindai higashi Ajia sekai no keisei* (Tokyo: Shunjūsha, 1977); "Nihonshi

higashi Ajia shi sekaishi ni tsuite kataru: Tōma Seita Sensei no rekishi kenkyū no ayumi," in *Kumamoto Gakuen Daigaku keizai ronshū*, 3:1–2 (1996).
14. Ishimoda Shō, "Kiki ni okeru rekishigaku no kadai" (1951), in *ISC*, 14:175–6 (1989).
15. Kitayama Shigeo, "Nihon ni okeru eiyū jidai no mondai ni yosete" (1953), in Ueda Masaaki (ed.), *Ronshū Nihon bunka no kigen* (Tokyo: Heibonsha, 1971), vol. 2, p. 308.
16. With regard to the notion of "race," Ishimoda stated the following: "Race is of course nationality and includes other conceptual, supra-historical features." See Ishimoda Shō, "Kiki ni okeru rekishigaku no kadai," pp. 175–6.
17. Ishimoda Shō, "Yowasa o ikani kokufuku suru ka" (1953), in *ISC*, 14:307.
18. Kadowaki Teiji, "Nihon Kodai: Kodai kokka no seiritsu to botsuraku ni tsuite no sho mondai," in *Rekishigaku no seika to kadai san: 1951 nen rekishigakkai nenpō* (Tokyo: Iwanami Shoten, 1952), p. 14.
19. This point attains further credence through the relationship between the theory of "discourse" propounded by Michel Foucault and the Annal School's history of social thought. See also Patrick Hutton, *History as an Art of Memory* (Hanover, NH: University Press of New England, 1993), p. 116.
20. Ishimoda Shō, "Kodai kizoku no eiyū jidai," p. 21.
21. *Ibid.*, p. 19.
22. *Ibid.*, pp. 53, 12.
23. *Ibid.*, p. 15.
24. *Ibid.*, p. 19.
25. G. W. F. Hegel, *Aesthetics: Lectures on Fine Art*, trans. T. M. Knox (Oxford: Clarendon Press, 1975), vol. 1, p. 180 (first published 1820).
26. Ishimoda, "Kodai kizoku no eiyū jidai," p. 12.
27. *Ibid.*, pp. 20, 24.
28. See, for example, G. W. F. Hegel, *The Philosophy of History* (New York: Dover Publications, 1956) (first published 1837); and *The Philosophy of Right*, trans. and ed. T. M. Knox (Oxford: Oxford University Press, 1942), pp. 170–1. For commentary on Hegel, see S. Gallagher (ed.), *Hegel, History, and Interpretation* (Albany: State University of New York Press, 1997); and H. White, *Metahistory: The Historical Imagination in Nineteenth-Century Europe* (Baltimore: Johns Hopkins University Press, 1973), chap. 2.
29. Ishimoda, "Kodai kizoku no eiyū jidai," pp.14–22.
30. For prewar theories on epic poetry and the Heroic Age, see Saigō Nobutsuna, "Eiyū jojishi e no michi," *Bungaku* (1949), 17:10.
31. Ishimoda, "Kodai kizoku no eiyū jidai," p. 84.
32. Ishimoda Shō, *Chūseiteki sekai no keisei* (1946), in *ISC*, 5:253 (1988).
33. Ishimoda, "Kodai kizoku no eiyū jidai," p. 21.
34. Ishimoda Shō, "Rekishigaku ni okeru minzoku no mondai," in *ISC*, 14 (1989).
35. Ishimoda, "Kodai kizoku no eiyū jidai," p. 21.
36. *Ibid.*, p. 94.
37. Ishimoda, "Rekishigaku ni okeru minzoku no mondai," p. 113.
38. *Ibid.*, p. 124.
39. Hegel, *Aesthetics: Lectures on Fine Art*, vol. 2, p. 1045.
40. Ishimoda, "Kodai kizoku no eiyū jidai," p. 37.

41. *Ibid.*, p. 23.
42. *Ibid.*
43. *Ibid.*
44. *Ibid.*, p. 82.
45. *Ibid.*, pp. 35–6.
46. Takagi Ichinosuke, "Nihon bungaku ni okeru jojishi jidai" (1933), in *Yoshino no ayu* (Tokyo: Iwanami Shoten, 1941).
47. Hegel, *Aesthetics: Lectures on Fine Art*, vol. 2, pp. 973–4.
48. J. Knappert, "Is Epic Oral or Written?," in L. Honko (ed.), *Religion, Myth, and Folklore in the World's Epics: The Kalevala and Its Predecessors* (Berlin: Mouton de Gruyter, 1990), p. 394; and, in the same volume, L. Honko, "The Kalevala: Problems of Interpretation and Identity," p. 570.
49. Kitayama, "Nihon ni okeru eiyū jidai no mondai ni yosete," p. 301.
50. *Ibid.*, p. 306.
51. Ishimoda, "Yowasa o ikani kokufuku suru ka," p. 307.
52. For "logocentrism," see Jacques Derrida, *Of Grammatology*, trans. Gayatri Chakravorty Spivak (Baltimore: Johns Hopkins University Press, 1997), p. 71. For further discussion on "logocentrism," see works by and about Jacques Derrida.
53. For criticism of logocentric intellectual history, see M. Foucault, *The Archaeology of Knowledge*, trans. A. M. Sheridan Smith (New York: Pantheon Books, 1972); M. Jay, "Should Intellectual History Take a Linguistic Turn? Reflections on the Habermas–Gadamer Debate," in Dominick LaCapra and Steven L. Kaplan (eds), *Modern European Intellectual History: Reappraisals and New Perspectives* (Ithaca: Cornell University Press, 1982); and T. Adorno, *The Jargon of Authenticity*, trans. Knut Tarnowski and Frederic Will (Evanston, IL: Northwestern University Press, 1973).
54. Ishimoda, "Kodai kizoku no eiyū jidai," p. 39.
55. *Ibid.*, p. 59.
56. *Ibid.*, p. 54.
57. *Ibid.*, p. 52.
58. Ishimoda Shō, "Rekishigaku no hōhō ni tsuite no kansō " (1957), in *ISC*, 14:99.
59. Ishimoda, "Kiki ni okeru rekishigaku no kadai," p. 176.
60. Suzuki Ryōichi, "Haisengo no rekishigaku ni okeru ichi keikō: Tōma Ishimoda shi no shigoto ni tsuite" (1948), in *Rekishi kagaku taikei*, vol. 29 (Tokyo: Azekura Shobō, 1983), p. 209.
61. Ishimoda, "Kodai kizoku no eiyū jidai," p. 90.
62. Kōnoshi Takamitsu, "Kotomuke," in *Kojiki no tassei: Sono ronri to hōhō* (Tokyo: Tōkyō Daigaku Shuppankai, 1983).
63. *Nihon shoki* ; *Nihongi: Chronicles of Japan from the Earliest Times to A.D. 697*, trans. W. G. Aston (Tokyo: Charles E. Tuttle Company, 1972), p. 206. Translation slightly modified.
64. Inoue Mitsusada, "Kabane, ikai, kanshoku" (1982), in *Inoue Mitsusada chōsakushū* (Tokyo: Iwanami Shoten, 1986), vol. 5; Katō Akira, "Waga kuni ni okeru kabane no seiritsu ni tsuite," in *Zoku kodaishi ronshū* (Tokyo: Yoshikawa Kōbunkan, 1972), vol. 1.

65. *Nihon shoki; Nihongi: Chronicles of Japan from the Earliest Times to* A.D. *697*, p. 207. Translation slightly modified.
66. Ichimura Hiromasa, *Zōho "nazuke" no seishinshi* (Tokyo: Heibonsha, 1996), p. 140.
67. Ichimura, pp. 134–40. With regard to the act of naming in myths, see T. W. Adorno and M. Horkheimer, *Dialectic of Enlightenment* (1944), trans. John Cumming (London: Continuum, 1996), chapter 1.
68. On cultural difference as produced by reading and writing, see B. Stock, *The Implication of Literacy: Written Language and Models of Interpretation in the Eleventh and Twelfth Centuries* (Princeton: Princeton University Press, 1983), chap. 3; and E. Gellner, *Nation and Nationalism* (Oxford: Blackwell, 1983), chap. 2.
69. Hani Gorō, "Gengo oyobi moji to kaikyū" (1929/1930), in *Hani Gorō rekishiron chōsakushū* (Tokyo: Aoki Shoten, 1967), p. 205.
70. Rekishigaku Kenkyūkai, *Minzoku no bunka ni tsuite: Rekishigaku Kenkyūkai 1952 nendo taikai hōkoku* (Tokyo: Iwanami Shoten, 1953), p. 39.
71. Tōyama, *Sengo no rekishigaku to rekishi ishiki*, chaps 2 and 3.
72. Ishimoda, "Kiki ni okeru rekishigaku no kadai," p. 176.
73. Michel Foucault, "Power and Sex", in *Politics, Philosophy, Culture: Interviews and Other Writings 1977–1984*, ed. Lawrence D. Kritzman (New York: Routledge, 1990), p. 118.
74. Ishimoda Shō, "Koe naki koe" (1951), in *ISC*, 16:50 (1990).
75. *Kojiki*, trans. Donald L. Philippi (Tokyo: University of Tokyo Press, 1968), p. 246. Translation slightly modified.
76. Saigō Nobutsuna, *Kojiki chūshaku*, vol. 3 (Tokyo: Heibonsha, 1988), p. 344.
77. Ishimoda Shō, "Kodai bungaku seiritsu no ichi katei: Izumo Fudoki shoshū 'kunihiki' no shishō no bunseki" (1957); "Kunitsukuri no monogatari ni tsuite no oboegaki: Kojiki no seikaku to no kanren ni oite" (1957); and "Nihon shinwa to rekishi: Izumo kei shinwa no haikei" (1959), in *ISC*, 10 (1989).
78. Ishimoda Shō, "Kaisetsu: Nihon shinwa to rekishi," in Ishimoda et al. (eds) *Nihon shisō taikei: Kojiki* (Tokyo: Iwanami Shoten, 1982), vol. 1, p. 648.

Index

Abe Yasurō 24
academic essays 9, 31–2
aesthetic empathy 14, 108–9, 112–16, 121, 123
Age of the Gods, see Divine Age
Aizawa Seishisai 92
"Alleged books' records" 40–9, 50–3, 55–6, 58
Amaterasu Ōmikami
 ancestor of the emperors 20, 56, 111–12
 birth of 51–2
 and Susanowo 38–9, 42–7, 48–9
Ame-no-Murakumo, see Kusanagi sword
ancient myths (kuji), see teiki and kuji
ancient nobility 134–44, 147
ancient understanding 117–21
Ancient Way (kodōron) 110–17
Anesaki Masaharu 33
Antoku, Emperor 82
Arai Hakuseki 86–92, 96
archeology 90–1, 98, 100, 103
Asaka Tanpaku 92
Association of Democratic Scientists 128, 129
Atsuta shrine 24–5, 68, 70, 74–5, 77–83
authenticity of records 18, 26–34, 48, 55–6, 61–2, 85–107, 134–44
Awa Province, Fudoki of 71
Azumi clan 22, 59, 118

Bar, James 3
Bible 2–3, 5, 8, 19
biographical records 150
Buddhist influences 27–9, 76, 153

canon
 canonization 3–4, 7, 19, 50–65
 interpretation of 4–5
 and its variants 35–65
 Kiki as 32–3, 151
 role and social function 7–8
canonic laws 63
capitalism 103, 105
Chartier, Roger 3
Chikamatsu Monzaemon 29
Chinese influences 6, 56, 64, 84, 85–6, 90–2, 96, 123, 153
Chronicle of Ancient Matters 58, 66, 72–3, 119; see also teiki and kuji
Chronicle of Japan, see Nihon shoki
Chūai, Emperor 73, 88, 94, 100, 101, 103
Chūsei Nihongi 24–9, 30, 85
Chushi, teachings of 86, 92, 96
clan
 genealogies 41
 history 1, 7, 12, 18, 19, 21–2, 26, 118–19
 names 59–60, 61, 148–50
 records, see teiki and kuji
 relations to the imperial house 21–3, 53–60, 75–6, 118–19, 148–50
 status of 41–2, 53–60, 83–4, 148–50
 structure 54–5, 57
class-based society 60–1, 104, 136–8, 140, 143, 146
commentary 4–5, 8–9, 31–2, 35–6, 50, 60
common-sense approach 93–5
communal memory 20, 30
communality 136–44
communism 130, 132
comparative Kiki studies 2–7, 85–90, 100–7
comparative mythology 38, 42–9
Confucian influences 13–14, 86–98, 100, 115–16, 121

Confucian Shintō 34, 113
contemporary Kiki studies 121–5, 133
context, word alterations and 47–9, 69, 88
creation myth 19–20, 38–9, 47, 51–3, 88, 108–25
cultural hegemony 147–55
cultural identity 101–5, 153

Dainihonshi 86, 91–2, 96, 98
Dannoura, battle of 82
dating of the Kiki 32–3, 48
Davis, Jon 5
debates, Heroic Age 109, 129–33, 138
demarcating myths 40–9
discursive historical research 152–5
dissemination of texts 28, 120
dissertation style of interpretation 9, 31–2
divergence of myths and texts 24–8
Divine Age
    archetypal theory of 96–8
    Buddhist influences 27–9
    Confucian interpretation 13–14
    as historical fact 33
    as origin of the imperial family 100–2
    records 27–8, 35, 49, 51–3, 87–92, 94–5
divinity, concept of 20, 29, 87, 115–16
dualism 37, 86

early-modern Kiki interpretations 85–98
Edo period 33, 34
education, history 30–1, 98–9, 128
emotionality 108–9, 113–14
emperor, status of 20, 29–30, 44–5, 49, 111–12, 117–19
emperor system, *see tennō* system
Engi period 72
Engishiki (ritual text) 23–4
Enryaku period 59
epic literature 134, 139–41, 144, 147–8
epistemological systems 150, 153

essays, academic 9, 31–2
essentialism 8, 13, 138
ethnic memory *(minzoku)* 29–34

feudal system 86, 92
forgeries, of clan writings 119
foundation myth, *see* creation myth
fudoki 1, 35, 70–2, 79, 85, 149, 151
Fujitani Mitsue 93
Fujiwara Arizane 73
Fujiwara clan 60

Gadamer, Hans-Georg 10
gender and the Susanowo myth 43–5, 47
genealogies, *see* clans, genealogies; imperial genealogies
Genjō, Emperor 61
Genmei, Emperor 67
Genshō, Emperor 67
geographic name records 1, 35, 70–2, 79, 85, 149, 151
Gleanings from Ancient Stories, *see Kogoshūi*
God, understanding 85–107
government use of the Kiki 30–1, 128
Graham, William A. 2
grass-fires 68–70, 74, 77, 78–9, 81
gunki (military tales) 26, 28

Hakarutama 47
Hakusonkō, battle of 54
Hani Gorō 151
Harima no Tarōhime 69
Hegel, G. W. F. 17, 134–8, 140–1
Heian period 20–3, 25, 27, 33–4, 58–60, 72–6, 85
Heidegger, Martin 1
Henderson, John B. 4, 123
Heroes of Japan, characteristics 135–6, 147
Heroic Age 15, 126–55
Heroic Age debates 109, 129–33, 138
Hino Tatsuo 114–15
Hirata Atsutane 97–8, 121–2
historical authenticity 18, 26–34, 48, 55–6, 61–2, 85–107, 134–44

Index

historical interpretation 3–5, 8, 36–7
historical origins of Japan 10, 11, 15–16, 97, 138, 144, 152
historical research 105–7, 126–9, 132, 133, 141–2, 144, 146, 152–5
historical texts, loss of 18
historiography 16, 92, 110, 129–32, 138–9
history education 30–1, 98–9, 128
Hitachi Province, Fudoki of 71
Hizen Province, Fudoki of 71
Hobsbawm, E. J. 117
Honchōtsugan 86, 91–2, 96, 98
Honji, see *teiki* and *kuji*
Honji Suijaku doctrine 28–9
Hononinigi 20, 28, 38, 39, 49, 112
human emperors 92, 96, 98, 100–1
humanity of the gods 87–92, 94
humans and myth 117–25

Ibuki, Mt. 67, 69, 70, 73, 80, 81, 154
Ichijō Kanera 36
Ichikawa Hiroshi 127
Ichikawa Tazumaro 86, 94, 95–6, 97
identity, of self 106
ideological interpretation 93–5, 100–3, 105
Ienaga Saburō 102
Imbe clan, *Kogoshūi* of the 119
imperial chronicles, see *teiki* and *kuji*
imperial edicts 40, 41, 50, 59, 63
imperial genealogies
 authenticity of 48, 50, 56, 94, 100
 and clan structure 41–2, 45, 91
 lineage 73, 101, 111–12, 117–21
 see also *teiki* and *kuji*
imperial primacy 38–9, 102–4, 106, 136–7, 139–42, 148, 152; see also Yamato Court / kingdom
imperial records (*teiki*), see *teiki* and *kuji*
imperial regalia 28, 68, 74, 76
 see also Kusanagi sword
imperial system, see *tennō* system
Inatane-no-Kimi 80, 81
Inbe clan 21, 22, 59, 75
Inbe Hironari 75, 77

individuality 135–7
Ingyō, Emperor 57, 61, 63, 64
Inoue Kiyoshi 131
intellectual history 124–5, 153–5
interpretation, historical 3–5, 8, 36–7
interpretations, Taishō 100–5
interpreters' perceptions 1–2, 8–10, 23, 34, 61–5, 105–7, 109–12, 117, 124–5, 143–4
Ise Sadatake 97
Ise Shintō 18, 76, 81
Ise Shrine 22, 24, 67, 77–8, 83
 see also Yamatotakeru legend
Ishimoda Shō 7, 15, 17, 104–5, 109, 126–55
Issho (variant of the *Nihon shoki*) 35
Itō Masayoshi 24
Izanagi and Izanami 20, 38, 51–3, 111–12

Japan, historical origins of 10, 11, 15–16, 97, 138, 144, 152
Japanese archipelago, creation of 38–9, 51–2, 53, 148–50
Japanese Chronicles, see *Nihon shoki*; *Nihongi*; *Nihongi kōsho*
Jauss, Hans Robert 108
Jindai, see Divine Age
Jingū, Empress 67, 100
Jinmu, Emperor 91, 100, 101, 103, 139, 140, 147
jisha engi 26, 28, 30, 31
Jitō, Emperor 67, 85

kachō 19, 21, 26
Kagutsuchi 52
Kakubutsuchichi 96
Kamakura period 33, 66, 76–8, 146
kami 20, 29, 87, 115–16
Kamiyo no maki 27, 28
Kamo no Mabuchi 86
Kan'ei era 120
kanji 6, 69, 88
Kanmu, Emperor 63
Karatani Kōjin 109
Kawasaki Tsuneyuki 129
Kazamaki Keijirō 31

Kazuo Miyake 7
Keikō, Emperor 24, 67, 68–70, 71, 72, 74, 76, 78, 80
Kikan riron journal 130
Kiki
    ancient function of the 19–24
    ancient mythology in the 11–12
    collapse of the study 132
    compilation of 35–6, 54–6, 84, 94
    interpreting 1–2, 6–9, 11, 15–17, 32, 84
    origin of 17, 42, 103
    as a symbol of power 98–9
    unification of texts 7, 62–3
    variations 35, 51–3, 58
    see also *Kojiki*; *Nihon shoki*
kingship myths 117–21
Kinki region 17
Kinoshita Jun'an 96
Kitabatake Chikafusa 25, 81
Kitayama Shigeo 131, 142
kodōron 110–17
Kogoshūi 21–2, 58, 64, 66, 73–5, 77–8, 82–3, 87
Kojiki
    establishment of 1, 6
    modern-day affinity for 109
    ranking below the *Nihon shoki* 58, 63
    selection of records 50
    as variant of the *Nihon shoki* 21
    see also Kiki
Kojiki uragaki 79
Kokki 56, 57–8, 61
Kokugaku, see Nativism
kokushi 21–3, 24, 26–7, 59, 75–6
Kokusuishugi, see Nationalism
Kōninshiki 58, 63
Kōnoshi Takamitsu 7, 8, 17, 19, 37
Konta Yōzō 120
kuji (ancient myths), see *teiki* and *kuji*
Kujiki 58, 66, 72–3, 119
Kumaso, pacification of the 67, 68, 69, 72
Kume Kunitake 98–9
Kuni-Tokotachi-no-mikoto 18, 27

Kurano Kenji 104
Kusanagi sword 13, 24–6, 66–83
Kyūri ideology 96

Land of the Dead 38, 46, 51–3
language as power 147–52
laws, canonic 63
lectures on commentary, see *Nihongi kōsho*
Levering, Miriam 2
Lévi-Strauss, Claude 42
Levinson, Bernard M. 5
literal interpretation 8, 11, 13, 27, 93, 105

Maruyama Masao 8, 114, 127
Marxist influences 17, 103–6, 126–32, 138, 141, 151
Masuda Katsumi 151
materialism 103–5, 128, 134, 136, 141, 143
Matsumoto Sannosuke 121
medieval function of the Kiki 24–9
medieval Heroic Age 137–8
Medieval Japanese Chronicles 24–9, 30, 85
Meiji period 32, 98, 102
military tales *(gunki)* 26, 28
Minshushugi Kagakusha Kyōkai 128, 129
Mishina Shōei 36
Miyake Setsurei 98
Miyazuhime 74, 79, 80
Mizoguchi Mutsuko 41
Mizubayashi Takeshi 17
modern era 29–34, 98–9, 121–5
mono no aware 14, 108–9, 112–16, 121, 123
monogatari 83
Mononobe clan 66, 72, 119
Mori Ōgai 99
motifs, mythological 26, 38, 42–9
Motoori Norinaga 14–15, 19, 33, 46, 88, 93–5, 96, 108–25
Murasaki Shikibu 76, 113
Murata Harumi 93, 97
Muromachi period 33, 66

Musuhi-no-kami 115–16
mythological motifs of the Kiki 26, 38, 42–9
mythology, Japanese
　approaches to 17–19
　as a concept 33, 34
myths, analysis of 117–21

Naka Michiyo 32
Nakatomi clan 29, 59, 75
names 59–60, 61, 69, 71, 148–50
Nara period 20, 55
national culture 129–31, 151
national historical research 152–3
national identity 15, 101–4
national memory, Kiki as 18–19, 29–34
national spirit 126, 135–8
Nationalism 10, 31, 108–25, 128, 129–32, 143, 146
Nativism 13, 14, 36, 66, 84, 93, 108–25
netherworld, the 38, 46, 51–3
Nihon shoki (Chronicle of Japan)
　authority of 58, 83
　coherence within 53
　establishment of 1, 63
　lectures on commentary 20, 27, 32, 36, 56, 73
　modern-day distance from 109–10
　as official state history 75-6, 83
　see also Kiki; Yamatotakeru legend
Nihongi 24–9, 30, 85
Nihongi kōsho 20, 27, 32, 36, 56, 73
Nintoku, Emperor 107
nobility and the Heroic Age 134–44, 147
non-ruling classes 114–22

objective criticism 88–103, 105
Occupation Army (U.S.) 127, 130
Ōjin, Emperor 87, 94, 107
Ōnamuchi 39
oral traditions 2–3, 6, 12, 88–91, 141, 144, 150–1, 154
original past, authority of 122–5

Oshihomimi 44–5, 49
Ōtsuka Hisao 127
Ōusu 68, 80
Owari Province, Fudoki of 71, 79

patriarchal systems 54–5
personal identity 106
poetry 73, 80, 126, 134, 140–1, 148
　see also songs
politics
　authority of the Kiki 11, 58, 63–4, 98–9, 100–5
　historical research 37
　identity 101–3
　influences 99
　layers within the Kiki 37
　loss of power by the Court 119
　solidarity 152–3
　structures 53–4, 63–4, 118–19, 124, 130–2, 145–7, 152–3
　see also Ritsuryō state; tennō system
popular culture 114–16, 151
positivism 132–3, 144, 147
postwar interpretation 17, 36, 104–6, 126–55
printing, importance of 120
psychological interpretation 37, 93–5, 100–3, 105

rationalism 13, 85–107
reconstruction of records 35
Record of Ancient Matters, see Kojiki
Record of the Emperor 56, 57–8, 61
Records of the Country, see Kokki
Rekishigaku Kenkyūkai 129, 130
Rekishō shinsho 88
research, historical 105–7, 126–9, 132, 133, 141–2, 144, 146, 152–5
research methods, current 18
Richū, Emperor 87
rikkokushi 21, 22–3, 28, 58, 75
Ritsuryō state 17, 19–23, 29, 54–5, 58–9, 63–4, 76, 135–9
ritual texts 23–4
rituals 3, 23–4, 29, 75
Ryōbu Shintō 28

sacred texts, artificial selection of 3–4, 7–8, 12, 83, 87–8, 94
Saga, Emperor 61–2
Saigō Nobutsuna 129
Sakamoto Tarō 37
Scrolls of the Divine Age 27, 28
Seimu, Emperor 67, 73
selfless view of society 111–14
Sendai kuji hongi 58, 66, 72–3, 119
Senmyō 35
sequential alterations of myths 36
Shinbetsuki 58
Shinsen shōjiroku 21, 23, 58, 59–60, 61, 62
Shintō 18, 30–1, 34, 88, 99, 113, 116
Shintōsho (texts) 18, 26, 27–8, 30, 82
Shizuki Tadao 88
Shoku Nihongi 72, 78
Shōwa era 103
shrine histories 26, 28, 30, 31; see also Atsuta shrine; Ise shrine
silent reading 3
Six National Histories 21, 22–3, 28, 58, 75
Smith, Jonathan Z. 4
Smith, William Cantwell 3
social standing, notion of 57
social status 41–2, 53–60, 83–4, 148–50
social structures 53–5, 60, 123, 130–2
Sōhei period 58
solidarity movement 152–3
songs 139–40, 144; see also poetry
state histories 21–3, 24, 26–7, 59, 75–6
State Shintō 30
state system 17, 19–23, 29, 54–5, 58–9, 63–4, 76, 135–9
structural characteristics of the Kiki 37–9
subjectivity 58–9, 126–9, 130, 134–8, 145–7
Suika Shintō 18, 88, 113
Suiko, Empress 56, 57
Suinin, Emperor 76, 77
Suishu (Book of the Sui Dynasty) 56
suppression of material 104

Susanowo myth 20, 38–9, 42–9, 51–3, 67
Suzuki Ryōichi 146

Taishō Democracy 100–7
Taishō era 31–2, 33
Takagi Ichinosuke 140
Takagi Makoto 26
Takagi Toshio 33
Takahashi clan 21, 22, 59, 118
Takahashi ujibumi 21, 22, 41, 57, 58, 59, 64, 151
Takeuchi Yoshimi 127
Tale of Genji 76, 113
Tale of Heike 25–6, 82, 84
teiki and *kuji* (imperial chronicles)
    kujiki 56, 66, 72–3, 119
    selection of 20–1, 61
    unification of 50–1, 53–4
    variations of 35, 39–49, 63, 64
temple origins 26, 28, 30, 31; see also Atsuta shrine; Ise shrine
Tenchi, Emperor 54
Tenmu, Emperor 36–7, 40–9, 50, 54–5, 61, 94
tennō system
    modern view of 105–6, 126–8, 133, 152
    Nativist view of 124
    rationalist view of 97–9
    subjective view of 136–8, 139, 144
Tennōki 56, 57–8, 61
texts
    artificial selection of 3–4, 7–8, 12, 50–1, 83, 87–8, 94
    historical perspective of canonized 3–4
    literal interpretation of 11
    re-interpretation of 12–13
    textual interpretation 1–2, 9
Tō Teikan 90, 91, 97
Tokugawa period 31, 86, 92, 121
Tōma Seita 17, 109, 129–30
transitional periods 134, 135–7, 141–2, 151
Tsuchihashi Hiroshi 42

Tsuda Sōkichi 7, 13–14, 35–7, 39, 63, 99–105, 123, 128
Tsukiyomi 20, 47, 51–2, 56

Ueda Akinari 88, 93, 97
Uehara Senroku 132
ujibumi 1, 7, 12, 18, 19, 21–2, 26, 118–19
Umemoto Katsumi 127
unification of Japan 67, 95–6, 148–50, 152
unification of *teiki* and *kuji* 50–1
unification of texts 62–3
universality 135–6, 141
Urabe Kanekata 78–9

variations of *teiki* and *kuji* 35, 39–49, 63, 64
variations on mythology 35–65
variations on Yamatotakeru legend 66–84
verbal declarations, importance of 154–5

Watanabe Yoshimichi 103–4
Watarai Yukitada 78
Watsuji Tetsurō 6, 102, 103, 105, 124
way of sincerity (*kodōron*) 110–17
Western influences 2–5, 13, 17, 33, 34, 88, 98, 103, 153
Wollaston, Isabel 5
words changing context 47–9, 69, 88
world history and its relation to Japan 134
worldviews

coloring interpretation 1–2, 23, 34, 39, 61–5, 94, 105–7, 109
of the literate coloring records 151
of non-ruling classes 114–16, 123
projection into the texts 124–5
writing, introduction of 6, 87–9, 95, 150–1

Yamagata Bantō 86, 88–9, 91, 95–6
Yamato Court / kingdom
 consolidation of 71
 as creator of the Kiki 1, 101–2
 history through Kiki 17, 38, 66, 151
 kingship myths of 56, 118
 legitimized through Kiki 14
 loss of power 54, 83, 85
 unification of Japan through 67
 as users of the Kiki 20–1
 see also imperial primacy
Yamatohime 24–5, 67, 68, 70, 74, 76–8, 80, 82
Yamatotakeru legend
 ancient / medieval versions 12–13, 66–84
 as conqueror 147–50
 death 67–81, 154–5
 Kusanagi sword 13, 24–6, 66–83
 Motoori Norinaga's interpretation 108–9
 postwar interpretations of 129–30
Yayoi period 60
Yoshida Kanetomo 27, 81–2
Yoshida Shintō 31, 81
Yoshimi Yoshikazu 18, 29, 88